trim healthy future

trim healthy future

the trim healthy **future** of **our kitchen** & **yours**

Rashida Simpson

(with Serene Allison and Pearl Barrett)

WELBY STREET
PRESS

Trim Healthy Future

©2020 by Rashida La'el Simpson, Serene Allison & Pearl Barrett

Published by Welby Street Press

Cover Design: Welby Street Press

Interior Layout and Design: PerfecType, Nashville, TN

Food Photography: Rashida La'el Simpson (@rashidala'elphotography)

Cover & Lifestyle Photography: Autumn Barrett (@autumnrosephotography)

B-Roll Photography: Polly Lohrmann (@picturepollyphotography)

Food Styling for Book Cover: Savanna Honaker (@savsdish)

ISBN: 978-1-7923-5020-7

Table of Contents

PART ONE: Let's Chat First

PART TWO: Let's Eat Now

CHAPTER 1

From Serene and Pearl
(Introducing . . .)

From the time she could crawl she could cook. Don't believe us? We wouldn't stoop to such exaggeration. Us??? Never! This tale is roughly ninety-something percent kinda truth. We figure she was probably cooking in the womb and stirring with the umbilical cord (okay . . . okay . . . some slight exaggeration on that one but it's family folklore).

The "she" we're talking about here is of course this gorgeous Mama on the cover . . . our 24 year old niece Rashida. Actually, growing up here on the Hilltop alongside our own children, she's always been more like a daughter to us than a niece but she does put the word "Aunty" before our names.

In these last eight years since the release of our first Trim Healthy Mama book . . . we feel like we've lived life with so many of you . . . it's like we're family. So now we want you to get to know another family member. If we've had the privilege of playing a role in making a positive difference to your food and health world, we've got a feeling Rashida is about to infuse your future with even more! If you're new to this whole Trim Healthy Mama thing, perhaps this is the first THM book you've picked up . . . huge "hi" and welcome! You're going to love these recipes and love this lifestyle. We couldn't be more thrilled to have you join us on this freeing and joyful trim and healthy journey.

If you don't mind, we want to tell a few stories about Rashida … and ourselves … and just have a little yarn session with you before you crack open the rest of this book and jump headfirst into the recipes.

Rashida's new to you … no viral YouTubes or Facebook posts. She's never blogged or had any kind of Instagram following. She doesn't selfie any glamorous life events or vacations (heck … she barely checks her social media accounts). She works part time, but most days she's at her cute little house with her three little children, having fun creating healthy and tasty recipes in her kitchen or doing some sort of landscaping/garden project. But Rashida smiles a lot, laughs a lot, and is in absolute love with her very normal life.

Don't let us give you a completely wrong picture here though. While she is no kind of public celebrity, she does have a crowd of mega fans. Her family members here on the Hilltop make for a pretty big bunch. (BTW … Hilltop? It's our nickname for where we live—about an hour outside of Nashville, TN on a hill surrounded by thick woods). But here on the few hundred beautiful acres that we all own a piece of, we're all devoted followers, tasters and die-hard lovers of her recipe creations. Rashida captured our fan-ship as a toddler when she started with her elaborate mud pie creations and is now at legendary level in our family for her incredibly delicious yet healthy and … thankfully … slimming food.

Rashida's most famous event in our family history was when she was seven years old, drying edible wild flower petals to top a clove infused spice cake which she was planning to serve after her mint and raisin marinated venison chops, for her visiting Great Granddad from Kiwi Land. The meal was 5 courses, all designed by her and made from scratch with no adult input for any part of it. We still have the menu she wrote out for him (seven-year-old spelling and all) in our family keepsakes. On this occasion, the eighty-year-old food connoisseur was brought to tears with pride as he watched the little round-faced, curly head girl, maneuver nimbly around the kitchen and climb up the tall stool to stir the vibrant salad topped with wild Hilltop onions that she picked (probably with the help of forced labor from other littler cousins … she also knew how to give orders early on).

If we may shamelessly brag for a minute … being famous in our family for food is no small feat. The love of food has been woven into the fiber of our family for generations. We love to gather and we love to yarn … tall tales of course as we are mostly a bunch of lengthy Hilltoppers (in every sense of the word—tall genes run strong). And when we spin our yarns, we love to eat … and when we eat … we love to oooh and aaah … and when we oooh and aaah we also love to verbalize the wonder of each mouthful with extroverted demonstrations and descriptions and long and dreamy inhales and exhales. If you've ever seen the movie *What About Bob*…think about that scene where Bob "mmmms" his way through his first meal at Dr. Leo Marvin's house…yeah…lots of us doing just that with maybe even more gusto.

When everyone . . . we mean everyone . . . aunties, uncles, cousins, grandies, great grandies, stray friends and their dogs gather together here on the Hilltop we're a huge, boisterous group of hungries and a few hangries (there are no less than 80–90 of us at Thanksgiving and Christmas). The food goes on long plastic tables that are all shoved together to form one ginormous train banquet of foodie art and love in our parent's walkout basement slash church building slash family shindig gathering place. Certain family members can't get their act together and arrive on time so once grace is finally being said, you have superior spiritual powers if you can manage to keep your eyes shut through the prayer for fear of losing sight of the food and someone else getting ahead of you.

The hordes are ravenous. This forces the necessity to make a plan.

"Pregnant and nursing mamas first!" Granddad (our Dad, but everyone calls him Granddad) yells over the ruckus.

"No, make that Uncle Steve goes first," says Uncle Steve (one of our brothers) chuckling as he shoves the other uncles aside and grabs the first piece of roasted lamb. (He's somehow made himself head of the "Plan of Food Attack" committee…although he's the only one left in the committee, as all the others left, because he doesn't allow their vote.)

The better-behaved uncles usher anyone who's pregnant to the front of the food line and work hard to keep the throngs of teenage grandies (who are swarming like zombies toward the food table) at bay. At this point, Nana (our mom and grandmother to 43 grandchildren also great grandmother to 17) attempts to raise her voice above the din to make her special speech about not taking more than you can eat.

Know why she has to give that spiel every single time? Cuz everybody's eyes are way bigger than their stomachs and we get worried about getting our share. This is no well-mannered Baptist-type potluck, let us tell ya'! Growing up in a large family does something to your brain wiring. It makes you say things like…"I have dibs on that piece first" or "I don't care if you licked it…it's mine…give it back!"

Fending for your perfectly roasted and seasoned sweet potato or making sure there is a piece of Aunty Simone's cheesecake left after all the cousins have swarmed in line before you, brings out this "food maniac" in a way that only sharing a meal with 80 other crazy family members can do.

But don't get us too wrong. We are not quite the miserable wretches you might be picturing. This kind of food warring is fun for us ... it's family sport tradition ... good-hearted competition. In the end, there is always more than enough food on that long plastic table train. We all usually end up saying ... "I'm as full as a double-yolked egg ... Here, have my slice ... Actually, take that whole extra cake of mine home with ya' mate!"

But back to Rashida ... got indulgently rabbit trailed for a wee bit (we enjoyed ourselves at least). There is only one official way our huge family gatherings end ... with crowning the winner for the dish of the day. Over the years . . . family gathering after gathering ... we've all worked hard to grab that title but the reigning queen ... the one who's won the most times ... the one who ends up bringing a round of applause and agreeing pats on the belly, from all the now satiated hordes of Hilltoppers is this girl on the cover here. And on the occasions that she didn't win ... she's always been in the running. We can't remember a gathering in the last decade plus some where we haven't all raised our glasses to honor her food.

If it wasn't for us pushing and prodding her to make some of her yummy food creations available to you, Rashida would never have dreamed of publishing a glossy book with her face and food photographed throughout. You'd think with all the talent and gifted ideas that ooze from her pretty little head, she might be a tad proud.... but she's not. Well, we are not so bashful. We'd love to take the credit for her "yum" ability but that would not be exactly truthful (although growing up she did spend a lot of time in our homes ... mostly in our kitchens with us ... so round of applause to us for that). But the truth is, we need to praise her talented mother, our sister Vange.

Vange and her hubs Howard recognized Rashida's extraordinary passion and creativity in the kitchen when she was barely tall enough to reach the door on their refrigerator with a stepping stool. Our sister, who is actually a splendid cook herself and loved to create wonderful family meals in her kitchen, saw this rare and special ability Rashida had with food so she gave the whole kitchen domain over to her little girl who basically turned their home into a Hilltop restaurant ... (no charge, but with a long waiting list). And this time we are not kidding or exaggerating even slightly. When we say Rashida had ruling kitchen domain ... we do mean she was the literal creator and cook of all their family meals ... from the time she was about 6. And this was not forced child labor. This was her joy and passion.

So, no more keeping her to ourselves. This book is titled "Trim Healthy Future" because we believe in passing this baton of healthy eating on. Trim Healthy Mama may have started with us but God has allowed it to go far further than where we could ever take it. It certainly won't end with us.

Rashida is shooting out a branch that is all her own into the future of our Trim Healthy brand with our big-time blessing. But it only feels natural ... we might have been the faces on our book covers and the voices on our Poddy, but THM has always been a full family affair. At first it was just all of our family cheering us on as we wrote that original Trim Healthy Mama book. Then after that book launched it was Meadow (Pearl's daughter ... a young teenager at the time) who had the first official THM job of packaging up books as the orders started to come trickling in. Then it was Charlie (Pearl's husband) who realized he had to leave his job and help Meadow package books full time as the orders started flying in. Then it was Sam (Serene's husband) who needed to come on and work full time too. Then, that's when things got crazy. They took on a life of their own as this message spread like wild fire and we could barely keep up. We have hired cousins, uncles, aunties, parents, long lost relatives of all kinds and plenty of friends and strangers ... all working alongside us to help spread this THM message.

We've always wanted to pass along anything to you that has blessed our own lives. If something makes our lives better it feels like a crime to keep it to ourselves. So, we're giving you our niece ... well her recipe book anyway. With sniffing noses, a couple prideful tears and ridiculous facial expressions that only proud Aunties can make, we're ushering her forward before you and offering you all that she has come to mean to us. ... food wise at least. Just like some of our recipes such as Pearl's Chili or Lazy Lasagna, or Serene's Good Girl Moonshine, Fat Stripping Frappa, or other crazy okra or baobab-laced creations you never thought you'd make but ... well, you are ... we know Rashida's favorites will be made over and over in your homes for years and generations to come as they are in ours.

Pulling off all the work that goes into creating a recipe book while pregnant is a big deal (we know) and taking all the beautiful pictures herself, on top of her busy home life, is a tribute to this capable woman who makes complicated things look easy. But be assured that the recipes, tips, and tricks which she brings to you in these pages, will be fast and simple enough even if you consider yourself a kitchen klutz. Rashida's recipes are tasty, but with a home-style feel, so basically anyone can make them. Everything inside these pages has been stamped with our approval ... well, not just ours ... there are many more eager mouths in our big extended family that have sampled and approved her recipes.

Can we indulge in one last story before we pass you fully into Rashida's capable hands? We sit at the back at our Hilltop Church (which is mostly made up of all the family members we've been talking about here along with some Hilltop neighbors and stragglers). Our Pastor Dad is 80 now but he can still preach up a storm. Anyway ... we don't sit at the back because we're backsliders ... Hehe. ... we do it because we are usually watching babies and Grandbabies (no nursery in our church) and well ... because lately the back of the church makes for a good opportunity to test out Rashida's latest treats for this book. Hey ... the good fuel helps us concentrate more on the sermon!

There was one time at church recently when we brought some of Rashida's Strawberry Gummy Worms (page 300) along with us. We passed some out to other family and friends sitting close by and suddenly a bunch of "Amens!" to our Dad's sermon got really expressive. These worms were sooo yummy and sooo awesome nobody could keep their excitement down. Dad really got into it as he thought we were digging his preaching ... and we were ... but the worms, too! Soon all sorts of other hungry church attending Hilltoppers were nudging their hands across the aisles for a try ... until half of the church was getting way louder on their hallelujahs ... all boosted by ... gummy worm revival!

Saying goodbye now because at this stage you're probably just being polite by reading through to the end of this and you're beyond ready to dig into the meat of this book. But as we leave, we want you to know that the name "Trim Healthy Future" also has a far deeper meaning. It represents fresh starts and new healthy tomorrows for you. If unhealthy food addictions are generations deep in your family . . . if you and your family have been snared by the epidemics of obesity and high blood sugar let this title be your declaration. Trim Healthy Future calls hope and new beginnings into your present but also into your future generations. It plants a pioneer flag of ground breaking new healthy food habits into the soil of your family's future. We believe Rashida's recipes will help you and your family get there . . . with much joy and licking of lips.

So, open these pages and let your future be lit up with fresh discoveries in flavor and health. This is the first, but we are sure not the last, of Rashida's offerings of love through healthy, joyful food to the world. There now . . . we went and got ourselves all choked up with aunty pride and sentiment . . . sniff sniff . . . enjoy . . . and be kind to her!

Love,
Serene and Pearl

P.S. Okay, truth be told, as you turn these pages, you'll notice we couldn't keep ourselves out of this book. Sure, you might get another "just Serene and Pearl" cookbook at some point in the next few years, but we couldn't help chiming in here, too. We're each giving you 12 of our latest and greatest recipes. And, well . . . you'll be able to tell they're ours not Rashida's because we're being our usual, true natured, long winded selves in our recipe intros. We're making these 12 each really count and giving you teaching sessions along with some of our recipes, sharing our new thoughts and

discoveries that have recently blessed our own lives in the hope they will bless yours too. Like we said . . . you're family now, so you're probably used to us being long winded and most of you just forgive us for it. You'll probably love Rashida's shorter, more to the point millennial style of introducing her recipes, but please know . . . she would have been even shorter if we didn't cajole her into giving any intros at all. She somehow missed the long-winded family gene even though we tried to pull it out of her! Here's a list of our recipes if you want a reference to them . . . all the other 170 or so are from our amazing niece.

PEARL'S RECIPES:

SERENE'S RECIPES:

CHAPTER 2
From Rashida (A "Truer" Tale)

Well ... I just read my aunties' letter to you. They made me out to be some sort of child prodigy slash humble saint. You'll be wondering why if I'm so humble, I boast so much about my recipes all through this book. I sent all my recipes one by one to my aunts to edit before publishing and they pretty much sent each one back saying something like ... "SELL THIS RECIPE, RASHIDS (their nickname for me)!!! WRITE AN INTRO THAT WILL MAKE EVERYONE WANT TO GO MAKE IT!!!"

So, I don't sound even remotely humble as I "sell" you my recipes all throughout these pages. But, if "selling" them gets you making them then I'll be happy. They'll slim you down and health you up ... it'll be worth it. But honestly, I am no virtuoso ... I'm just a young woman who loves to cook, loves to eat healthy and loves to merge the two.

Now for my own version of the story ... (I love my aunts but their version of the truth is sometimes a little larger than life.)

My aunties got the first part right. I grew up on a hilltop, deep in the Tennessee woods with nine siblings and far too many cousins to keep count. Seriously. All thirty something of us ran barefoot together through the woods to one another's homes every day of our lives, more like sisters and brothers than cousins. Hold on ... I guess I'm making it sound like we had moonshine stills, no education or electricity and thick accents LOL ... it wasn't like that.

These cousins I grew up with? Yeah you already figured . . . they were my Aunty Serene's and Aunty Pearl's children. My Mom (Vange) and her two sisters Serene and Pearl grew up down under in New Zealand and Australia so all of us children developed a mixture of their accents mingled with our American fathers' ones. And in case you're still worried . . . we all finished school and put on shoes occasionally—wink. And . . . well, in case you're the super-duper worried type . . . check out where I painstakingly put that apostrophe on that word "fathers'". Our Moms did have their own husbands—ha! Trying to set your mind at ease here.

At an early age, I discovered a love for cooking and experimenting with food. When I was around 5 years old, I had perfected my mud pie, mud cookie, and mud cake recipes . . . so much so that I would make elaborate versions of these, fully decorated with real icing and trimmings, and then would proudly bring them to cousins' birthday parties. The only issue was that I never told anyone they were made of mud until everyone started eating them!

My parents noticed how much I was obsessed with cooking with mud so they started to let me do some real cooking . . . brave of them! I always loved watching my mom and my nana cook. My mom taught me how to make bread and other easy foods to prepare when I was around 5. I was only around six or seven when my Aunty Serene was hard into her raw, vegan-only food stage, and I was always mesmerized watching her prepare her dishes. After homeschool, I would tear off through the woods to go watch her in her kitchen where she was dehydrating and juicing food all day. She made pizza crust out of carrot pulp! It was like watching a live cooking show! Meadow (Aunty Pearl's daughter) became my regular after school cooking companion. We loved making all kinds of treats together, and we would finish up with a royal tea party!

By the time I was eight (my Aunties said I was 6 . . . yes, I made lots of family meals at that age but I didn't really take over until I was 8), I became chief cook for my big family of two parents and a huge bunch of kids. Mom is a big believer in making room for one's talents so she let me take full reign. We always had a bunch of visitors over too so my passion for entertaining and making people happy through yummy food started early. This love for having people over and serving them my latest kitchen creations has only grown as I've reached adulthood and started my own family. It is a true love language for me, but these days my life is so busy . . . so as I hope you'll notice through my recipes, I like to keep things as quick and simple as possible.

I was a teenager when my aunties released their first book Trim Healthy Mama. My mom suggested I should read it for one of my required health books in high school. Well, it changed my life . . . and changed the way I cooked for my family. We had always used mostly healthy ingredients growing up but reading Trim Healthy Mama took my focus on healthy cooking to a whole new level. My family all loved the THM recipes I started to create but something else not quite so great happened. I became very passionate about THM . . . a little too much . . . then lots too much. I turned into a "THM Freak". All of the principles made so much sense to me and being the all-or-nothing person I was, I became very strict . . . almost to an unhealthy point. If I cheated, I would get down on myself and make myself work out extra hard the next day. My family members (especially my aunties) constantly told me to relax and live a mindset of "Food Freedom" but somehow, I couldn't hear it.

Thankfully, after meeting my husband (Jack), God used him to help me come out of being too obsessive over health. I am definitely still a Trim Healthy Mama enthusiast; I still believe in making wise health choices to honor my body and as a certified THM coach, I love helping others lose weight and get healthier using the THM principles, but being perfect doesn't consume me anymore. I tend to do the plan differently now . . . my strict rules approach is far behind me. The simplicity I've found feels so natural. I have had three healthy pregnancies eating the THM way and nursed my babies with plenty of milk. This means I include plenty of Crossovers in my eating plan (but I also enjoy lots of E meals and S meals, too . . . if you're new to this plan and don't know what these letters mean, they are explained on page 30).

These days I even let myself splurge on a date night and perhaps eat something off-plan on those occasions. Maybe to some that doesn't sound like a big deal, but in my pre-freedom approach to THM, I would not know how to forgive myself for choices like that. These days I enjoy all my Trim Healthy Mama meals, but I refuse to harbor shame or guilt if I make different choices for a meal or two. I know that it makes my husband happy to see me enjoy something special with him and not be a stuck-up health prude. Hehe!

Speaking of my husband, you'll hear a lot about him in this book. I created some of these recipes to replace the ones he loved from his childhood . . . extremely yummy, but unhealthy southern-style, Tennessee food. He has been such a good sport about my endeavors and showers my efforts with compliments when I get it right. When I don't . . . he'll eat them anyway!

Now that I have my own family, I have a love affair with making us all healthy, delicious food. It's really a form of art for me. That being said, I don't spend all day in the kitchen (you'll see that most of my recipes are not too time consuming), although this past year I spent a whole lot of time tweaking and perfecting all these recipes. I guess I am a cross between my Aunties Serene and Pearl. I have some Drive Thru Sue tendencies like Aunty Pearl because I want my recipes to be quick to whip up but Aunty Serene's purist ways still inspire me. I still love her out-of-the-box, passionate methods of getting more and more nutrients and hidden veggies into almost every recipe.

I have never been the type of person to write down my recipes until I decided to write this recipe book. They all just stayed in my head and I'd wing them every time. The same goes for photographing food. Photographing people and nature are what I have done since I was a young teenage girl, but this food photography thing has been a crazy fun, new adventure that I plan to continue to pursue.

I hope you enjoy all these mud pies! Err … I mean … recipes as much as we do in my home.

May your future be trim and healthy!

Love,
Rashida

CHAPTER 3

From Jack (Awww!)

This is to the woman who has held my heart (and my appetite) since I first laid eyes on you (and first tasted your omelet). You are a woman of true duality who possesses total love and devotion to your husband and family, and extreme passion and drive to see dreams fulfilled and stomachs stuffed. Your place on this spectrum of womanhood sits not in the middle, you exist uniquely on the ends of each extreme—loving devotion and fierce persistence.

You have supported my soul, stomach, and mind every step of the way in our journey through my medical training, schooling, moving, working long nights, rushed dinners, and lunches on the phone, all out of love. Never, and I mean never . . . as in not once, did you ever let me go unloved, unappreciated, or hungry (my cardinal emotion) during my long days in the hospital or in class. I still stand in admiration to have watched you rise so early every morning to prepare all the meals for yourself, our darling little wildcat daughters, and for of course, myself. Only then did you begin working laboriously on your prodigious recipes and photographs.

To finish without commenting on your consistency would be most despicable of myself. It took you approximately 15 months to write this book from start to finish. Not once did I see you falter in your commitment to the dream, or to your tediously consistent rate of recipe production and finalization. Not once did I hear you complain or despair (but if you did, I couldn't hear it over my obnoxiously loud chewing from the food you had just served me). Finally, not once did I see you ever give up on your vision nor place it above your love for your family.

The level of commitment and consistency I am highlighting here is but a glimmer of the whole woman that you are. You are a preeminent wife, a luminous mother, and a prestigious cook. You are the love of my life and the patron of life to my taste buds and stomach.

Sincerely,
Your loving, lustrous, hungry husband,

Jack Simpson

CHAPTER 4

Important Stuff!
(THM Nutshell & Vital Recipe Info)

HOW TO EAT THE THM WAY.

I suggest you purchase (or borrow) one of the THM books if you don't already know how this plan works. The *Trim Healthy Starter* book is a great way to learn the plan and it also has 50 easy starter recipes to get you going. Or you could get *Trim Healthy Table,* which has a quick-start guide plus hundreds more recipes. For a more in-depth dive into how and why the plan works for long term health and weight control, grab *The Trim Healthy Mama Plan* book.

　　The following is my summary of what THM is: (You still need to know the "why's" of Trim Healthy Mama so please do a little extra reading to fully understand the concepts.)

Trim Healthy Mama includes all food groups. It doesn't leave out either carbs or fats as our bodies were created for both and require both for optimum health. Weight loss happens when you focus on one fuel in your meals at a time, either carbs or fats … with a nice, healthy amount of protein to stabilize your blood sugar.

That's basically it!

Here's what the abbreviations mean after my recipes:

S means Satisfying. This recipe celebrates fats. *(weight loss)*

E means Energizing. This recipe celebrates healthy carbs. *(weight loss)*

FP means Fuel Pull because we are pulling the fat and carb fuels way back. This recipe is likely focusing on lean protein and/or non-starchy veggies or berries. *(weight loss)*

XO means Crossover. This recipe combines both fats and healthy carbs in ample yet safe amounts. *(not for weight loss)*

SUBS FOR SPECIAL INGREDIENTS:

These days the term "special ingredients" is a bit outdated. In the last couple of years most grocery stores have become excellent about stocking blood sugar friendly baking and cooking ingredients. For this reason, I am not labeling any of my recipes with an NSI (no special ingredients) sign since things that used to be "special" in the early years of the Trim Healthy Mama world are really more commonplace now. The majority of these recipes just use basic, old fashioned ingredients you are already used to. If I do call for ones you are less familiar with, just know that any recipe can pretty much be made NSI with the easy subs I've listed below.

On the whole, I use the Trim Healthy brand in my ingredients. And since I'm in the family, I'll be listing those here in my book. Please don't be mad at me for this . . . I've actually tried others, but I prefer the THM brand. It's important that you don't think you *have* to use THM items if you prefer others though. My aunties have always made it clear that you can use any other healthy item brand of your preference if you love it. I can honestly say Trim Healthy Mama has the highest quality and I do pretty much use them on a daily basis, but if you have other preferences here's what you'll do when I list the following THM items in my recipes:

- **Mineral Salt**—Use a high quality, unrefined Himalayan or Celtic sea salt

---

- **Baking Blend**—Make your own frugal blend using ⅓ each of coconut flour, almond flour, and golden flax meal. Those are all easily found at any grocery store. THM's Baking Blend is

FP and this frugal flour option is S, but it can still work in most recipes though I can't promise results will be exactly the same. You can also sub some oat fiber in that blend if you want to purchase some online (it is not usually in stores). If you want to get even closer to THM's Baking Blend you can look up copycat recipes online, although they are not usually any less expensive to make yourself-vs-buying.

———

Sweeteners—Note: when it comes to sweeteners, I like to have all three of THM's sweeteners on hand. I use the Pure Stevia Extract Powder and the Super Sweet Blend and Gentle Sweets for different things. To me, they shine in different recipes and sometimes I find things even taste better when they are combined . . .

- **Gentle Sweet**—Find a grocery store stevia or monk fruit plus erythritol sweetener blend that has a mild, sweet strength. It may or may not be stronger or weaker than Gentle Sweet though so you might have to play around with it and check out the Sweetener Conversion Chart on www.trimhealthymama.com.
- **Super Sweet Blend**—Find a grocery store stevia or monk fruit plus erythritol sweetener blend that is powerful in strength. It may or may not be stronger or weaker than Super Sweet Blend (probably not as strong) so you might have to play around with it and check out the Sweetener Conversion chart on www.trimhealthymama.com.
- **Pure Stevia Extract Powder**—Honestly . . . there's nothing out there like THM's for taste and quality in my mind, but feel free to shop around to find your own favorite extract. Stevia extract is the most economical way to sweeten as a little (a doonk which is 1/32 of a tsp.) goes a long way and can last you many months.

———

- **Baobab Boost Powder**—You can find baobab elsewhere online or even in some grocery stores sometimes. But, be sure to watch out for quality, which can vary greatly. Darker colored powders often mean they are less fresh.

———

- **Integral Collagen**—Find collagen elsewhere online or in stores, but please try to make sure it is grass-fed (collagen made from cows that are not grass-fed has shown to have too high levels of glyphosate).

———

- **Just Gelatin**—You can find unflavored gelatin in grocery stores which is porcine (from pigs). THM's is bovine (from pasture-raised cows) but you can use porcine if you'd rather . . . just fewer health benefits, but still works in recipes.

- **Gluccie**—This is konjac root powder with zero carbs and calories that I often use for thickening. Its official name is "Glucomannan" because it helps stabilize blood sugar, but my aunties have a thing for nicknames. While not offering the same slimming and blood sugar improving effects, xanthan gum (found at any grocery store) can be a good starch-free thickening sub.

- **Pristine Whey Protein**—Best to find a cross-flow micro-filtered whey isolate with only 1 carb and no other fillers. You can use a pea or hemp protein if you can't do dairy at all, but find one with only minimal carbs if possible.

- **Nutritional Yeast**—This can now be found at many grocery stores (even Walmart), but sadly, many of these brands contain synthetic B vitamins. Folic acid is a synthesized B vitamin that many experts believe can interfere with methylation for those with MTHFR genetic markers. So, it is best to try to find an unfortified nutritional yeast (like the THM brand is) that only contains naturally occurring folate which is excellent for those with MTHFR issues and pregnant women.

- **Natural Burst Extracts**—These THM extracts seem to be more powerful than regular so yes, you can use any brand of extract found in grocery stores but perhaps just use slightly more. It is best to find natural ones, but that is not a deal-breaker if you don't care about that sort of thing. THM does not currently have orange or peppermint so I use pure versions of those found at any grocery store.

- **Trim Healthy Chocolate Chips**—Use any stevia-sweetened chocolate chips you like. Do be careful about some that are in grocery stores with inulin in the ingredient list. There is nothing unhealthy about inulin, but it can cause a lot of people major bloating and gas.

- **Whole Husk Psyllium Flakes**—Although this ingredient isn't called for quite as often as some of the others here in this book, it is still a good idea to grab a bag if you can because you can always use them for my aunties' Wonder Wraps or PPP recipes (look those up on their website www.trimhealthymama.com as they have videos). You can find psyllium flakes in health stores if you don't want to purchase off the Trim Healthy Mama website, but be sure to buy the whole husk version, which is ground much coarser than psyllium powder. The powder is super fine and works differently.

- **Oat Fiber**—I haven't seen this in stores yet, but you can find it elsewhere online.

Note: There are lots of other products that THM has (or has on the way) that you may want to check out ... slimming cookies, bars, brownies, crackers, bread mixes, pizza crusts, and more that can make your THM life so easy and doable. But hey, if you prefer to stay super simple, shop only at your local grocery store, and give THM products the old shun-a-roo ... that is perfectly fine, too! My aunties will still luv ya' with muchness! I will, too.

THREE PECULIAR GROCERY STORE ITEMS

I list citric acid, pectin, and natural food colorings in some of my recipes. Citric acid and pectin are usually in the same place in your grocery store ... in the canning area with all the jars. I use liquid pectin as powder pectin has dextrose added to it and we don't want that! Save leftover liquid pectin in small Ziploc bags in your fridge. You can usually find natural food colorings right along-side the regular, dye-filled ones in the baking aisle.

DAIRY-FREE RECIPES

I have a ton of them in here! Look for the DF sign at the top of the recipe page. I don't use mayon-naise either as I have a strange aversion to it. If you're mayo-free, you're in luck.

R'S RECIPES

You'll notice I name some of my recipes as simply R's. That's because there are other versions of these recipes out there … not pretending I invented such staples as French toast, salsa, or granola! My aunties even have versions of some of these in their books and some THM bloggers surely have some great ones, too. Maybe you'll like somebody else's version, maybe you'll prefer mine, but just know that if you're making any of my recipes with an R in front of it, it is one of my major go-to recipes. I can count on it to work for me day in and day out and I included it in this book because I have a feeling it will really bless your life.

FROZEN-VS-FRESH MEAT AND FISH

Any time I call for meat items in my recipes e.g. 2½ pounds boneless, skinless chicken breasts … this means it needs to be either fresh or thawed from frozen. If starting from frozen, I will always mention the word "frozen".

WHAT'S A DOONK?

A doonk is ⅟₃₂ of a teaspoon—the measurement for a serving of Pure Stevia Extract Powder.

5

DANGEROUSLY DELICIOUS DRINKS

Just Like Orange Juice (FP)

Just Like Grapefruit Juice (FP)

Super Swig (FP)

Sparkling Cran-Ginger (FP)

Creamy Piña Colada (FP)

Tummy Soother (FP)

Iced Chaga Coffee (S)

Immunity Apple Cider (FP)

Winezalla (Adults Only)

Sparkling Strawberry
   Lemonade (FP)

Indian Cardamom Tea (FP)

Anytime Chai (FP)

Vanilla Caramel Coffee
   Creamer (S) or (FP)

Flying Flamingo (All-Day
   Sipper) (FP)

Cardinal Has Landed (All-Day
   Sipper) (FP)

Bird of Paradise (All-Day
   Sipper) (FP)

Parrot Punch (All-Day
   Sipper) (FP)

Spa Sip (All-Day Sipper) (FP)

Hydrated Hummingbird (All-Day
   Sipper) (FP)

This chapter comes first for a very important reason … it is my favorite! I absolutely love making and serving drinks. It's a total passion of mine as drinks are such an integral part of my life. Technically, they're a part of everyone's daily life, but no need for semantics! (Hehe) When I am in my master lab (aka "my kitchen") concocting new drink recipes, I often recite to myself, *"I am the drink-master!"* Whether this title actually does anything for me or not, it sure resonates well inside my head!

I love having something special to sip on prior to or after eating. They help me close a meal, they help me between meals, they help me stay full for longer and, most importantly, they keep me hydrated, healthy and happy. For some women, it might be jewelry that brings delight but for me … drinks bring on the happies.

I'm big on having company over and always look forward to serving drinks for them. It only takes a few minutes to whip up one of my latest concoctions and voila, they are an instant hit! Drinks have this amazing ability to go from tying a special meal together, to softening the atmosphere for a lovely chat when a friend stops by.

They also work wonders for my husband Jack who as a health care provider, is constantly around sick people. I just pack his lunch bag up with an immune boosting loaded drink and off he goes … amazingly, he stays so healthy … even in the midst of pandemics!

My girls love them too. These drinks are especially important in their diets since I don't buy them juice (aka sugar water). Having a healthy drink that keeps them hydrated and that they love is a win, and I know it can be for your kids too. I also make popsicles for them with a lot of these drinks. They think it's so much fun, and it's a good reward for them after they (attempt) to clean their room.

You can choose a decaf option for any of the teas mentioned in these recipes if you prefer. This is what I normally do since I like to get my caffeine from my coffee and I want to be able to drink them at any time of the day. I truly hope you enjoy making and drinking these just as much as I do!

Note: I have split this Dangerously Delicious Drinks chapter into two sections. The first section is just for drinks that you have with a meal or a snack (or even as your full snack, if you prefer). The second section is for my "All-Day Sippers". Yes, I'm keeping the family tradition my aunties started for all-day sipping alive and kicking here! These sippers all make about two-quarts, which is a huge amount! You can use them as sippers just for you for a day or two, or share with family members.

JUST LIKE ORANGE JUICE

Makes Multiple Servings (about 4–6)

Do you miss orange juice with breakfast or just any time? It's back, baby! But now it's better than ever because this "juice" balances your blood sugar, boosts your immune system, and provides you with oodles of antioxidants…far more than orange juice does. This is all thanks to baobab, which you might notice due to how often I use it, is one of my absolute favorite healthy foods and the slimming and immune-boosting star ingredient in this drink. Baobab has more antioxidants than any other food on the planet and has a unique fiber which has shown in studies to melt belly fat off ya'!

½ cup Baobab Boost Powder
1½ tsp. citric acid
5–7 doonks Pure Stevia Extract Powder
2 pinches Mineral Salt
2 quarts water
2½ tsp. pure orange extract
Optional 5–6 drops natural orange food
  coloring

1. Add everything minus the water and natural coloring to a pitcher. Then slowly add half the water while whisking any clumps that form. Add remaining water and natural food coloring.
2. Serve chilled or add ice.

JUST LIKE GRAPEFRUIT JUICE

Makes Multiple Servings (about 4–6)

I have always loved grapefruit juice but I never drink it because it's loaded with sugar. I decided to make a healthy knock off version and it worked. Not only does it not have sugar, it has wonderful health benefits! The collagen adds a nice amount of protein so it is perfect to have with a lower protein meal such as a bowl of oatmeal or a sprouted bread sandwich.

Pearl Chimes In MAMAS!!! THIS IS ME IN ALL CAPS SHOUTING ABOUT THIS DRINK!! (Okay, I'll calm down.) Rashida brought this over to my house and since then I've been nuts about it ... I can't get enough! Trust me on this. If you are a 100% grapefruit juice lover like I am and have really missed it since you realized juice is not great for your blood sugar ... this hits the spot ... in fact, Rashida is such a genius, I think this is even better than the real thing! Never been a grapefruit juice lover in the past? Jump on board! You'll thank me for the push!

¼ cup Gentle Sweet
¼ cup Integral Collagen
⅓ cup Baobab Boost Powder
8 oz. hot water
2 Tbs. Super Sweet Blend

1 Tbs. citric acid
¼ tsp. Mineral Salt
optional 2 – 4000 mg vitamin C*
6 cups cool water (or more if needed)
Optional natural red food coloring

1. Add everything but the cool water and natural coloring to a blender. Blend until smooth then pour into a pitcher. Add cool water then add drops of natural food coloring until a pinkish/grapefruit color is obtained. This juice is quite tart as written (the way I prefer it) so serve over plenty of ice or add more water as needed for your tastes.

*Note: I buy vitamin C tablets as they are the least expensive that I can find. I crush them with the bottom of a jar before adding to drinks, but you can use vitamin C powder, if preferred.

SUPER SWIG

Makes 1–2 Servings

I've always been on a mission to get more fresh greens into my husband Jack. I'd sometimes pack salads for him to take to work, but he let me know they took far too long to eat on his short lunch breaks. (I can eat my salad super-fast, but we are all talented in different ways.) I know my

Aunty Serene created her Earth Milk drink as a way to get more greens in, but my husband is not the type to carry around a big mason jar by that name (wink) and he'd just rather get a green drink over and done with than sip it all day.

I quickly whiz Super Swig up in the morning for him to take to work and drink on the drive there ... or to swig before he sees his first patient. He loves how it fits perfectly into his fast-paced lifestyle and he actually likes the taste! He'll sometimes gulp it down with his breakfast before he even leaves the house. He even drinks it with dinner sometimes, if he's not in a salad eating mood in the evening. Even though I came up with this recipe for Jack, we all drink it now. I feel extra energized when I have it and our girls love it as well (I slightly dilute it for them). If you have toddlers who can't eat greens without choking, this is perfect for them! This can be a side to any meal or snack if you are tired of salads or just don't have time for them. Or, put a little collagen or whey in it for protein and it can be your complete snack.

2 cups water	5 frozen strawberries
3 large handfuls fresh kale or spinach	2 tsp. Super Sweet Blend

1. Throw everything into a blender and blend until smooth.

Note: You can add 1 tsp. Dynamic Duo Greens Powder, which boosts nutrition even more (spirulina and moringa are two of the most powerful greens on earth). But I created this before THM made this powder available, so you sure don't have to. It is still super health boosting simply as written.

SPARKLING CRAN-GINGER

Makes Multiple Servings (about 4)

I can barely express how much I love this and how it has saved me from many dismal days! I created it when I was just a few weeks pregnant with my first baby and feeling miserable. The ginger and bubbles helped with my nausea and the cranberries made it taste so delightful that it helped me make it through the worst of those "blah" feeling days. Since cranberries are loaded with polyphenols and antioxidants, they super charged my health while pregnant (and beyond). During pregnancy, a woman can be more susceptible to UTI's so the cranberries are also a great preventative against that. But don't just drink this when you're pregnant. Anytime is the perfect time . . . even my husband loves it!

Note: Buy heaps of cranberries when they are in season and then save in your freezer to use in lots of my recipes.

2 cups fresh or frozen cranberries
3 cups water
2 Tbs. ginger powder
2 Tbs. Super Sweet Blend
2 pinches Mineral Salt
Optional 4000 mg vitamin-C *
24 oz. sparkling water

1. Place cranberries in a pot with the 3 cups of water and ginger powder. Place a lid on the pot-and bring to a boil.

2. When cranberries have all started to pop, remove lid, stir then let simmer on low for 3–5 minutes. Let the mixture cool off then pour it through a cheesecloth or super fine strainer. Now add the Super Sweet Blend, salt, vitamin-C, and sparkling water. Best served over ice.

*Note: I buy vitamin C tablets as they are the least expensive I can find. I crush them with the bottom of a jar before adding to drinks, but you can use vitamin C powder, if preferred.

CREAMY PIÑA COLADA

Makes Multiple Servings (about 4)

This tastes so indulgently creamy yet it's a FP! How cool is that? Keep some in your fridge and you can have a big glass on the side of your lunch, dinner or snack, or even as an after-dinner dessert style drink. This helps fill you up so you stay more satisfied after your meal and it brings balance to your protein intake with much needed glycine and proline amino acids from the collagen. Those amino acids are very important for the health of our immune systems, our skin, hair and nails but they are sadly missing from our modern diet.

4 cups unsweetened almond or cashew milk	3 Tbs. Super Sweet Blend
1 Tbs. MCT oil	½ tsp. Mineral Salt
1 Tbs. citric acid	1 tsp. Gluccie
2 Tbs. Integral Collagen	2 tsp. Coconut Natural Burst Extract
2 Tbs. Unflavored Pristine Whey Protein	2 tsp. Pineapple Natural Burst Extract
3 Tbs. Baobab Boost Powder	2 cups water

1. Make your choice. Want to use up this whole drink now? (Perhaps you have company over or your whole family wants some.) Or would you rather enjoy one glass at a time?

2. If using all at once, put all ingredients except water in a blender and blend smooth. Then pour into a pitcher. Put water into blender along with 3½–4 cups ice and blend until ice is in tiny, fun-sized pieces then add to pitcher. For just one serving, blend all ingredients and then pour into pitcher and refrigerate. When ready to have a drink, blend a cupful in blender with 1 cup of ice . . . or just pour over ice.

TUMMY SOOTHER

Makes Multiple Servings (about 6–8)

You know what happens when you eat a lot of those sulfuric veggies like cauliflower or cabbage, right? Or perhaps, the beans, or legumes are kicking in… Haha! Tummy Soother to the rescue! The 3-star ingredients in this drink… chamomile, fennel and ginger are all brilliantly talented at soothing a bloated, gassy belly. But this creamy drink has such a nice flavor, don't save it for just when you are feeling gassy. The taste and health benefits are fantastic for no trouble tummy times too. My little girls really love this.

> **Note:** Don't worry if this drink slightly separates, just give it a little stir and voila!

1 Tbs. ground fennel	1 tsp. Maple Natural Burst Extract
2–3 tsp. Super Sweet Blend	Optional 2 Tbs. Integral Collagen
1½ tsp. ginger powder	2 cups water
¼ tsp. Mineral Salt	5 cups unsweetened almond or cashew milk
Optional 1 tsp. blackstrap molasses	3 chamomile tea bags
1 tsp. Vanilla Natural Burst Extract	

1. Add everything except tea bags to a large pot, whisk well then add tea bags. Cover pot with a lid and bring to a boil. Pull off heat. Discard tea bags and enjoy hot or over ice.

ICED CHAGA COFFEE

Makes a Single Serve

My Dad gave me some of his special stash of chaga powder and told me I should make a creamy iced coffee drink with it to put in this recipe book. He's crazy about chaga (which is a super healthy mushroom) and all the wonderful health benefits it contains. It lowers inflammation, boosts immune and brain function and is loaded with minerals and vitamins. Well, thanks, Dad . . . you've given me the replacement for one of those sugary coffee drinks at Starbucks . . . but this is way healthier and super kind to my waistline. For more info about chaga mushrooms just look them up on "Dr. Google". MedicalNewsToday.com has some great info on them.

Note: Dad actually found his Chaga at a discount store, but you can find it online . . . just look around for the best deal.

1 cup chilled coffee
1 cup ice
⅓ cup of coffee creamer from page: 53
¾ tsp. chaga powder

1. Place everything into a blender and blend until smooth.

IMMUNITY APPLE CIDER

Makes Multiple Servings (about 4–6)

This literally tastes just like the cider you get offered at every fall and Christmas party, but that stuff causes waistline explosions! This is slimming, super healthy, and immune-boosting . . . WHAT??? Keep this drink around during cold and flu seasons and the next time you go to a gathering, bring this along to help keep you and your friends healthfully indulged! You can thank me later!

8–9 cups water
3 cinnamon sticks
20 cloves
¼ tsp. Mineral Salt
1 tsp. blackstrap molasses
¾ tsp. cinnamon
½ tsp. pure orange extract
2000 mg vitamin C*
1 Tbs. Super Sweet Blend (or more to taste)
¼ cup Gentle Sweet
⅓ cup + 2 Tbs. apple cider vinegar
Optional 2 Tbs. Integral Collagen
Optional ¼ cup Baobab Boost Powder

1. Add everything but the collagen to a large pot, cover with a lid and cook on high to bring to a boil. Reduce heat to medium-low, whisk in the collagen. You can continue to let it simmer if you want an even bolder flavor and your house will smell even more amazing!

*Note: I buy vitamin C tablets as they are the least expensive I can find. I crush them with the bottom of a jar before adding to drinks, but you can use vitamin C powder, if preferred.

WINEZALLA (ADULTS ONLY)

Makes 2–4 Servings

You know those sparkling sweet wines that are horrible for your waistline? They're back on plan! (Well, not those actually . . . but this is!) I can definitely enjoy a glass of dry wine which has always been a part of the THM plan, in moderation, but I gotta admit . . . I missed girly wine sometimes . . . you know . . . sweet and sassy wine with a hint of bubble? The sort that so many of us females delight in. This is perfect for when I feel like more of a dessert drink or if I want a lighter taste than dry wine. You also get to drink two full glasses using only 4 oz. of wine. BOOM! I like to serve this in a glass with a few frozen berries added . . . makes it extra cold and gives it more color and pizzazz. Great for girls' nights or book clubs . . . just use moderation, of course!

8 oz. dry red wine (Cabernet, Merlot, Pinot, or Shiraz)
1–2 doonks Pure Stevia Extract Powder
⅓ cup Gentle Sweet
½ tsp. citric acid or juice of 1 lemon
24 oz. plain or naturally flavored sparkling water (chilled)

1. Mix wine in a 2-quart jar or pitcher with everything but the water, stir until sweetener and citric acid have dissolved for the most part, then add sparkling water.

Note: I am not labeling this with S, E, or FP because alcohol doesn't really have a fuel type on THM as it burns differently to food fuels. You can drink this with any meal type though as it is low in carbs.

SPARKLING STRAWBERRY LEMONADE

Makes Multiple Servings (about 4)

This is so refreshing . . . especially in the summer time. If I'm going to have company over, I like to have this pre-made in the fridge. I just wait to add the sparkling water and ice until right before they walk in the door, so it's nice and sparkly on everyone's tongues. You'll notice there is actually no lemon juice in this drink, the lemon extract and citric acid give it a lovely lemony taste without you having to juice a bunch of lemons. They are nice to use as a garnish though if you want to take that extra step.

5 fresh or frozen strawberries
1 tsp. citric acid
5–7 doonks Pure Stevia Extract Powder
2 pinches Mineral Salt
½–1 tsp. pure lemon extract
Optional few drops natural red food coloring
2–3 cups ice
24 oz. sparkling water

1. Cut strawberries into tiny pieces (like the size of peanuts) add to a pitcher along with everything but the water, stir then add the water.

INDIAN CARDAMOM TEA

Makes Multiple Servings (about 4–6)

Don't let the title of this drink deter you if you are not familiar with cardamom. This hot, creamy tea is very delicious and soothing to the body, taste buds, and mood. The health benefits of Carda-mom are crazy amazing! I love Indian food and my favorite drink at Indian restaurants is their sweet, cardamom tea. Now I can have it healthfully at home or take it on the go in a stay warm mug.

---

6 regular or decaf black tea bags
3 cups water
1½ tsp. ground cardamom
4½ cups unsweetened *vanilla almond or
   cashew milk
⅛ tsp. Mineral Salt
1 Tbs. Super Sweet Blend

1. Add tea bags and water to a large pot, bring to a boil then stir in cardamom, fol-lowed by all remaining ingredients, con-tinue to heat until nice and hot. Remove tea bags and run through a sieve before serving.

Note: If using plain, unsweetened almond milk, add 1 tsp. Vanilla Natural Burst Extract.

ANYTIME CHAI

Makes Multiple Servings (about 4–6)

I love this chilled and poured over ice for hot summer days or hot and cozy in the winter…AMAZ-ING! The ability to use decaf black tea bags also makes this a drink you can have day or night. See where I was going with the name? No, this is not an all-day-sipper due to the amounts of almond milk in it but it is an any-time-drink!

4 cups water	2 doonks (¹⁄₁₆ tsp.) black pepper
4–6 regular or decaf black tea bags	5 doonks Pure Stevia Extract Powder
2 cups unsweetened almond or cashew milk	1 Tbs. ground cinnamon
1 tsp. Coconut Natural Burst Extract	⅛ tsp. Mineral Salt
⅛ tsp. ground cloves	

1. Bring water and tea bags to a boil in a large pot, then start whisking in each spice and sweetener but be careful not to rupture tea bags. (You can take them out and put them back, if you're not a very careful person.)

2. Add almond milk and continue to simmer until it's a beautiful drinking temp. Or chill, if preferred, and have over ice. (Top with Fat Free Reddi Wip if desired.)

VANILLA CARAMEL COFFEE CREAMER OR

Makes Multiple Servings

Ladies and Gents!!! (Even though I doubt there are many men reading). Here you go . . . a healthy but absolutely delicious, perfectly sweetened creamer. One of the hardest things for people to give up on a sugar-free lifestyle is flavored creamers. I have seen many of you on the THM Facebook groups asking (not so gently . . . hehe) for a THM one. So, if you're mourning over your dearly departed coffee creamer, I dedicate this recipe to you. Yes, you can even have it when you're doing Deep S! My favorite way to have this is with iced coffee; tastes like a coffee from your favorite coffee shop. Use just a tablespoon or two in your drink for FP needs or with your E meals, but feel free to enjoy more for S. Oh . . . and if you prefer a plain coffee creamer without flavors just omit the extracts.

1½ cups unsweetened almond milk
½ cup MCT oil
¼ cup Gentle Sweet
¼ cup Unflavored Pristine Whey Protein
¼ cup Integral Collagen
½ tsp. Vanilla Natural Burst Extract
½ tsp. Caramel Natural Burst Extract
⅛ tsp. Mineral Salt

1. Add all ingredients into a blender, blend until smooth.
2. Pour into a jar with a lid, refrigerate.

Note 1: To make this dairy-free, you can replace the whey protein with ⅛ cup collagen and also add ½ teaspoon Sunflower Lecithin . . . it won't look as white in color, but still tastes good.

Note 2: To lighten this up further calorie wise, use just ¼–⅓ cup MCT oil . . . if you are post-menopausal and struggle to lose pounds, or if you burn fat fuels very slowly for other reasons, you might want to try that trick.

ALL-DAY SIPPERS

FLYING FLAMINGO

All-Day Sipper—Makes about 1½–2 quarts, can be shared with other family members or use for a day (or two!) worth of sipping for yourself.

If you've scrolled through this chapter, you're probably wondering why the heck all the bird names for my sips??? Crazy, I know, but it runs deep . . . Aunty Serene got the bird theme going with her infamous "Singing Canary" sipper . . . I'm just grabbing the family baton from her and offering you more ways to rock your health and your taste buds. These bird related names just kept flying out of my brain (pun intended), so I have to say they come to me honestly. Oh, and I have always loved birds . . . I even had a pet parrot growing up, and yes, it talked a lot . . . so that could be part of the reason, too! This sip is such an excellent way to enjoy drinking all those stupendous green tea antioxidants that you know you should, but you probably don't often get around to doing . . . if you're anything like me.

4 regular or decaf green tea bags	1½ tsp. Natural Burst Pineapple Extract
1 large coffee mug just off boil water	2 pinches Mineral Salt
Optional 2 tsp. Integral Collagen	½ tsp. citric acid
3 Tbs. Baobab Boost Powder	4½ cups water
2½–3 Tbs. Super Sweet Blend	½ cup lemon juice (fresh or bottled)

1. Steep tea bags in boiled water for five minutes, remove and discard tea bags and add collagen if using. Stir well and then transfer to a pitcher or 2-quart jar.
2. Stir in the baobab powder, whisking out any clumps that form, then add all the other ingredients. Pour into your 2-quart jar or pitcher and then fill to the top with ice.

CARDINAL HAS LANDED

All-Day Sipper—Makes about 1½–2 quarts, can be shared with other family members or use for a day (or two!) worth of sipping for yourself.

Why this name??? Well, just follow me here in my bizarre train of thought. Here in Tennessee, we see cardinals all year. The mint in this sip slightly reminds me of winter, but the lemons remind me of summer. Black tea can be enjoyed in spring or fall. So, just like Tennessee's cardinal . . . you can delight in this drink all year round. How's that for logic? Growing up, whenever we went to one of our dear family friend's (Peggy Fitzpatrick) house, she would always have a big pitcher of mint laced, hint of lemon, black tea out for everyone to enjoy. I always loved it, I think that's what inspired me to try and replicate it.

6 decaf (or regular) black tea bags
1 large mug just off the boil water
¾ cup fresh or bottled lemon juice
3–3½ Tbs. Super Sweet Blend
½–¾ tsp. pure peppermint extract
1½ quarts water

1. Steep the tea bags in boiled water for 5 minutes while you add all other ingredients to a pitcher or 2-quart jar. Discard tea bags then pour brewed tea into pitcher or jar with other ingredients. Serve chilled or over ice.

BIRD OF PARADISE

All-Day Sipper—Makes about 1½–2 quarts, can be shared with other family members or use for a day (or two!) worth of sipping for yourself.

I originally thought to call this "Put the Lime in the Coconut Sip". You know, the lyrics from that song . . . "Put the lime in the coconut and shake it all around," at least I think that's how it goes. But now that I have this bird theme going, Bird of Paradise suits this really well . . . especially if you imagine yourself on a tropical island, sitting on the beach with the sun shining down while you sip this right out of a coconut.

Juice from 5–6 medium limes
¼ tsp. Pure Stevia Extract Powder
¼ tsp. Mineral Salt
2 tsp. Coconut Natural Burst Extract
7 cups water

1. Squeeze the limes into a 2-quart mason jar or pitcher then add all remaining ingredients. Stir it up and serve over ice.

PARROT PUNCH

All-Day Sipper—Makes about 1½–2 quarts, can be shared with other family members or use for a day (or two!) worth of sipping for yourself.

The first time I made this drink my husband was like … "This is good, it tastes like Hawaiian Punch!" My girls devoured it too; they also love it when I make popsicles with it (just pour it in popsicle molds). If you have hibiscus tea you can use that in it as well, just don't use the citric acid or natural food coloring because hibiscus is naturally tart and has a beautiful crimson red color.

A bit off topic but that parrot I mentioned in another intro to one of my sippers? I had her when I was in high-school. Every time you walked by, she would say, "Praise the Lord!" She lived in my room along with my three sisters, so it was a good reminder to get our praise going.

3 Tbs. lemon juice, fresh or bottled
½ tsp. Natural Burst Pineapple Extract
½ tsp. Natural Burst Cherry Extract
¼ tsp. Natural Burst Coconut Extract
1 Tbs. Baobab Boost Powder
1 Tbs. Super Sweet Blend

3–5 doonks Pure Stevia Extract Powder
½ tsp. citric acid
2 pinches Mineral Salt
Optional 3–5 drops red natural food coloring
 (or 4 hibiscus tea bags)
2 quarts water

1. Add all ingredients minus the water into a pitcher, stir up until you have no clumps.
2. Add the 2-quarts of water and chill or serve over ice. (If you'd rather use hibiscus tea, remove 1 cup of water from the 2-quarts. Brew 3–4 tea bags for five minutes in the 1 cup of boiled water.)

Note: Don't do the hibiscus-version if you're pregnant or nursing . . . or just reduce to 1 cup a day.

SPA SIP

All-Day Sipper—Makes about 1½–2 quarts, can be shared with other family members or use for a day (or two!) worth of sipping for yourself.

Okay, time to ditch the bird names. This can be an All-Day Sipper, but I wasn't feeling birdie when naming this one. Cucumber, one of the star ingredients here is so cleansing to both the digestive system and skin and ginger (the other star) gets your body burning fat and reduces bloat in your digestive system. With these benefits in mind, I feel so healthy whenever I make this drink…feels like I'm giving myself a spa-like treatment (well, that's what I tell myself). It's also absolutely delicious! My good friend/boss (Lisa) did not like any green veggie-based drinks until she tried this. She loved it so much that I now make it for her regularly at work.

4 medium cucumbers
4 lemons
4–5 oz. fresh ginger
7–8 cups of water
2 Tbs. Super Sweet Blend
Optional ⅓ cup apple cider vinegar

1. Cut cucumbers, lemons, and ginger into chunks (if the skin is not too thick don't worry about peeling lemon and don't bother taking seeds out if your blender is powerful enough to blend them).
2. Put ⅓ of the chopped ingredients into the blender with 1½ cups of water. Blend until smooth and then strain through a cheesecloth or other fine strainer into a large bowl or pot. Repeat process two more times until the chopped ingredients are used up.
3. Add remaining water, sweetener, and apple cider vinegar (if desired) to the strained liquid. Serve chilled or over ice.

HYDRATED HUMMINGBIRD

All-Day Sipper—Makes about 1½–2 quarts, can be shared with other family members or use for a day (or two!) worth of sipping for yourself.

Oh my, this sipper is wonderful for keeping you hydrated! It's packed with vitamins and super foods... and it tastes great, if I may boast. My aunties Serene and Pearl don't usually love the idea of putting berries in All-Day Sippers, as they don't want all of us sipping on fuel all day... but I showed them this recipe and they said the berries are such a small amount, most people should do fine with this as a sipper. Just assess how you do... if the slight amount of fruit sugar in the berries proves too much for your own unique body to burn while drinking this all day... use this as a drink with your meals instead. But they doubt that will happen... all that ginger in here is just going to rev your metabolism!

1 medium cucumber, chopped	2 pinches Mineral Salt
3 stalks celery, chopped	6 cups water
3–4 ounces fresh ginger, chopped	2–3 Tbs. Super Sweet Blend
2 lemons	¼ cup frozen raspberries

1. Chop veggies, ginger, and lemons into chunks (You can remove skin from the lemons if you want, but I seldom do. If the skin is not too thick, I leave it on.) Throw them into a blender (I don't even bother taking out the lemon seeds... all of it goes in) with 2 cups of the water. Blend until everything is completely smooth.
2. Strain pulp out by pouring through a cheesecloth or a very fine sieve.
3. Add the remaining 4 cups of water, plus the rest of the ingredients. Stir and serve over ice.

Note: Feel free to add 1 tsp. Dynamic Duo Greens Powder to this sipper if you want.

6

SIMPLY SPLENDID
SHAKES & SMOOTHIES

Raspberry Coconut Smoothie **FP** or **E**

Piña Colada Smoothie **S**

Kiwi Strawberry Smoothie **E**

Mint Chip Ice Cream Shake **S**

Chocolate Covered Strawberry Shake **E**

Chocolate Banana Smoothie **E**

Strawberry Banana Smoothie **E**

Pumpkin Shake **S**

Strawberry Lemon Seed Shake **FP**

Almond Blueberry Oat Shake **E**

Greenie Meanie Yuck Yum **FP**, **S**, or **E**

Pre, Pro, & Post Shake **FP** or Light **E**

Aaahhh....so delicious, slimming, and healthy! Shakes and smoothies are fast, out-the-door options that have everything you and I need in them to start the day (or even to end the day as a delightful evening snack or dessert if you want to share with a family member or two). They're perfect as speedy, sweet and super refreshing afternoon snacks or lunches in the summer....or any time of the year if you don't mind drinking cold things when it's 10 degrees outside! I've been known to put on a heavy sweater and go for it!

But the thing I like best about shakes and smoothies? I get to hide so many awesome, health building foods in them that my family might otherwise turn their noses up at. My little girls and husband usually have no idea about some of the sneaky ingredients. They just chug them down and what they don't know only helps them!

Most of these shakes and smoothies make a large amount and I created them that way because my girls love sharing them with me. So, I'll end up with half a shake (they share the other half) and I'll have that with a light meal or snack. But okay, let's be honest...sometimes I hide in the bathroom and drink the whole thing myself . . . a girl's gotta do what a girl's gotta do.

Note: For the shakes and smoothies that are rather large, I have noted on the serving size that you can share (they make close to a quart or more). The ones that just say "Makes 1 Serving" might not be enough to share unless you just want a cupful or so each.

RASPBERRY COCONUT SMOOTHIE

 FP OR **E**

Makes 1 Large Single Serve (or can be shared with a family member for 2 smaller servings)

This one is a family favorite in my house. The kefir compliments the raspberries well since they're both tart, then the coconut extract balances that tartness out making this one of my favorite smoothies. (If you're not into raspberries you can sub them out for strawberries and it tastes great too.)

If buying low-fat kefir from the store and using it straight from the refrigerated bottle, this drink would be considered E-ish as store-bought kefir still has a few carbs left over in the form of milk sugars. You can double ferment your kefir to reduce milk sugars and make this more of a FP drink. To do this, use homemade low-fat or fully skimmed kefir and do a double ferment or use low-fat, store-bought and leave it out on the counter (still sealed) for another 12 hours at room temperature before refrigerating.

1 cup frozen raspberries
1½ cups plain, low-fat kefir
½ cup ice
2 pinches Mineral Salt
1½–2 Tbs. Super Sweet Blend
½ tsp. Vanilla Natural Burst Extract
¾ tsp. Coconut Natural Burst Extract
Optional 1 Tbs. Integral Collagen or 2
  Tbs. Unflavored Pristine Whey Protein
  (optional for added protein)
Optional: unsweetened coconut flakes

1. Blend everything up but the coconut flakes until smooth. Top with coconut flakes, if desired.

PIÑA COLADA SMOOTHIE

Makes 1 Large Serving (or can be shared with a family member for 2 smaller servings)

Nothing better than a good creamy tropical tasting smoothie in my mind! This one hits the spot every time I make it and there's no dairy involved so I take my curtsy to all you dairy-free-ers! My girls love it, too . . . even more so on hot summer days. You get such tropical vibes from this, but without the fuss of waiting for your pineapple to ripen or making sure you have frozen pineapple. It's a smoothie that almost entirely comes from your pantry!

½ cup canned coconut milk*
1 cup unsweetened almond or cashew milk
1 Tbs. plus 1 tsp. Super Sweet Blend
2 Tbs. Baobab Boost Powder
1½ Tbs. Integral Collagen
¼ tsp. citric acid
1 tsp. Pineapple Natural Burst Extract
½ tsp. Gluccie or xanthan gum
2 pinches Mineral Salt
1½ cups ice
Optional: unsweetened coconut flakes

1. Blend everything up but the coconut flakes until smooth. Top with coconut flakes, if desired.

*****Note:** I use Imperial Dragon Coconut Milk, which I find at Walmart. If you use another brand such as Thai Kitchen it will likely be much higher in calories and fat, so best to stick to ⅓ cup for that brand.

KIWI STRAWBERRY SMOOTHIE

Makes a Single Serve

I guess I love "kiwis" so much probably because I'm related to a whole bunch of them. Get it??? People from New Zealand are called Kiwis. (It's bad when you have to explain your jokes.) But even if you don't have Kiwi family members or friends, you too can love kiwis as much as I do through this smoothie. Kiwis are super high in vitamins (including C, K, & E), folate, and potassium. If you look them up, you'll find even more amazing reasons why you should eat more of them. I won't go into them all; just go make it!

2 peeled kiwis
12 frozen strawberries
1 cup unsweetened almond or cashew milk
2 pinches Mineral Salt
½–1 Tbs. Super Sweet Blend
Optional 1½ Tbs. Integral Collagen
1 cup ice

1. Throw everything into the blender and blend until smooth.

MINT CHIP ICE CREAM SHAKE

Makes 1 Large Serving (or can be shared with a family member for 2 smaller servings)

Aunty Serene started the okra-in-smoothies craze a few years back, but I'm not about to let her have all the glory! Around that time, I was still a teenager and was making my own okra ice cream. My parents would often have people over and I would very proudly make them "Okra Mint Chip Ice Cream" for dessert. But I have to be honest, while I loved it and reeeeaaalllly wanted everyone else to love it too, I got a lot of mixed reviews. Some people dug it and some people … well, you know … they just thought it was weird. So, I decided to tone it down and make an ice cream shake. This toned-down version worked … no more weird reactions!

So, sorry, Aunty Serene … those Secret Smoothies you put in your cookbooks? They're okra wussies compared to this one. You had only a measly ¾–1 cup okra in your recipes. Dear, Sweet Okrafied Aunty … I challenge you to try this 2-cup version! If you can taste the okra in this, I'll buy next time we go out for coffee. I'm pretty confident you'll be paying for your own … ha!

But … I'm not finished with this intro yet … my aunties told me to "sell" my recipes to you. Well, I'm fired up about this shake. Not only is it filled with okra, but it also contains spinach … what??? Yes, this is literally packed with healthy, slimming veggies and my family is none the wiser. Although this can be a single serving, I like to share it and have it on the side of our lunch with my girls. Both girls love it; they consider it like an ice cream/shake treat and I have even made popsicles with it for them. They both gag when eating cooked, plain okra so this is a great way to get this gut-healing and vitamin C rich veggie into them.

---

2 cups frozen chopped okra
1 cup unsweetened almond or cashew milk
1 cup fresh spinach
1½ tsp. Super Sweet Blend
2–3 Tbs. Gentle Sweet
¼ tsp. pure peppermint extract

½ tsp. Vanilla Natural Burst Extract
1½ Tbs. Integral Collagen
1 Tbs. Unflavored Pristine Whey Protein Powder
2 large pinches Mineral Salt
2–3 Tbs. Trim Healthy Chocolate Chips or
   85% dark chocolate chopped up

---

1. Place everything but the chocolate chips into a blender. Blend until smooth, then add the chocolate and blend for a few seconds or until they have broken up enough to fit through a straw.

Note: Feel free to add 1 tsp. Dynamic Duo Greens Powder to this but try without the first time you make it.

CHOCOLATE COVERED STRAWBERRY SHAKE

Makes 1 Large Serving (or can be shared with a family member for 2 smaller servings for a snack or part of your meal)

You may be wondering why I label this an E when it only contains frozen strawberries rather than other higher sugar fruit. Well, the amount of strawberries here is large . . . about 2 cups worth so that goes beyond FP amounts. At the very most it is a light E but whatever fuel it is . . . even if it is in no man's land, it is super healthy and super delish!

1½ cups unsweetened almond or cashew milk
Optional ½ tsp. pure strawberry extract
½ cup low-fat cottage cheese
12 frozen strawberries
2 pinches Mineral Salt
½–1 tsp. Gluccie

3 Tbs. cocoa powder (I use extra dark)
2 Tbs. Super Sweet Blend
Optional 1–2 Tbs. Unflavored or Strawberry
    Pristine Whey Protein Powder (if using
    strawberry, cut back on the sweetener)

---

1. Add everything to the blender and blend until smooth.

CHOCOLATE BANANA SMOOTHIE

Makes a Single Serve

My little girls and husband all love this drink! Don't tell, but it features spinach! If I want to drink this alone, I need to not let my girls see it! It's usually hard going to get them to eat fresh spinach, so this drink comes in handy for them as it is completely disguised by the intense color and taste of the cocoa and banana. If sharing with my girls and we all want plenty, I'll make up a double serving so we can all get a good amount. Just one serving gives us a small amount each and we'll have it as a side for our lunch.

1 small to medium banana
2 pinches Mineral Salt
2–3 tsp. Super Sweet Blend
¼ cup cocoa powder
1 cup unsweetened almond or cashew milk
2 cups fresh spinach
4 Tbs. Unflavored Pristine Whey Protein Powder
1 cup ice

1. Add everything to a blender and blend until smooth. Taste, if you need extra sweetness due to a not powerfully ripe banana, add a little more Super Sweet Blend and then blend again.

STRAWBERRY BANANA SMOOTHIE

Makes a Single Serve

---

12 frozen strawberries

1 banana

1 Tbs. Baobab Boost Powder

2 Tbs. Unflavored Pristine Whey Protein Powder

1 Tbs. Integral Collagen

1 Tbs. Super Sweet Blend

2–3 doonks Pure Stevia Extract Powder

1 cup unsweetened almond or cashew milk

2 pinches Mineral Salt

---

1. Blend it all up, baby!

PUMPKIN SHAKE

Makes a Single Serve

I like pumpkin stuff, but I'm not usually crazy for it like I know so many of you are. So, with all my love, I made this up for you to enjoy when that pumpkin craving hits. I had my cousin (Autumn, Pearl's daughter) and sister-in-law (Stephanie) over while I was testing this out and they both went nuts over it so I hope you love it just as much. But actually, in the process of perfecting this pumpkin shake I actually REALLY began to enjoy it, I'll be making it for myself again … looks like I'm hopping on the crazy-for-pumpkin train with you now after all!

1½ cups ice
1 cup unsweetened almond or cashew milk
½ cup canned pumpkin puree
2 Tbs. ⅓ less fat cream cheese
2 tsp. Super Sweet Blend
¼ tsp. pumpkin pie spice
3 pinches Mineral Salt
¼ tsp. Gluccie or xanthan gum
1 tsp. MCT oil
½ tsp. Maple Natural Burst Extract
3–4 Tbs. unflavored Pristine Whey Protein Powder

1. Combine all ingredients in a blender and blend until smooth.

STRAWBERRY LEMON SEED SHAKE

Makes a Single Serve

Pearl Chimes In I'm sitting here going through all of Rashida's recipes as she sends them in to me and I see this title. I immediately call her...

"Rashida... what on earth? You feature lemon seeds in this shake? Are there health benefits to lemon seeds somehow that I've never heard of? Wouldn't they taste terrible????"

Rashida: "Huh? I don't remember putting lemon seeds in any of my shakes... they're in the ingredient list?"

So, I look through ingredients and no lemon seeds... there are poppy seeds though. Somehow, she tied poppy seeds and lemons together and thought the combination worked as a great title. Back to the phone call... she can't stop laughing and puts it down to pregnancy brain (she is 6 months pregnant at this time), but I'm not buying that. This is something Rashida would do pregnant or not... ha! She wants to come up with a new title, but I am not allowing it. This needs to go down in history as Strawberry Lemon Seed Shake... sort of a ring to it and I won't be able to help but smile every time I see the title.

Juice from 1 lemon
1 cup unsweetened almond or cashew milk
½ cup low-fat cottage cheese
1 Tbs. plus 1 tsp. Super Sweet Blend

5 frozen strawberries
½ tsp. pure lemon extract
⅛ tsp. Mineral Salt
1 tsp. poppy seeds (not lemon seeds! lol)*

---

1. Put all ingredients minus the poppy seeds into a blender and blend well. Stir in poppy seeds.

*Note: If you're having a drug test done, just leave poppy seeds out! They just give this shake a nice, slight crunch, but it will still taste great without them.

ALMOND BLUEBERRY OAT SHAKE

Makes a Single Serve

Yep, if you scroll down these ingredients, you'll see this has a full teaspoon of Gluccie! You can use xanthan gum, but Gluccie has way more slimming and blood sugar healing benefits and it helps keep you soooo full! In this shake this amount does not make it slimy in my opinion due to the combination of ingredients used but you can always try ½ teaspoon of Gluccie if you're a 'fraidy cat'—winky.

1 cup frozen blueberries	1½ Tbs. Integral Collagen
1 cup unsweetened almond milk	¼ tsp. pure almond extract
¼ cup old fashioned rolled oats	2 pinches Mineral Salt
1 cup ice	1 tsp. Gluccie or xanthan gum
1–1½ Tbs. Super Sweet Blend	

1. Go down the list, throwing everything into the blender ending with the Gluccie. Blend until smooth.

GREENIE MEANIE YUCK YUM

Makes a Single Serve

Serene Chimes In There's no way I could not make an appearance or two in this chapter. Smoothies have always been my thing; in fact, I would go as far as to say…my main thing. As a busy mom of 14 children, they are the way I have lived and thrived on my THM journey. They're so quick to whip up and can pack such a health punch, I truly don't know how I could have endured my crazy life without them by my side.

So, in the same amazingly yummy, yet deliciously yucky vein of my original Yuk Yum I brought you in our Trim Healthy Table book…I present you with my latest precious offering. Rarely does a day go by that I do not savor every drip in the jar of my new favorite Greenie Meanie Yuck Yum! It is freakingly exploding with potent nutrition and fills you with a zing in your step and a zap of electricity in your cells (well, that's what I imagine). If you need to pep talk yourself into partaking, then read up on all the mind-blowing benefits of spirulina in my Greenie Meanie Balls recipe (page 314). I actually created that recipe before this one, so the explanation of the name is over on that page, too. Here in smoothie form, adding in the health recharging power of double fermented kefir gives you even more crazy good reasons to dig in or slurp up.

12 oz. kefir (homemade double fermented from raw whole milk [S] or store-bought double fermented from low-fat milk [FP])

1 handful raw spinach (or 2 Tbs. frozen spinach)

2 tsp. Dynamic Duo Greens Powder (or 1 tsp. spirulina and 1 tsp. moringa powder)

1–2 Tbs. Baobab Boost Powder

2–3 Tbs. fresh lemon juice (not from concentrate for this recipe, all about potent nutrition here)

1–2 doonks Pure Stevia Extract Powder

1 Tbs. Integral Collagen

Optional 1 Tbs. unflavored Pristine Whey Protein Powder

Optional 1–2 tsp. MCT oil for S (only use for store-bought kefir)

Optional 1 Tbs. green banana flour* (along with the Crunchy Additions for a super Light E)

Optional Other Superfood Additions:

(If you have them laying around. I ask for them for Christmas and birthdays or special treats … but I'm a quirky girl that way.)

- ½ Tbs. maca powder
- ½ Tbs. açaí powder
- 1 tsp. camu camu powder

Optional Crunchy Additions for S:

- 1 Tbs. raw whole flax seeds
- 1 Tbs. cacao nibs
- 2 Tbs. unsweetened coconut flakes

Optional Crunchy Additions for E:

- 2 Tbs. R's Granola from page 96 or Pearl's Crunchy Granola from Trim Healthy Table
- 1 Tbs. either Dried Cranberries from page 243, golden berries, or goji berries

1. Put all ingredients except for Crunchy Additions into a blender or use a hand blender in a wide mouth mason jar. Blend well until no little bits of spinach can be seen then stir in your crunchies, if using.

Notes: To learn about double fermenting your own homemade or store-bought plain kefir, read page 459 of Trim Healthy Table or Google it on the internet. (If you have store-bought … all you do is leave it out on your counter still sealed for another 12-hours before refrigerating.)

Your low-fat, store-bought kefir once double fermented will yield an FP Yuck Yum. Adding the optional E ingredient and/or the E crunchy additions will turn your FP Yuck Yum into a Light E.

Homemade kefir from whole raw milk is by far the most delicious in my opinion. It is a little more superfoody and will make an S Yuck Yum. (This is the one I indulge in most regularly along with the S Crunchy Additions.) Don't add the optional oil to it as it doesn't need it, the MCT oil is only for the store-bought option if you want to turn it into an S.

I buy Superfoods by MRM brand of green banana flour online which has only 3 net carbs per tablespoon. I use this flour all the time in my smoothies now and a couple of my other recipes here call for it.

PRE, PRO, & POST SHAKE

 **FP** OR LIGHT **E**

Makes a Single Serve

Serene Chimes In   Why this title? Let me explain . . . probiotics are important for your health, but we all know that. Prebiotics are not quite as widely talked about but are just as important as they set the stage for probiotics to thrive and without them a healthy inner ecology is just not going to happen. But postbiotics . . . these are a relatively new term in the world of gut health. If you have gut goals . . . postbiotics are what you ultimately want, but until recently not many people knew much about them. Probiotics in themselves can't do much for your health. Here's how it actually has to work . . . basically, probiotics must feed on prebiotics and give birth to postbiotics. I like to think of them as probiotic babies (even though technically they're the waste products of probiotics but let's not get into schematics). Postbiotics are the desired end result of probiotics . . . the things that actually regulate every organ in your system including your immune system, your brain and they have a huge influence over how well you burn foods so you don't store too much fat.

So, let's break it down into nutshell language . . . this gut circle of life . . . it starts with the pre . . . that feeds on the pro . . . that results in the post. Postbiotics make your gut stronger the second time around so it can process prebiotics more effectively. When things are working in this manner, the cycle will repeat and repeat until vibrant health is flourishing with healthy gut bacteria. This ecosystem inside of our bellies is called our microbiome and when it is not cycling properly—we suffer.

The shake below is fertilizer for all the pre/pro/post diggity. Think of it as a fertility drug for your microbiome so you can hatch a billion postbiotic babies. Drink up and get baby bug making.

---

1 cup unsweetened almond or cashew milk

1 Tbs. green banana flour (for FP) and/or 1 pre-sliced and frozen very green banana (for Light E)

1 Tbs. Baobab Boost Powder

4 pinches Mineral Salt

4 doonks Pure Stevia Extract Powder

½ tsp. Vanilla Natural Burst Extract and/or ¼ tsp. Banana Natural Burst Extract

2–4 Tbs. unflavored Pristine Whey Protein Powder (or 1–1½ Tbs. Collagen for DF)

Optional ¼ tsp. nutmeg

Optional ¼ tsp. Gluccie (While optional, it adds another gut-healing fiber to the mix. It does thicken it slightly, so leave it out if that is not your desired texture.)

1. Put all ingredients into a blender and blend until perfectly creamy.

Note 1: If you're wondering how I can label this as FP … Green banana flour, unlike regular bananas, is usually low in carbs. But brands vary. So, check that the brand you use is low in carbs per tablespoon. If you add the green banana, or just use it in place of the banana flour, you'll still be close to FP … but probably closer to a very Light E. That is because most (about 80–90%) of the starch in green bananas cannot be digested. This indigestible, or what is known as resistant starch is the fertilizer your gut needs for good bacteria to feast upon as it ferments in your intestines … Yes, that is a good thing. Both the flour and the fresh green banana prevent and treat insulin resistance and lower post meal blood sugar levels. You will also notice that I have only included Pure Stevia Extract Powder as the sweetener. My reason is to keep bloat to a minimum when including so many fermentable fibers. Some may bloat a little at first when beginning this shake … but, it's a healing and healthy bloat. Ride with it until your body gets use to it. Combining the fermentable fibers with natural sugar alcohol sweeteners may be too much toot power … ya' get my stinky drift?

Note 2: You can easily turn this into a Frisky, which is colder and creamier and WAY hugier … (I know that's not a word, but I prefer it) without any added calories. It's like a HUGE SNOW YETI that's sweet on your gut! To create this, make sure you include a full green frozen banana, 2 extra doonks of stevia, and then add 1½ cups of ice before including the whey and blend until smooth. Add the whey at the end and whip for a few seconds more until creamy and Yeti creature-like.

P.S. *I know this is Rashida's book, but hopefully she won't mind me taking over and being extra-long winded here. This Yeti creation I mentioned above is soooo massive that something might happen. Just like the "If You Give a Mouse a Cookie" story, you might get the idea to add another half ice cube tray-worth of ice to make a delicious ice cream. But once you do that, you might get the idea to shoot for ice cream from the very begin-ning next time … a Pre, Pro, & Post Ice Cream, by golly! You can do this by omitting the ice and using the same measurement of straight water (definitely using the Gluccie) and pouring it all into ice cube trays to freeze. Once frozen, divide the frozen cubes into two separate baggies in the freezer for two single servings. Or, if you will be making it for two, just chuck it all in together. When ready to make your Pre, Pro, and Post deliciousness … place your frozen cubes in a food processor and process into snow powder … stopping the machine and pushing the unprocessed bits back down where the blades are, if needed. (Yes, those of you who are familiar with Tummy Tucking Ice Cream will be nodding heads at this process.) Now, add just enough unsweetened almond milk … tinsy bits at a time until the powder whips into a thick ice cream. My favorite thing to do is to actually replace the tinsy bits of almond milk for tinsy bits of Nut Pods Original Unsweetened Coffee Creamer. It doesn't have a lot of fat, but tastes super-duper creamy and adds that extra bit of lusciousness.*

Over and Out,
Serene

7

BRILLIANT BREAKFASTS!

Happily Ever After Omelet **FP** or **S**

Thermo Boost Omelet **S**

Rad Hash Brown Casserole **S**

Overnight Cinnamon Squares **XO**

Overnight Biscuits **XO**

Top & Tail Yogurt Cups **E** or **XO**

R's Granola **E**

Handy Breakfast Burritos **S**

Chocolate Banana Waffles **E**

Berrylicious Oatmeal **E**

Super Slimming Porridge **S**

Zucchini Bread Oatmeal **E**

Mini Quiches **S**

R's French Toast **E**

Cauli Tots **S**

Breakfast Bread Pudding **E**

I was never much of a breakfast person . . . I mean I ate it but never gave breakfast the honor it deserves. Sure, I had a couple of omelet recipes that I really enjoyed but I'd eat them more often for lunch than I would for breakfast. When I was first married to Jack, he would walk into the kitchen and raise his eyebrows to see me having salad or even leftover chili for breakfast. It was just a meal to get over and done quickly so I could start my day.

It was Jack who got me on the breakfast food kick. His passionate love affair with breakfast was something I'd never encountered before! I loved seeing his face light up over a good breakfast and that inspired me to start creating more meaningful breakfast creations. . . . of the Trim and Healthy kind of course. I can honestly say breakfast has now become one of my favorite meals thanks to the influence of my handsome husband. Jack also had good instincts, studies show that we burn food fuels faster and more efficiently in the morning than we even do at night. We humans are built for breakfast!

I hope you start enjoying your day by revving up your metabolism with these breakfast recipes as much as I've learned to do.

HAPPILY EVER AFTER OMELET

 OR

Makes a Single Serve

This has been my go-to omelet for years. I love the fact that I can make it an FP or S, depending upon my needs and it is delicious either way. Cilantro (one of the ingredients here) is so incredible for the body, it is considered to be the King of all heavy metal and virus cleansing foods. If you don't love cilantro, try fresh parsley instead or in a pinch... if you don't have those ingredients or don't have the time... just sprinkle in some dried cilantro or parsley... still a good tasting omelet.

A story behind this omelet ... when we first started dating, Jack came out to my parents' house for the first time and I made him a really big S version of this. He loved it so much that he asked very sweetly if I could make him another (he's very tall with a high metabolism so the guy can EAT!!!) I said NO!!! Of course, I'm kidding! I kindly made him another, he devoured it again, and we were married and lived happily ever after. (Not all in the same day... but, still.)

3–4 egg whites (or about ½–¾ cup liquid egg whites) for FP or 2–3 eggs for S
Optional ¼ cup chopped cilantro
⅛ tsp. creole seasoning

3 Tbs. low-fat cottage cheese for FP or ¼ cup grated cheddar for S
2 Tbs. salsa
1–2 pinches black pepper
Optional small sprinkle cayenne pepper

---

1. Mix egg whites, cilantro, and creole seasoning in a bowl. Spray a skillet with coconut or olive oil and place over medium-high heat. Pour mixture into skillet, cook with a lid until it goes from clear to white.

2. Flip omelet, then add cheese, salsa, and spices on top. Fold omelet so one side covers the other. Place the lid back on and reduce heat to medium-low until cheese is all melted.

THERMO BOOST OMELET

Makes a Single Serve

Welcome another of my favorite omelets into your life . . . hoping you love it as much as I do! Peppers (otherwise known as capsicums) raise your metabolism by boosting the thermogenic temperature of your body. Studies have also shown that they help you stay full for longer and are literally packed with vitamin C . . . They have 3 times the amount of vitamin C than oranges. Did you know that vitamin C is not only so important for your immune system but also for losing weight? Yes! It's a scientific fact . . . vitamin C deprived people can't shed fat properly, so load up on the peppers and get thermo-boosting!

1 medium bell pepper (any color), chopped	1 egg + 2 egg whites (or 1 egg plus ¼ cup
Optional, but yummy . . . 1–2 tsp. diced,	liquid egg whites)
pickled jalapeño peppers	1 Tbs. water
2 Large pinches Mineral Salt	⅛ tsp. creole seasoning
⅛ tsp. black pepper	¼ cup grated sharp cheddar cheese

1. Spray a non-stick skillet with coconut (or olive) oil and place over high heat. Add the chopped bell pepper, salt, and pepper. Allow the edges of the peppers to get a little dark color to them, not to the point of burnt, you just want a nice roasted edge. Stir in the diced, pickled jalapeños then cook another 2–3 minutes, tossing frequently.

2. Set peppers onto a plate. Spray skillet again then reduce heat to medium-high. Mix eggs and egg whites with water and creole seasoning then pour into the skillet. Flip as soon as it appears just cooked through then add the cheese and pepper mixture.

3. Let cheese melt then flip half the omelet over to other side. This is lovely sprinkled with Italian seasoning and a little Parmesan cheese if you so desire.

RAD HASH BROWN CASSEROLE

Makes 6–8 Servings

This goes perfectly with an egg or two on the side and perhaps some sliced tomatoes and/or a couple pieces of turkey bacon for breakfast or any meal . . . even dinner! You can share it with family members, or bake ahead and store pieces in the fridge or freezer for when you want to have some. I really wanted to create a healthy hash brown type casserole recipe because it is pure comfort food. I asked my good friend/boss (Lisa) to give me her opinion on this recipe since she loves hash brown casserole—usually made with real potatoes of course. She gave me super positive feedback and said I should put it in the book. So, if you end up thinking it does not taste like the one you're used to, you can call her, not me! I do want to make this with golden potatoes sometime for a fun XO breakfast. I know my husband will be extra happy if I do that.

Note: If you want this to look like a regular hash brown casserole, it is best to peel the radishes first, that way you won't get a pink tinge in the final product. However, if you don't care about that, you can save a step or two and buy pre-shredded/matchstick-size radishes in the produce department of most grocery stores.

2 lbs. radishes (pre-shredded or whole)	8 oz. grated, sharp cheddar cheese (divided)
2 Tbs. unflavored coconut oil	2 eggs
1¼ tsp. Mineral Salt	½ tsp. parsley flakes
1 tsp. Italian seasoning	⅛ tsp. black pepper
½ cup sour cream	

1. Preheat the oven to 425°F. Spray a 9x13 baking dish with coconut or olive oil and set aside.
2. If using whole radishes, peel and then run them through the food processor with the grating blade on it. Add shredded radishes to a non-stick skillet with the coconut oil, and salt. Cook on high for 10–15 minutes or until they're soft (tossing frequently so they don't stick or burn).
3. Now add the Italian seasoning, sour cream, and half the cheese (4 oz.) to the radishes and give a good stir then stir in the two eggs.
4. Spread the mixture onto the sprayed baking dish, sprinkle on the remaining 4 oz. of cheese and spices and bake for 20–25 minutes. Top with chopped green onions if desired.

OVERNIGHT CINNAMON SQUARES

Makes About 8–10 Servings

I have been doing a bunch of experimenting with soaking einkorn flour (which is a wonderful ancient grain) in kefir to make it gentler on blood sugar and more digestible. I had this wonderful

dream of making beautiful fluffy cinnamon rolls that we could enjoy for breakfast . . . well . . . the dough wouldn't obey me! Try-after-try, it just wouldn't do the things I needed it to. My results tasted so great each time and the texture was soft and lovely but they looked nothing like fluffy rolls! So, I gave up on the rolls and decided to embrace what this wanted to be since my little girls and I enjoyed it so much. I was not planning for this to even go in this book, but I ended up sending some home with Aunty Pearl on a whim, and what do you know!? She loved them, so here we are. You can even have them as an afternoon treat if you prefer, they don't have to be break-fast . . . just enjoy!

Pearl Chimes In You bet they're going in the book! There is a place for Crossovers in Trim Healthy Mama . . . we all need them some-times. These squares are too good not to be in your life. I enjoy them with a little collagen in my coffee for some added protein.

2 cups einkorn flour (or you can try any other on-plan flour such as a sprouted wheat flour) (see Note 1)

1½ Tbs. water

1 cup low-fat kefir

1 packet of active yeast (see Note 2)

1 Tbs. warm water

½ Tbs. Super Sweet Blend

1 tsp. Vanilla Natural Burst Extract

1 tsp. Butter Natural Burst Extract

1 tsp. Mineral Salt

1 tsp. baking powder

½ tsp. baking soda

½ cup Baking Blend

1 cup Gentle Sweet (divided)

1 tsp. molasses

1 stick (½ cup) butter (melted)

1½ Tbs. ground cinnamon

1. Mix flour, water, and kefir in a medium glass bowl, cover with clean dish towel and let it sit for 10–14 hours or overnight.

2. Preheat the oven to 375°F when getting ready to bake.

3. Add active yeast and hot water together in a small bowl and stir.

4. Now add the Super Sweet Blend, extracts, salt, baking soda, baking powder, Baking Blend, 3 tablespoons of the butter, ½ a cup of the Gentle Sweet, and the yeast mixture to the soaked flour. Mix well!

5. Place a large piece of parchment paper onto a large cookie-sheet then spray with coconut or olive oil, place the dough on it, then spread out with your hands (wash and damp them so the dough won't stick to your hands and it will spread better). Spread it out to approximately ⅓ of an inch thick.

6. Mix the remaining butter, Gentle Sweet, molasses and cinnamon together then spread out all over the flattened dough. Now roll it up, (it will look like one big floppy cinnamon roll that has not been cut yet). Bake for 18 minutes then cut into squares before serving.

Note 1: For more on einkorn flour, see pages 94 & 262.

Note 2: If you don't have yeast, don't sweat it, just don't add the extra water. It will still come out lovely! Honesty, I found out after writing this recipe that honey helps the yeast activate. If you want to try adding a little honey to the yeast and water go ahead, but it may turn out totally different and not look like what's in the picture.

OVERNIGHT BISCUITS

Makes About 10–12 Biscuits

Another one of my mad scientist experiments with soaked einkorn flour mixed with Baking Blend. I love the texture the two of these bring when combined. I did use regular baking einkorn flour for the biscuits in this picture . . . you can use whole grain einkorn, which would be even more optimum, but the soaking does help the regular einkorn be friendlier to blood sugar. I consider it a pretty much on-plan, but not a precisely perfect option that I like to choose. The end result is great either way though.

I can eat two of these biscuits, but if you have a husband like I do who loves biscuits then he's probably going to want three . . . or five. Ha! These go great topped with my Berry or Apricot Wow-Spreads (pages 366) or just with butter on the side of scrambled eggs and perhaps sautéed veggies like spinach or mushrooms, for a wonderful weekend breakfast.

1½ cups einkorn flour (or try another on-plan flour of your liking)	1 tsp. baking soda
	⅔ cup Baking Blend
1 cup low-fat kefir	1 stick (½ cup) melted butter
2 tsp. baking powder	½–¾ tsp. Mineral Salt

1. Mix the flour and kefir in a medium glass bowl, cover with clean dish towel and let it soak for 10–14 hours or overnight.

2. Preheat the oven to 375°F. Place parchment paper on a baking sheet.

3. Add the remaining ingredients to the bowl and stir together. Then, shape into biscuits and then place them on the lined baking sheet.

4. Bake for 18 minutes.

TOP & TAIL YOGURT CUPS

 OR

Makes 4 Servings

For treats growing up, we would have the "Brown Cow" yogurts with the fruit on the bottom. I always loved them, so I wanted to make them without sugar and take it even a step further and put crunch on the top … my kind of treat! They're great for fast breakfasts since you can just grab one out of the fridge and be on your way but they're also awesome for snacks.

1⅓ cups Apricot or Berry Wow-Spread from pages: 366 or 369	3 Tbs. Super Sweet Blend
	1½ tsp. Vanilla or Maple Natural Burst Extract
4 cups 0% Greek Yogurt (or use full fat for an extra treaty XO)	2 large pinches Mineral Salt
	2 cups R's Granola from (page: 96)

1. Take four pint-sized mason jars and add ⅓ cup of Wow-Spread of your choice to each jar.
2. Mix up the yogurt with sweetener, extract and salt. Add one cup of the yogurt to each jar then top each with ½ cup of the granola.

R'S GRANOLA

Makes Multiple Servings

I told myself I could not finish the book without coming up with a very crunchy granola recipe, so here you are! I know my aunties had a granola in one of their cookbooks but we all like different things so if that one didn't float your boat . . . try this! They're not the type to be offended if you like mine better . . . Haha! Or even if you don't . . . change is fun. The main thing I love about this granola is that you can have over a cup of this without even coming close to your E carb limit . . . no stingy portion sizes! This goes great with Greek yogurt, or just with some unsweetened vanilla almond milk in a bowl. If you're having it with almond milk and not yogurt, have some lean protein on the side like a little collagen in your coffee or tea as this doesn't have a lot of protein on its own.

---

4 cups puffed brown rice
6 cups puffed millet
2 cups old fashioned rolled oats
1 cup water
1 cup Gentle Sweet (Xylitol-Free)*
½ Tbs. unflavored coconut oil
1–2 Tbs. blackstrap molasses
2–3 Tbs. Super Sweet Blend
2 tsp. Mineral Salt
2 tsp. each Vanilla and Butter Natural Burst Extract

Optional 1 tsp. each Caramel and Maple Natural Burst Extract
2 Tbs. ground cinnamon (divided)
3 egg whites or ⅓ cup liquid egg whites
Optional ⅓ cup sliced almonds, chopped walnuts, or pecans.
Optional ⅓ cup raisins, 1 cup freeze dried strawberries, or dried cranberries from page: 243

---

1. Preheat oven to 350°F and line 2 large and 1 small-medium cookie sheets with parchment paper.
2. Put first three ingredients into a large bowl.
3. Add everything after that down to half the cinnamon to a medium-sized saucepan and cook on high for 5 minutes stirring throughout this time.
4. Beat egg whites in a bowl until stiff peaks and set aside.
5. Add ⅔ of the contents of saucepan to the large bowl containing oats and puffed grains, stir well. Add the rest and stir well again with the nuts, if using.
6. Now mix in the beaten egg whites and spread granola mixture onto your cookie sheets. Bake for 18–20 minutes (you'll need to do it in 2 batches as most ovens don't fit 3 trays). Sprinkle the remaining Tbs. of cinnamon onto the trays and let granola sit out for 1–2 hours to dry out and get all crunchy. Add raisins, freeze dried strawberries, or dried cranberries from page 243, if desired!

*Note: I like to use the Xylitol-Free Gentle Sweet for this recipe because it tends to get crunchier that way (xylitol tends to inhibit the crunch, but original Gentle Sweet can still work).

HANDY BREAKFAST BURRITOS

Makes 8–12 Burritos (great for freezing)

Do yourself a favor and make these super handy but ultra-hearty burritos! They're great to have ready in the freezer for those busy mornings when you need to get out the door fast. Perfect to heat up before church or work, or whatever else you've got going … and your kids and hubs won't taste the cauliflower … promise! Wrap them as I have demonstrated in the photo where I've used parchment paper (or just wrap in paper towels) and then stick in a big Ziploc bag to freeze.

1 (12 oz.) bag frozen cauliflower rice
1 Tbs. unflavored coconut oil (divided)
1 tsp. Mineral Salt (divided)
1 tsp. black pepper (divided)
½ tsp. Italian seasoning
14 oz. ground turkey sausage
8 eggs

8 egg whites (1 cup liquid egg whites)
¾ cup low-fat cottage cheese
1 cup grated sharp cheddar cheese
Optional hot sauce, fresh spinach, and
    cilantro for add ins.
Low-carb tortillas (I use Extreme Wellness
    Low Carb Tortillas)*

1. Put cauliflower rice in a large skillet set to medium-high heat with ¼ teaspoon of the salt, ½ teaspoon of the black pepper, and 1 teaspoon of the coconut oil. Cover with a lid and cook for 7–10 minutes (stirring occasionally). When fully cooked transfer into a bowl or just dump on a paper plate (what I do).

2. Brown and crisp the sausage until cooked in the same skillet then add to the bowl of cauliflower rice.

3. Put eggs, egg whites, cottage cheese, and the remaining salt and pepper into a big bowl and whisk around with a fork. Now add the remaining 2 teaspoons of coconut oil to the skillet and pour in the egg mixture. Stir eggs every minute or so and cook to your preference.

4. Add in a ½ cup of the cheese and give it a little stir and then add in meat, cauliflower rice, and the remaining ½ cup of cheese. (Another way to make all this is to cook the cauliflower rice first in the skillet with all the oil, keep it in skillet but shove it to one side, brown the turkey sausage on other side of skillet and then add the cottage cheese and egg mixture. Cook . . . stirring very frequently (so bottom doesn't stick) until done.

5. Now fill up the tortillas with the mixture and add options, if desired. Roll them up and then serve or freeze to reheat later. To reheat from frozen, you can microwave if you are the Drive Thru Sue type or heat in the oven if you're a purist.

***Note:** You can use Wonder Wraps if you can't do wraps with gluten . . . my aunties have a video showing how to make them on www.trimhealthymama.com.

CHOCOLATE BANANA WAFFLES

Makes a Single Serve

FOR THE WAFFLE:
1 small ripe banana
3 Tbs. Gentle Sweet
3 Tbs. Baking Blend
3 Tbs. cocoa powder
2 pinches Mineral Salt
¼ tsp. baking soda
¼ tsp. baking powder
¼ tsp. each Vanilla and Butter
   Natural Burst Extract
1½ tsp. Super Sweet Blend
2 egg whites (¼ cup liquid egg whites)

FOR PEANUT BUTTER DRIZZLE:
3 Tbs. Pressed Peanut Flour
1 Tbs. Gentle Sweet
2½ Tbs. unsweetened almond milk
⅛ tsp. Vanilla Natural Burst Extract
2 large pinches Mineral Salt

1. Spray waffle maker with coconut or olive oil (Hint: this works better if you plug in the waffle maker, ask me how I know! Hehe) Mash the banana in a bowl and then add everything else and stir together. Cook in a waffle maker.

2. While waffles are cooking, stir up the ingredients for the peanut drizzle in a small bowl. Then drizzle it all over cooked waffles.

Note: If you're using a baby waffle maker, this will make 4 little waffles. For a regular-sized waffle maker, it would probably make 2 big waffles. (Sorry, I don't have a big regular one so I don't know for sure!)

BERRYLICIOUS OATMEAL

Makes a Single Serve

This is one super antioxidant loaded and gorgeously colored oatmeal . . . baobab and berries together . . . about the healthiest way you can eat it! Aunty Pearl called me to say she's eaten this 5 days in a row and calls it her Pink Porridge.

½ cup quick oats (or ¼ cup each quick and old fashioned oats)
Optional, but recommended, 2 Tbs. Baobab Boost Powder
Optional 1 Tbs. Integral Collagen
¾ cup frozen mixed berries

1 Tbs. Super Sweet Blend (or 1 Tbs. Gentle Sweet plus 1 rounded doonk pure stevia)
2 pinches Mineral Salt
1 cup water (add another 1/2 cup for more volume)

1. Add everything to a small pot. Bring to quick boil and then cook on medium heat for five minutes (squish some of the berries to release their color during cooking). Top with Greek yogurt or 1 tsp. almond butter for E (more for crossover) or unsweetened almond milk.

SUPER SLIMMING PORRIDGE

S

Makes a Single Serve

Pearl Chimes In I was so torn over which twelve of my latest recipes should go in this book. Sounds ridiculous but I literally lost sleep over it . . . I'd wake at night mulling over which recipes have been the most blessing to my life so they could bless yours, too. But on this one I had no doubts. It was GOING IN!!! I might be more excited for you to try this recipe than any of my others here. It can rev up your health, decrease your inflammation and powerfully slim you.

I was actually going to call this Weirdo Porridge because honestly, the first time you try this, the texture might seem well . . . perhaps . . . the slightest bit weird. But wow . . . once you start digging into this, it does wonders for your life and any thoughts of weirdness fade away! It truly is delicious in my opinion . . . like a comforting hug that greets you in the morning. I do

have to give credit to my friend Karen though. She's an inspirational Trim Healthy Mama, a breast cancer survivor. After chemo she's had to tweak her THM journey to make it work for her new hormone altered body as her former way of doing THM didn't work as well for her new needs. She eats less fat overall now and does a lot of plant-based THM meals. We talk a lot online about our latest healthy meals and recipes. I sent her this recipe to try and it was honestly a lot weirder at the time. She tweaked it ... added the maple extract, the chia and psyllium, all of which helped with taste and texture, so thanks to her it is now much lower on the weirdo scale.

The star ingredient is flax here and one of the most awesome things about this humble seed is that it retains all of its health benefits even after cooking. I used to eat a lot of flax when I first started my THM journey but then somehow, I kinda forgot about it. I recently read about its incredible fat shredding and health boosting abilities in the book "How Not to Diet" by Dr. Michael Gregor so I've been eating a lot more of it again. (While I think that book is fantastic, this doesn't mean I agree with all aspects of it. He promotes avoiding animal products which is something I did for 12 whole years earlier in my life. I have no desire to fully return to that, but we can learn from everyone and I learned much from his excellent book). This porridge is a boon to my digestion (but drink lots of water before eating it), it helps me be super happy with my weight and I have less pain and stiffness in my body when I eat it several times a week due to the way it reduces inflammation. Give this a go and let me know what it does for you. Oh ... and read my notes and tweaks below the recipe.

3 Tbs. flax meal	1 Tbs. Gentle Sweet
3 Tbs. Baking Blend (or just coconut flour can work)	1 pinch Mineral Salt
1 tsp. Whole Husk Psyllium Flakes	¾ cup unsweetened almond milk
1 tsp. Baobab Boost Powder	½ cup water
1 tsp. chia seeds	Dash each of Maple and Vanilla Natural Burst Extracts
1 doonk Pure Stevia Extract Powder	⅓ cup frozen wild blueberries

1. Put all ingredients (except blueberries) in a small saucepan set to high heat, whisk well, and bring to a quick boil. Turn heat to low/medium and allow to bubble/simmer for a couple minutes, whisking much of the time. Take off heat.

2. Put blueberries into breakfast bowl and with the help of a spatula, scrape porridge into the bowl and over top of the blueberries. Allow porridge to sit on blueberries for a few minutes. As it sits it will thicken up further and thaw the blueberries. You can eat this as two layers, almost like a cobbler (as I do) or stir in if preferred.

NOTES

- As written this breakfast doesn't have massive amounts of protein ... close to 10 grams and that seems to be enough for me for breakfast sometimes in my particular season (various meals on THM will be naturally higher or lower in protein but it all balances out). As written, I usually find this filling enough and it sustains me until lunch with no blood sugar dips or highs. But you can always add a teaspoon or two of collagen to your coffee or right into the porridge if you need more protein as I sometimes feel I do depending upon the day.

- I actually prefer to grind my own flax for this. I put 2 tablespoons brown or golden flax in my coffee grinder and do a coarse grind ... not grinding it all the way smooth. This yields 3 tablespoons of a crunchier flax meal texture and that's how I prefer it. But to save time, using pre-ground flax is fine.

- You can use any blueberries but the little wild ones are healthiest and they take the least time to thaw. I get the huge bag of them at Walmart, Kroger, or Publix. If you don't have blueberries, any other small berry can also work.

- I understand putting these ingredients together in the morning takes a few minutes. It is a good idea to take 15 minutes on a weekend to take all ingredients out and fill small Ziploc baggies with the dry ingredients so you have single serve amounts already made up. Then all you have to do is dump into your saucepan and add liquid. Or take with you to work and cook in a microwave (just don't tell Serene). I am so excited about this recipe though that hopefully at some time in the future we can manufacture it so Drive Thru Sue's like me can just buy it pre-mixed in packets rather than having to put it together ourselves.

*I also make a fantastic E porridge in a similar way to this. I call it PPP which stands for Perfect Poop Porridge, but you can certainly call it something else if you hate that name. But it does do fantastic things for your bowels and your waistline! In a small saucepan, put 2 tablespoons quick-cook steel cut oats, 4 tablespoons old fashioned rolled oats, 1 slightly rounded teaspoon each of Whole Husk Psyllium Husks and ground flax, 2 doonks Pure Stevia Extract Powder (plus more sweetener of choice, if you like things sweeter), 2 pinches Mineral Salt, and 2 cups water (or try 1½ cups if you prefer less goopy texture and don't need to eat as big a bowl full). Bring to a quick boil and then turn down a little to let boil vigorously for another 5 minutes, stirring several times. Take off heat and stir well with a fork for about 30 seconds (it will look goopy, but don't worry, that will go away). Pour over bowl of frozen wild blueberries in the same manner as directions for S porridge. Cover bowl and then let sit for about 15 minutes to set into a cobbler-type breakfast before eating. (**Note:** If you don't have the quick cook steel cut oats, just use a full half cup old fashioned rolled oats). I have a video for this PPP recipe on www.trimhealthymama.com if you want to see Serene and I make it.

R'S FRENCH TOAST

Makes About 4 Servings

This is such a fast, easy breakfast but even better, it tastes amazing! Top with on-plan, sugar-free syrup to keep it in E-mode. If you want to turn this into a XO, have it with a smear of butter and some raw honey or maple syrup on top. If you want to make a single serving, just use ¼ of the ingredients … if you're math challenged, that is 1 egg white, 1½ tsp. cinnamon, 1 Tbs. Gentle Sweet, dash of vanilla, and maple, pinch of salt, and 2 pieces of the bread … you're welcome!

---

4 egg whites (½ cup liquid egg whites)
2 Tbs. cinnamon
4 Tbs. Gentle Sweet
1½ tsp. Vanilla or Maple Natural Burst
    Extract
⅛ tsp. Mineral Salt
8 pieces sprouted bread

---

1. Add everything minus bread to a medium bowl and whisk to mix.
2. Spray nonstick frying pan or griddle with coconut or olive oil and set to medium-high heat.
3. Roll each piece of bread in the wet mixture, cook a few minutes on each side until slightly crispy.

ZUCCHINI BREAD OATMEAL

Makes a Single Serve

Pearl Chimes In You've heard Serene and I encourage you to eat veggies with every meal over and over again right? But we always had this exception … "You don't have to with your oatmeal, of course." Well, now you can … you still don't HAVE to … but this is delicious so you might WANT to. Including non-starchy veggies in your first meal of the day helps set the tone for your blood sugar, it boosts your health, and helps you make great food choices the rest of the day through.

Note to read before making: Best to start with the ½ cup amount of grated zucchini listed here, but if you want to use more in future, be as zucchini crazy as you want!

½ cup zucchini (grated and tightly packed)
1½ cups water
¼ cup old fashioned rolled oats
¼ cup quick oats
Optional ½ tsp. Whole Husk Psyllium Flakes
   (I love this addition and use a full tsp.)
¾ tsp. ground cinnamon

1–2 doonks Pure Stevia Extract Powder
1 rounded Tbs. Gentle Sweet
2 pinches Mineral Salt
12–14 raisins
Dash each of Pecan and Maple Natural Burst
   Extracts (or any extract of your liking)

1. Put grated zucchini and water in a small saucepan set to high. Bring to a quick boil then allow to bubble furiously for 2 minutes.

2. Take pot off heat, add all other ingredients and stir well. Return to medium heat and allow to gently bubble for 2–3 minutes. Stir well once again then pour oatmeal into your bowl and go do something else while you let ingredients rest for 10 minutes. As the oatmeal cools a little it will thicken into a lovely texture during this stage. Top with a little unsweetened almond or cashew milk.

NOTES

- If you desire further protein, add a tablespoon or two of Pristine Whey Protein Powder while cooking (Vanilla Whey is a lovely addition). Or simply have a teaspoon or two of collagen in your coffee.

- If you are a volume eater and this doesn't feel like enough food for you … add another ½ cup of water plus another ½ teaspoon Whole Husk Psyllium Flakes and ¼ teaspoon Gluccie while cooking. During the rest stage (after cooking) it will thicken up nicely and create a larger bowl of oatmeal without adding any more actual food fuel (this is what I do). This extra fiber addition often helps those who have blood sugar trouble with raisins, too.

MINI QUICHES

S

Makes 48 Mini Quiches or 12 Regular Muffin-sized Ones (Serves about 6 if you're having them as a main protein source for a breakfast or other meal. If they're just for you, freeze whatever you're not going to eat within the next 3–4 days.)

While these are great for a tasty breakfast on the go, they're also awesome for parties! You can freeze them in Ziploc bags or sealed containers then pop back in the oven or microwave for a quick reheat.

FOR THE MINI CRUSTS:
¾ cup Baking Blend
¼ cup Oat Fiber
½ cup Parmesan cheese (green can is fine) or shredded mozzarella cheese
½ tsp. Mineral Salt
1 cup water
½ stick soft butter

FOR THE FILLING:
12 eggs
7 pieces bacon (precooked and diced)
½ cup Greek yogurt (any %)
1 tsp. Mineral Salt
½ tsp. black pepper
¼ tsp. parsley flakes
¼ tsp. red pepper flakes
½ tsp. Italian seasoning
Optional ¼ tsp. liquid smoke

FOR THE TOPPING:
1 cup sharp cheddar cheese, grated

1. Preheat oven to 375°F. Spray muffin trays with coconut or olive oil.
2. Put all dry crust ingredients in a bowl, stir around, then add water and softened butter and mix well again.
3. Add a small amount of crust mixture to each muffin hole, press dough down and around each hole. Par-bake crusts for 10 minutes. (You can use muffin liners if you want.)
4. While crusts are baking, crack eggs into a large bowl, then add all remaining filling ingredients and mix well.
5. Add a small amount of mixture to each par baked crust then top each one with about 1 teaspoon of the cheese. (If you're making the normal-sized muffin tins, sprinkle equal amounts of cheese on each one.) Bake uncovered for 10–15 minutes for the mini ones or 35–40 minutes for the regular sized ones.

CAULI TOTS

S

Makes 3–4 Servings as a Breakfast Side (or Other Meal Side)

Enjoy these at the start of a beautiful (or even not so beautiful) day or at any meal time! They're just so perfect as a side to scrambled or fried eggs, but you can have a few on their own for breakfast sometimes, too. Just enjoy collagen in your coffee for protein or have a small protein rich smoothie or shake on the side. Feel free to double the batch to have them ready to go in the freezer.

---

1 (12 oz. bag) riced cauliflower
¼ tsp. black pepper
¼ tsp. Mineral Salt or creole seasoning
2 Tbs. Whole Husk Psyllium Flakes

2 Tbs. Baking Blend
½ cup sharp cheddar cheese (grated)
1 egg white or 2 Tbs. liquid egg whites

---

1. Place riced cauliflower in a large non-stick skillet set to medium-high heat. Cover with lid and cook for 7–10 minutes. While that's cooking, mix the remaining ingredients (minus the egg white) in a bowl.
2. Once cauliflower is done, add it to the bowl then mix everything up along with the egg white.
3. Shape mixture into your desired tot-sizes, then spray that same skillet you used to cook the cauliflower with cooking spray and add tots. Cook with the lid on for 2–3 minutes, then remove the lid and flip tots from side-to-side until they're all slightly golden on every side.

BREAKFAST BREAD PUDDING

Makes 4 Servings

This bread pudding is yummy, yummy, in my tummy . . . Oh, and did I mention it's a delicious way to get those energizing carbs in to jumpstart your day! You can top this with a sugar-free syrup or the delicious Bread Pudding Sauce created for this found on page 374.

---

8 pieces sprouted bread
¾ tsp. Mineral Salt
1 Tbs. cinnamon
½ cup Gentle Sweet
3 doonks Pure Stevia Extract Powder

1 tsp. Maple or Vanilla Natural Burst Extract
4 egg whites (½ cup liquid egg whites)
¾ cup 0% Greek yogurt
½ cup unsweetened almond or cashew milk

---

1. Preheat oven to 350°F and spray an 8x8 baking dish with coconut oil.
2. Chop bread into small squares, add to a medium bowl, and combine with the rest of the dry ingredients.
3. Add all wet ingredients to another bowl and whisk with a fork until smooth.
4. Pour wet mixture into the dry mix, stir everything together, and add to your baking dish. Bake for 35–40 minutes and while it is baking make the sauce from page 374 to top your pudding with it.

8

SKILLET MEALS

Cancun Chicken

Sesame Chicken Fix

Cheesy Rice & Chicken Skillet

Chicken Stuffed Peppers

Cream of Chicken & Rice

Creamy Buffalo Chicken & Potato Skillet

Southern "Fried" Chicken or

Beef N Veggie Skillet

Shepherd's Pie Skillet

Great Wall Skillet

Salmon Avocado Skillet

Award-Winning Salmon

R's No Stress Tilapia

Happy Dance Fish Skillet

Fish Sticks

Eggplant Parm Skillet

Southwest Turkey Burgers

Quinoa Tuna Patties

Zucchini Fritters

Time for some smokin' hot, super sizzlin', yet super slimming skillet meals! Skillet meals have an uncanny balance of deliciousness and ease of cooking. They require few dishes ... aaannnnndd ... duh duh duh duh ... they are all LOADED with some sort of power veggie! Some of these recipes start in the skillet then go directly to the oven to become bakes and casseroles ... a skillet and a bake in one ... wahoo! Skillet dinners have been a relatively new adventure in cooking for me, but I've been loving how fantastic they turn out. Hope you will, too.

CANCUN CHICKEN

 WITH & OPTIONS

Makes 6–8 Servings (leftovers freeze well)

So easy!!! Just throw all ingredients in a skillet, cover and soon you'll have the most amazing fiesta flavored chicken. Eating this makes you feel like you are swept away to some restaurant in Cancun, Mexico...I think...I've never been there, but I can imagine it. If you love these sorts of spices, you can even double up on amounts! Best of all, this chicken can be used for so many meals.... any of the fuel types...S or E. To keep in FP-mode, eat over a salad or in lettuce wraps with added "Spiced-Up Mexican

Cauli-Rice"...page 259, R's Fresh Salsa from page 353, a dollop of 0% Greek yogurt and a garnish of cilantro. If you want an S meal, just add cheese, and "Hit the Spot Guac"...page 356 to the FP-version. For an E meal, add black beans, brown rice or even a small amount of corn kernels; pair whatever you want from the FP-version as well. For a XO, have with whatever fats you wish from the S-version along with a carb source from the E-version and/or maybe some blue corn chips.

2½ lb. boneless, skinless chicken breast
  (snipped or chopped into bite-sized pieces)
½ cup water
1 Tbs. ground cumin
2 Tbs. chili powder

1 Tbs. minced garlic
¾–1 tsp. Mineral Salt
¼ tsp. black pepper
Optional ¼ tsp. red pepper flakes
Optional ¼ tsp. liquid smoke

---

1. Add everything to a large skillet, then cover and cook on medium-high heat for about 15 minutes, stirring a few times.

SESAME CHICKEN FIX

 OR

Makes 6–8 Servings (leftovers freeze well)

Got an itch for sweet, saucy Chinese food? Yeah, I'm talking the kind that comes in white boxes, chop sticks on the side, and says ... "Fun food times are about to happen"! Well, that stuff literally explodes your waistline and drags down your health ... so nope, you don't want that tonight. But fun meals are still important and can easily happen on THM. How about tonight trying this Sesame Chicken Fix? It totally delivers! No, not to your door ... but to your taste buds! It is easy to make and goes great over some spiced up cauliflower rice, or noodles in the form of zucchini, konjac, or Dreamfield's for an S or brown rice for a XO.

FOR THE SAUCE:

1 cup water

4 Tbs. reduced-sodium soy sauce

3 Tbs. apple cider vinegar

1 Tbs. sesame oil

1 tsp. blackstrap molasses

½ tsp. ground ginger

½ tsp. black pepper

¼ tsp. Mineral Salt

¼ cup Gentle Sweet

½ tsp. Gluccie or xanthan gum

Optional ¾ tsp. Simply Sunflower Lecithin

1 Tbs. sesame seeds

FOR THE CHICKEN:

2 Tbs. unflavored coconut oil

2½–3 lb. skinless, boneless chicken breasts (chopped or snipped into bite-sized pieces)

½ cup Baking Blend

1. Make the sauce first. Add all sauce ingredients except Gluccie, sunflower lecithin (if using), and sesame seeds to a small saucepan. Cover with a lid until sauce comes to a boil, then reduce heat to low. Add Gluccie and sunflower lecithin and whisk them in like a mad woman so you don't get clumps. Let simmer on low for another 5 minutes. Finish with stirring in the sesame seeds, take off the heat and set aside.

2. Add coconut oil to a large non-stick skillet set to medium-high heat. While that's heating, sprinkle the Baking Blend all over the chicken pieces (cover both sides) then put them all squished in the skillet. Cover with a lid and cook for 10 minutes giving the pieces a few good tosses throughout that time.

3. Take the lid off to cook for another few minutes, turning chicken pieces again until they are fully cooked through and nicely browned. Turn heat off, pour the sesame sauce all over them. Place the lid back on for 5 minutes or so—BOOM!

CHEESY RICE & CHICKEN SKILLET

Makes About 4–6 Servings

Pearl Chimes In This is an easy, one pot family favorite in my home these days. It has become another of my "Sweat Pants Meals" (no think, no stress). My teens love it (especially the Taco-style way) so I end up making this once or twice a week as they enjoy having left-overs to just heat up and top with cheese or have over salad. Most of the rice here is of the vegetable origin but you don't need to tell your family members about that. I doubt they'll realize, mine don't seem to or if they do . . . they don't mind. This dish is super versatile, you can start with original flavors but try Taco, Asian or Cajun at other times for a change up and see which you like the most. You can enjoy a very generous sized amount in a bowl topped with the cheese sauce but I usually prefer to have this over salad. I love making the Taco-style version and putting a large sized amount of it over a big leafy salad (including cilantro). Before putting this on my salad, I simply toss the greens in juice from 1 lime and a squirt of Bragg Liquid Aminos . . . so simple, but it matches so well. Getting hungry right now thinking about it.

---

2 (10 ounce) bags frozen cauliflower rice
1 (12–16 ounce) bag frozen classic veggie medley (corn, carrots, peas and green beans)
2 cups quick cook brown rice (the 10-minute kind)
2 cups water
2–3 cups pre-cooked, diced chicken breast (or you can use canned chicken breast or replace some or all of the chicken with cooked or canned beans for plant based protein instead.)
1–1 ½ tsp. Mineral Salt
¼ tsp. black pepper
½–1 tsp. each onion and garlic powders
Optional 1–2 Tbs. Nutritional Yeast
Instant Cheese Sauce (page 380) for pouring over top or regular grated cheese for family members who prefer topping with that for Crossovers

---

1. Put cauli rice, frozen veggies, quick cook rice, and water into a large skillet and set to high heat. Stir ingredients then cover with a tight lid and cook on high for about 5 minutes. Stir, turn heat down to medium-high, replace the lid onto skillet and cook for another 10 minutes on medium-high heat.

2. Open lid, stir ingredients again, add seasonings and chicken or beans then turn heat down to medium. Cover with lid again and cook a few more minutes or until cauliflower rice and brown rice are fully cooked through and nice and tender and water is all absorbed. Stir ingredients a few more times while cooking so things don't stick to the bottom of the pan and burn.

TWEAKS:

Taco-style: Add 2 tsp. chili powder and 1 tsp. cumin powder

Asian-style: Reduce salt to ½ tsp. and add ¼ cup soy sauce, 1 tsp. ginger powder, and chili flakes to taste

Cajun-style: Remove salt and replace with 1½–2 tsp. creole seasoning

Notes: Feel free to add another bag of frozen veggies to stretch this to go further.

If you love fresh garlic, put 1 tsp oil or butter in skillet with 2–3 crushed garlic cloves and cook for a couple minutes before adding any of the other ingredients.

If you already have brown rice cooked, you don't have to use 2½ cups water. Only use ¼ cup water while veggies are cooking then add your 2–2½ cups of cooked rice after first 10 minutes of cook time.

CHICKEN STUFFED PEPPERS

S

Makes 6–8 Servings (leftovers can be eaten throughout the week or frozen for future use)

My husband doesn't even notice these stuffed peppers have cauliflower rice in them. They just taste like they're filled with creamy chicken and he just chows down. I always love when I can sneak another veggie in without him noticing. This is best served with a big salad, or my cucumber side salad from page: 261 and/or a steamed non-starchy veggie of your choice. Family members needing Crossovers can have fruit or whole grain bread on the side.

Fun pepper fact to remember: Peppers raise your metabolism and have super high amounts of vitamin C and other necessary vitamins. Peppers have even more vitamin C than oranges!

2 lb. boneless, skinless chicken breasts (chopped or snipped into small pieces)
1 medium onion (chopped)
3–4 garlic cloves (crushed)
1 tsp. ground sage
1 tsp. coriander
1 tsp. Mineral Salt
1 tsp. black pepper
optional ½ tsp. chili flakes
1 cup water
1 (12 oz.) bag frozen riced cauliflower
8 oz. ⅓ less fat cream cheese
4 large bell peppers
1½ cups grated cheese of your choice

1. Preheat oven to 400°F.
2. Spray a large skillet with coconut or olive oil and set to a medium-high heat. Toss chicken pieces with garlic, onion and spices for just a minute or two. Now add water, cover the skillet, and cook for 12–15 minutes . . . stirring occasionally or until chicken is cooked through. Add cream cheese and riced cauliflower and stir well.
3. While rice mix is cooking, cut peppers in half lengthways and take out seeds and stems. Once rice is cooked, fill peppers with the mixture and set them on a large plate or paper towels. Top each one with shredded cheese then set them all back in that same skillet again (if it is oven-safe . . . if not, use a different baking pan). Bake uncovered for 25 to 30 minutes (or longer if you don't like some of the life left in your peppers . . . I personally love them extremely wilted).

CREAM OF CHICKEN & RICE

Makes 6–8 Servings

You know those yummy, easy casseroles using just cream of mushroom soup, chicken and rice? Yeah, those. They speak comfort food to so many people, especially my husband. It was my father-in-law who perfected one of those "cream of" casseroles. He passed away unexpectedly a couple years ago but he made it for Jack all through his childhood. Jack has had such an emotional attachment to this dish. Of course, I was on a mission to healthify it as those "cream of" soups are full of unhealthy starches, chemicals and MSG but I didn't want Jack to miss out on

eating this childhood favorite. This hits my husband right in his cream of mushroom spot and it is so . . . so easy. If you already have the "Dream of Mushroom Soup" (page 188) made up, the rest of this recipe comes together in a few minutes then just throw 'er in the oven. This is great with any steamed and buttered non-starchy veggie and a salad. You'll notice this is a crossover and you might be thinking . . . why didn't she give us an S version using cauli rice? Trust me, I tried. I could never make it turn out despite several attempts. Sometimes I think Crossovers are there for a good reason and we should just stick with them on occasion.

---

1 Tbs. butter
2 garlic cloves (crushed)
2½ pounds boneless, skinless chicken
    tenderloins or sliced chicken breasts
1½ tsp. Mineral Salt (divided)
½ tsp. black pepper

2½ cups quick cook brown rice (the
    10-minute kind)
4 cups water
4 cups Dream of Mushroom Soup (from page:
    188)
Optional green onions (chopped)

---

1. Preheat oven to 375°F.
2. Add butter, garlic, chicken and ½ tsp. of the salt and all the black pepper to a large cast iron skillet set to high heat. Brown chicken in butter and garlic. Add all other ingredients (remember that final tsp. of salt) and stir well.
3. Bake uncovered for 45 minutes to an hour. You can top with chopped green onions, if desired.

CREAMY BUFFALO CHICKEN & POTATO SKILLET

Makes About 6–8 Servings

I don't feel like I need to do much explaining on why you should make this. If you like creamy golden potatoes (and who doesn't), if you like chicken and buffalo sauce (and again . . . who doesn't), it's such a no brainer! This is so fast to throw together, but then it takes a while to bake . . . almost a couple of hours. But don't let that throw you off, sometimes that's nice because you can just throw dinner in the oven while your children are still napping or go do some stuff around the home as your oven starts to waft out a delicious aroma. I pair this with some steamed green beans or broccoli on the side and a salad to stay in E-mode. For a Crossover, just put some nice butter on that non-starchy veggie or creamy dressing and cheese on the salad to keep things simple.

---

1 batch Creamy Buffalo Sauce from page 375
   (see instructions for cooking change)
6–8 medium golden potatoes (diced)
1 (8 ounce) bag of radishes (sliced into fourths)

2 lb. boneless, skinless chicken breasts
   (sliced into strips) or use tenderloins
1 cup water

---

1. Preheat oven to 400°F.
2. Rather than putting the ingredients for Creamy Buffalo Sauce in a saucepan as instructed on page 375, just put them all in a blender and blend until smooth. Pour sauce into a large skillet set to medium-high heat and cook for 5 minutes, stirring a few times. Add everything else but the water to the skillet and mix well.
3. Transfer skillet to the oven (or put in a baking dish if your skillet is not oven safe) and bake uncovered for 1 hour. Add the cup of water, flip chicken and stir mixture then place back in the oven for another 45 minutes or until everything is fully cooked and tender. Garnish with chopped parsley or cilantro if desired.

SOUTHERN "FRIED" CHICKEN

 OR

Makes 6–8 Servings (you can freeze whatever you don't eat)

As I've mentioned a few times, my husband grew up eating like a true southern boy so I've been on a quest to trim-healthify so many of his childhood comfort foods. He'll tell you that he is a healthier, happier man for the switch and now when I surprise him with this for dinner, his grin speaks everything. Jack's grandmother would make him fried chicken every week or even multiple times a week ... of course, it was deep fried and had lots of starch. This lightly skillet-fried version without the super starchy breading is so much healthier. Hot fried chicken is the big thing here in Tennessee. This has a mild spicy kick as a nod to what is known in these parts as Nashville Hot

Chicken but as written this is not super spicy; our girls love it as it has a very family-friendly temperature. So, if you love more heat … add a good sprinkle of cayenne pepper to the flour mixture!

Before THM came out with their Shameless Crackers, I would always make this as a Crossover using Wasa crackers and oats for the breading. Since that is a less expensive option, I often still do that, but I love having the S-option, too (tastes fantastic). I love this with a big salad, and a few Golden Fries on the side from page: 233. If you love fried chicken sandwiches, you can always use sprouted bread for a Crossover or make the S-version and put in a Joseph's pita (low-carb variety) or with any S friendly bread with mayo, lettuce, and tomato, etc … or, it goes great with coleslaw!

FOR THE CHICKEN:
2½–3 lb. boneless, skinless chicken breasts
   (sliced into strips) or use tenderloins
1 Tbs. hot sauce (any brand without sugar)
¼ cup water
2 eggs

FOR THE BREADING:
6–8 Light Rye Wasa or Ryvita crackers for
   XO or 1 bag Shameless Crackers-Classic
   Toppers for S

1½ cups ground oats (for XO) or 1½ cups
   Baking Blend (for S)
2 tsp. chili powder
1½ tsp. creole seasoning
½ tsp. black pepper
1 tsp. onion powder
Unflavored coconut oil for frying

---

1. Whisk hot sauce, water, and eggs together in a small bowl.
2. Put the Wasa or Shameless Crackers in a big Ziploc bag. Smash with the bottom of a cup or jar until you have some good-looking, gritty flour. Add ground oats or Baking Blend and spices and then pour onto a large plate or baking sheet.
3. Add a couple tablespoons of coconut oil to a nonstick frying pan set to medium-high heat. Dip chicken strips into egg mixture and then into the breading. Set into the frying pan.
4. Cook for about 5 minutes with the lid on and then flip and leave the lid off for them to cook on the next side for 3–5 minutes or until crispy. (These are perfect with the Real Thing Honey Mustard, page 358.)

BEEF N VEGGIE SKILLET

S

Makes About 6 Servings

Not only do we love having this for dinner, I really enjoy having leftovers for breakfast sometimes. Mushrooms are included here and for good reason since they are a literal superfood! But if you have mushroom haters in your family, don't fret! They're not going to know about them here . . . totally disguised . . . but their health benefits are still vividly apparent. Mushrooms are so great for your immune system, they're high in vitamins and minerals and have anti-inflammatory proper- ties. If possible, set your mushrooms in some sunlight . . . either on a window sill or outside for a couple hours before cooking . . . this takes their vitamin D level from a low amount to through the

roof! This dish is lovely with a side of green beans and/or some cauliflower mashed potatoes. For a Crossover option have with some Golden Fries from page 233 or a side of fruit.

1 medium onion (chopped*)	1 tsp. black pepper
2 Tbs. unflavored coconut oil or butter	Optional ½ tsp. ground sage
4 medium yellow squash (halved lengthwise and then thinly sliced)	1 lb. ground beef
	1 lb. mushrooms (processed in food processor)
½ cup water (divided)	¼ cup nutritional yeast
1 tsp. Mineral Salt	4 oz. Swiss or sharp cheddar cheese (grated)

1. Preheat oven to 375°F.
2. Put onion and 1 tablespoon of the coconut oil in a large, oven-safe skillet set to medium-high heat. Cook onion until caramelized, stirring several times. Add squash with ¼ cup of the water. Cover and cook for 10 minutes or until squash is soft.
3. Set cooked onions and squash aside on a plate or a bowl. Brown ground beef in the same skillet. Once meat is fully cooked, drain fat, put skillet back on heat and add ground mushrooms, remaining ¼ cup water, nutritional yeast, salt, pepper, and remaining 1 tablespoon of coconut oil. Cook on medium-high heat for 7–10 minutes.
4. Add back the squash and onions, stir into the beef mixture, cover with cheese then transfer to oven and bake uncovered for 20–35 minutes.

Note: If your children are not onion lovers . . . you can process the onion with the mushrooms and this will disguise them.

SHEPHERD'S PIE SKILLET

(S)

Makes About 6 Servings

As a child, I grew up making Shepherd's Pie for my family (the real thing with mashed potatoes on top). We would have people over a lot or lots of stray cousins who wanted to stay for dinner and this was a go-to meal if I couldn't think of anything else to make for the masses. I would make a huge amount . . . like 3 times as large as this and I would bask in the compliments from my nine siblings, my cousins and whoever my parents had over to gobble it up.

As I got into my teenage years and stopped growing taller, I kept making this for family and friends but I hardly ate it because it wasn't helpful to my waistline. I ended up creating this Trim Healthy version and it stuck. Everyone loved it. It is even healthier than the original with the cruciferous powers of cauliflower and the vitamin D immune boosting from the hidden mushrooms and my husband doesn't know the difference! No kidding . . . I made this the other night and we had leftovers for the next day. When I asked him if he wanted me to heat some up, he said . . . "Oh, I'll have some tomorrow . . . I've already had lots of carbs today." Yeah . . . he thinks this is topped with starchy white potatoes so please don't tell him if you ever meet him. I love this with a big salad or some fresh sliced veggies on the side (like sliced cucumbers and bell peppers). If you want a Crossover you can make my Overnight Biscuits from page 94 or just have some fruit on the side to keep things super simple.

FIRST LAYER: BOOSTED BEEF
1 lb. ground beef
1 lb. mushrooms (processed)
1 Tbs. chili powder
1 Tbs. paprika
1 tsp. ground cumin
1 tsp. garlic powder
½ tsp. Mineral Salt
1/2 tsp. black pepper
1/2 cup water

SECOND LAYER: TRICKED YOU MASHED POTATOES
3 (12 oz. bags) frozen riced cauliflower*
4 oz. ⅓ less fat cream cheese
1 tsp. Mineral Salt
½ tsp. black pepper

THIRD LAYER: THE SOUTHERN TOUCH
2 (14.5 oz.) cans cut green beans (drained) or 1 (15 oz.) bag frozen cut green beans (See Note*)
1½ cups shredded cheese

1. Preheat the oven to 375°F.

2. Brown ground beef in a large cast iron skillet. Once completely browned, drain fat, add ground mushrooms, water and spices, simmer on low for a few minutes.

3. While beef is cooking, steam riced cauliflower in a pot with 2–3 cups of water for 7–10 minutes on medium-high. Once cooked, drain the water then process with cream cheese, salt, and pepper until it looks as creamy as mashed potatoes

4. Spread your mashed cauliflower layer on the skillet of Boosted Beef, layer on the green beans then finally top with the cheese. Put in the oven and bake uncovered for 25–30 minutes.

*Note 1: You can use regular, frozen cauliflower in place of the riced cauliflower as it is sometimes less expensive, but you'll have to steam a bit longer to get it soft.

*Note 2: If you don't like using green beans from a can (like me), just steam (or microwave) a frozen bag of them until they're nice and soft … it is an extra step, but I prefer it.

GREAT WALL SKILLET

S

Makes 6–8 Servings (leftovers freeze well)

This super tasty, Asian-inspired skillet is amazing served in lettuce wraps or simply on top of shredded cabbage but you can just eat a big bowl of it any way you want! I hope I am taking you to the Great Wall of China in your mind as you sprinkle sesame seeds on top and enjoy extra soy sauce on the side (if needed and as shown in the picture). For young children who gag/choke on lettuce, or others who want Crossovers, serve with brown rice (I understand it would be white rice if you were truly eating this by the Great Wall of China, but let's still go for brown shall we?) and finely chopped cabbage.

- 1 large onion (chopped)
- 7 garlic cloves (crushed)
- ¼ cup fresh ginger (finely grated) or 1½ tsp. ground ginger
- 2 Tbs. unflavored coconut or olive oil
- 2 lb. 93% lean ground turkey or chicken
- 2 Tbs. apple cider vinegar
- 2 tsp. blackstrap molasses
- 2 cups chicken broth or stock (divided)
- ½ cup low sodium soy sauce
- 1½ tsp. Gluccie or xanthan gum
- 1 lb. mushrooms (finely chopped, or you can process to disguise if you want)
- 2 tsp. black pepper
- 2 tsp. garlic powder
- 1 tsp. Mineral Salt
- ½ tsp. chili flakes
- 2 tsp. sesame oil
- 2 Tbs. Gentle Sweet
- 2 Tbs. balsamic vinegar
- 2 (5 oz.) cans bamboo shoots (chopped)

1. Place the onion, garlic, ginger, and coconut oil in a large skillet. Cover with lid and set to high heat and cook for 3–5 minutes. Take off lid, add ground turkey, apple cider vinegar, molasses, and ½ a cup of the chicken stock.

2. Stir, then place the lid back on and cook until meat is fully done, stirring several times. Now add everything else (don't forget the remaining 1½ cups of chicken stock), stir it all up then reduce heat to medium-high, cover and cook for another 8–10 minutes.

SALMON AVOCADO SKILLET

Makes 6 Servings (I make all 6 and enjoy any leftovers for lunches throughout the week.)

We all need to eat more fish and this, along with the next few recipes, gives you easy and tasty ways to do it. This salmon goes great with a big salad and some steamed non-starchy veggies, or some fried up cauliflower rice to stay in S-mode. For a Crossover, I like to have it with my Toasted Corn & Pepper Salad from page: 258 and some R's Fresh Salsa from page: 353. Oh, and a few blue corn chips for the side. Delish!!!

6 (4–6 oz.) salmon fillets
½ tsp. garlic powder
½ tsp. black pepper
½ tsp. ground sage
½ tsp. creole seasoning
Optional ¼ tsp. chili flakes

Optional 2 bay leaves
2 Tbs. unflavored coconut oil, melted butter, or olive oil
3 limes
¼ tsp. Mineral Salt
1 avocado (thinly sliced)

1. Add salmon fillets to a large, dry skillet and sprinkle all spices onto the fillets. Drizzle the oil over them and squeeze the juice from one of the limes over the fillets. Now slice another of the limes and place the slices over the salmon.

2. Sprinkle the salt onto the avocado slices and then place them on top of the fillets. Turn the stove to high and cook for 7–8 minutes. Reduce heat to medium/low. Cover with a lid and then cook for another 3 minutes. Squeeze the juice from the last remaining lime over the salmon right before serving. (Keep the lid on the skillet until ready to serve.)

AWARD-WINNING SALMON

Makes 6 Servings (I make all 6 and enjoy any leftovers for lunches throughout the week.)

Okay . . . so maybe if I tell you that I'm the one who awarded myself with the name of this dish, you'll have a slightly different opinion of me. But my book . . . my names . . . haha!!!! And really . . . this is soooo good and deserves a few blue ribbons. . . . well that is what I tell myself but I have a feeling you'll think it worthy. This salmon pairs perfectly with a salad and some steamed broccoli, family members wanting Crossovers can simply have some brown rice, sprouted bread, a glass of whole milk or fruit on the side.

---

1 large onion (chopped)
5 garlic cloves (crushed)
2 Tbs. butter or unflavored coconut oil
½ tsp. black pepper
½ tsp. crushed, dried rosemary

1 tsp. Mineral Salt
1 cup water
6 (4–6 oz.) salmon fillets
Juice of 1 lemon

---

1. In a large skillet set to medium-high heat, caramelize onions, garlic, butter, and all the seasonings for about 7 minutes using a lid . . . but take it off to stir a few times.
2. Add water and cook for a further 3 minutes. Then submerge salmon fillets and cook for 7–10 minutes using the lid. Squeeze the lemon all over the salmon at the end. That's it!

R'S NO STRESS TILAPIA

(S)

Makes 6 Servings (I enjoy any leftovers for lunches throughout the week.)

My aunties have talked about "Sweat Pants Meals" in some of their Poddies . . . you know, those meals that are your go-to . . . no-stress . . . barely-have-to-think-about, throwing-them-together meals? They require nothing special and help keep you happily on plan. Well this for sure is one of my Sweat Pants Meals. I love that it is a lovely Light S and its simplicity is what keeps me from going crazy in my busy life! I keep plenty of frozen fish fillets in the freezer as fish thaws so quickly in a bowl of warm water and is then ready to cook up. If I can't think of what to have for dinner . . . I turn to this yummy and healthy protein source and have it with a salad and cooked up non-starchy veggies to stay in S-mode. If I want a Crossover, I'll enjoy it with brown rice, or another healthy carb such as a piece of fruit . . . like my high metabolism husband and little girls do.

   Note: I know some people don't love the idea of eating tilapia as it is farm-raised. This recipe works great with any white fish, but I do use tilapia because it is an affordable lean protein for my family.

---

6 (4–6 oz.) tilapia fillets (or other white fish)
¾ cup Parmesan cheese (green can works great)

½ tsp. black pepper
1 Tbs. unflavored coconut oil or butter
⅓ cup lemon juice

---

1. On a plate, mix Parmesan cheese and black pepper. Roll fillets in the mixture.
2. Heat oil in a large skillet set to medium-high. Put fillets in skillet and allow to brown for a minute or two. Turn fillets over, let brown for 1 minute on that side then pour lemon juice over fillets. Allow to cook for another few minutes with the lid on until fully done and until the Parmesan has a nice little crisp to it.

HAPPY DANCE FISH SKILLET

Makes About 6 Servings (leftovers work great for lunches or freeze well . . . so make this whole thing)

Imagine if eating fish played a bigger role in your life . . . your health would zoom upwards and your waistline would shrink . . . no, really . . . fish is actually that powerful a boon to your health and weight. This skillet recipe is my new, favorite invention and it can be yours, too! It is so fast to throw together and tastes so zesty, fresh, and delish. It makes a life of fish-eating so doable . . . even crave worthy! The flavors just make you want to do that happy dance! I love to have this with some finely sliced cabbage on the side or a salad with lean dressing to stay in E-mode. If you want a delicious

Crossover, have some sliced avocado on top or some shredded cheese and maybe even a few blue corn chips.

---

2 tsp. unflavored coconut oil
1 cup quick cook brown rice (the kind that's ready in 10-minutes)
1 cup water
½ tsp. Mineral Salt
1 (12 oz.) bag frozen pepper and onion blend
6 white fish fillets (I usually use tilapia because they're the cheapest, but any white fish works.)
1 (15 oz.) can black beans (drained)
1 (14.5 oz.) can petite diced tomatoes (not drained)

1 (10 oz.) can Rotel-style tomatoes and chilies (not drained)

FOR THE SAUCE:
1 bunch cilantro (chopped)
5 garlic cloves
1 tsp. Mineral Salt
1 tsp. black pepper
Juice of 6–7 limes (equaling about ¾–1 cup juice)
2 tsp. ground cumin
½ cup of water

---

1. Preheat oven to 400°F.
2. Add coconut oil, rice, water, salt, and frozen pepper and onion blend to a large, oven safe skillet. Mix around and cook for 3–5 minutes on high heat.
3. Set fillets on top as a single layer all around the skillet then dump the black beans all over the fillets. Add the petite diced tomatoes and the Rotel.
4. Blend everything from the sauce list and pour all over the skillet. Transfer to oven and bake uncovered for 40–45 minutes. Garnish with chopped cilantro or parsley if desired.

FISH STICKS

S

Makes About 6 servings

BOOM—healthy fish sticks! When I was younger, my dad loved to buy us fish sticks for a rare treat. My mom would almost always disapprove because she's a health nut and they're not healthy—but, Dad would always say, "It's fine, my Darling" and they got through it . . . Haha! My healthy version of these came out delicious, bringing back childhood memories, and my girls and husband devour them! I love serving these with ketchup or homemade tartar sauce (R's Tartar Sauce from page 359). You can enjoy a meal of these with cauliflower mash or steamed broccoli and a big salad to stay in S-mode. For a yummy Crossover, have some Golden Fries from page: 233 and/or some sliced veggies and Home Run Hummus from page 347.

FOR THE FISH FILLING:
2 lb. tilapia fillets (or other white fish)
2 eggs
1 tsp. Mineral Salt
½ tsp. black pepper
¼ tsp. citric acid

FOR THE COATING:
5 Light Rye Wasa Crackers or 1 bag
  Shameless Crackers-Classic Toppers

½ cup Parmesan cheese (green can works
  great)
½ cup Baking Blend
½ cup Oat Fiber
½ tsp. Mineral Salt
1 tsp. black pepper
1 tsp. onion powder
1½ tsp. garlic powder
Unflavored coconut oil for frying

1. Put the tilapia fillets in the food processor and pulse for a few seconds at a time. Then add the eggs, salt, pepper, and citric acid. Pulse again until fish is broken up into teeny tiny pieces . . . almost like fish mush.

2. Add the Wasa crackers to a gallon-sized Ziploc bag, then smash them with the bottom of a cup or a jar until broken up to a gritty flour.

3. Add the remaining coating ingredients to the Ziploc bag, seal, then shake together.

4. Pour coating mix onto a baking tray then put the tilapia mixture into the same Ziploc you used for the coating (reusing bags here). Cut about ⅓ of an inch in one of the bottom corners. Pipe a couple of inch fish mixture amounts onto the tray with the coating ingredients then roll each "fish stick" through the coating. Repeat until fish is all coated.

5. Put 2 tablespoons unflavored coconut oil in a large skillet set to medium-high heat. Once oil is hot, put fish sticks in the skillet (don't cram them in . . . you'll have to do two or three batches). Cook with the lid on for about 3–4 minutes on each side. Continue until you run out of fish sticks. You can serve with ketchup or homemade tartar sauce (R's Tartar Sauce from page 359).

*Note:** For DF use Nutritional Yeast in place of Parmesan cheese.

EGGPLANT PARM SKILLET

Makes About 6 Servings (Just go ahead and make the whole thing and freeze it in desired portion sizes, if you don't eat it all.)

This skillet version of Eggplant Parmesan saves you a lot of time and effort. You don't have to go through the steps of breading and frying the eggplant as you do with regular Eggplant Parmesan … that's an extra 30-minutes you shave off kitchen time … Hallelujah! I love having this with a super big salad dressed with balsamic vinegar and sometimes a glass of dry red wine for an extra Italian feel for my S meal. You can add buttered, garlic rubbed, and toasted sprouted bread for a Crossover.

1 lb. ground beef
Optional 8 oz. mushrooms (processed)
5–7 crushed garlic cloves
1½ tsp. Italian season
1 tsp. black pepper
1 tsp. creole seasoning
1 tsp. onion powder
½ tsp. dried rosemary

1 (15 oz.) can tomato sauce
1 (14.5 oz.) can petite diced tomatoes (not drained)
1 medium to large eggplant (thinly sliced)
1½ cups grated part skim mozzarella cheese
½ cup Parmesan cheese (green can is fine)

1. Preheat oven to 375°F.
2. Brown ground beef in a large oven-safe skillet, discard fat, then add everything but the last 3 ingredients and let simmer for 7–10 minutes on medium-high heat.
3. Place half the sauce/meat mixture into a bowl and set aside for a minute while you place half the eggplant slices all over the skillet.
4. Sprinkle ½ a cup of the mozzarella cheese onto the eggplant along with ¼ of a cup of Parmesan cheese. Now take the leftover sauce/meat mixture and spread it all over that bed of eggplant.
5. Take the remaining eggplant slices and make another layer. This time just sprinkle all the leftover cheese on top and an extra sprinkle of Italian seasoning, if desired, then transfer to the oven and bake uncovered for 45 minutes.

SOUTHWEST TURKEY BURGERS

Makes About 4–6 Servings (Make all of these because you can freeze leftovers in a Ziploc bag with parchment paper in between each one.)

These are super tasty burgers that contain a hidden veggie in the form of cauliflower rice, but your family members won't know it's there. These are also FP so they can work with so many meals. For a FP meal, you can wrap 2 or 3 patties (depending on how big you make them) in lettuce leaves and include salsa or a slice of tomato, cilantro, and a dollop of 0% Greek yogurt. Yum!!! S-mode . . . have with the list of above or have on a nice salad with Spiced-Up Mexican Cauli-Rice from page 259, grated cheese, toasted sunflower seeds, sliced avocado, or Hit the Spot Guac from page 356,

E-mode… have between two pieces of sprouted bread with everything listed for FP. You can even add 1-2 tablespoons of corn kernels to the burgers if you want to be eating these in E-mode. Or turn this E into a Crossover by putting guac and cheese on your sandwich.

1 lb. (96–99% lean) ground turkey or chicken	**1 medium bell pepper (chopped)**
2 egg whites or ¼ cup liquid egg whites	**1 medium onion (chopped)**
1–3 Tbs. hot sauce (use only 1 Tbs. if you are scared of heat)	**¾ tsp. Mineral Salt**
	1 Tbs. paprika
1 cup frozen cauliflower rice	**2 Tbs. chili powder**
1 cup canned or home cooked black beans (drained)	**2 tsp. cumin**

1. Put everything listed above in a big bowl, mix well, and then shape into thin patties.
2. Spray with coconut or olive oil and cook on medium for about 5 minutes on each side or until burgers are cooked through.

Note: Don't worry about the beans here for FP or S-mode. You won't be crossing over if you have these burgers with fats. Beans are a super gentle, slow-burning E fuel and THM allows up to ¼ cup in S meals, on occasion, so the amount used here is fine.

QUINOA TUNA PATTIES

Makes About 6 Servings (make them all . . . freeze leftovers for fast future meals)

These patties are a great way to enjoy that oh-so-healthy quinoa that's probably just sitting in your cabinet. I like to eat these patties as I have shown in the image to stay in E-mode (Joseph's Low-Carb Pita, sliced tomato, cilantro, cucumber, and hot sauce). To have this as a Crossover, just add some cheese or avocado. If you want, you can even have a smear of mayo. If you do include mayo, please don't invite me over. Hehe . . . (I hate it with a passion!) BTW . . . you'll notice cheese in the ingredient list . . . it is just a small amount that still fits in E guidelines.

2 cups cooked quinoa	4 (2.5 oz.) tuna pouches or 3 (5 oz.) cans of drained tuna
½ an onion (finely diced)	3 Tbs. Baking Blend or ground old fashioned rolled oats
1 tsp. creole seasoning	2 egg whites or ¼ cup liquid egg whites
½ tsp. black pepper	
1 tsp. dried oregano	
¾ cup grated part-skim mozzarella cheese	

1. Mix everything up and spray a non-stick skillet with coconut or olive oil.

2. Shape mixture into patties and then cook on medium-high heat for a few minutes on each side until they become slightly crispy. If you want to air fry them, set to 390°F and fry for 10 minutes. You'll need to do at least 2 different batches with both cooking options.

ZUCCHINI FRITTERS

Makes 6–8 Servings (great as leftover lunches or breakfasts)

I enjoy having these with lettuce, turkey bacon, cilantro, and avocado as shown in the image. I also love having them premade so I can have them on the side of my breakfast. It's such a fast way to get some veggies in the morning! You can also make a grilled cheese sandwich with them, basically using them as the bread. Just put sharp cheddar cheese on one of the fritters then place another fritter on top. Heat in a pan on medium-high heat and flip when the cheese is almost melted. So YUMMY! To enjoy this as a Crossover, have some fruit on the side or a baked sweet potato.

---

7 cups grated zucchini (about 4–5 medium zucchinis)
¾ cup Baking Blend
½ cup Parmesan cheese (green can works fine)
1 cup extra sharp cheddar cheese (grated)

½ tsp. Black pepper
1 tsp. Mineral Salt
3 eggs
Unflavored coconut oil or butter for cooking

---

1. Grate zucchini with a cheese grater or use a food processor. (It only takes me about 2 minutes to do it by hand and for me that's way better than trying to find the attachment to my food processor!)

2. Add everything to a large bowl and mix.

3. Set a large skillet to medium-high heat and put 2 tablespoons or so of coconut oil or butter in skillet. Shape mixture into fritter sizes with your hands and cook them until slightly crispy on each side. (You may need to do multiple batches.)

9

OVEN BAKED MEALS

No nifty, modern kitchen gadgets required here! If you like cooking with a magical device known colloquially as a good, ol' OVEN then this chapter has some mouthwatering recipes that I hope you and your family will adore! From casseroles to baked chicken and fish dishes … I really enjoyed making the dinner mains in this section. And if you don't mind me saying … I feel like each one is unique and flavorful in its own right. Enjoy!

ALL-PURPOSE CHICKEN ENCHILADAS

Makes 8 Servings (leftovers freeze well or are great for quick lunches)

Fast to make and everyone always loves them … Introducing my All-Purpose Chicken Enchiladas! These are big and hearty and can be created to fit any fuel type. When I'm going with FP (using a low-carb tortilla and keeping fats low) or E (using the sprouted tortilla and keeping fats low) I like having one alongside some fresh cut peppers and my salsa (R's Fresh Salsa from page 353) with a dollop of 0% Greek yogurt as I have shown in the image. If I'm planning on enjoying as an S (using

the low-carb tortilla and adding some fats), I still love that salsa on the side but I enjoy my serving with some sliced avocado or some Crazy Good Guac from page 356. When I'm having a Crossover (using either a low-carb or sprouted tortilla), I love having the Queso Dip from page 354 along with blue corn chips on the side. Oh, these are so good in so many ways!

Note: You'll see grated mozzarella called for in this recipe, amounts are low enough to fit into E and FP.

Cancun Chicken recipe from page 117
2 (12 oz.) bags frozen cauliflower rice
1 cup salsa
1 cup 0% Greek yogurt
1 Tbs. chili powder
8 low-carb tortillas for FP or S; 8 sprouted
   tortillas for E or XO
1–1¼ cups grated part-skim mozzarella cheese
   (can increase amounts for S if desired)

ENCHILADA SAUCE:
1 (15 oz.) can tomato sauce
1 tsp. garlic powder
1 tsp. smoked paprika
2 tsp. chili powder
½ tsp. onion powder
¼ tsp. black pepper
⅛–¼ tsp. Super Sweet Blend
1 Tbs. hot sauce

---

1. Preheat oven to 425°F. Spray a 9 x 13-inch baking pan with coconut or olive cooking spray.
2. Make the Cancun Chicken recipe from page: 117 and then add everything else from the first ingredient list, except for the cheese and the tortillas. Let cook for another 5 minutes on high heat.
3. Mix up the enchilada sauce in a small bowl and set aside. Fill the tortillas with the chicken and place them into the baking dish on their sides next to each other so the top folds do not come undone. Pour enchilada sauce over them and then sprinkle with the cheese and bake uncovered for 25–30 minutes.

BAKED ZAGHETTI

Makes About 6 Servings

My two-year old (Emory) absolutely loves this casserole! I love that what she thinks is simply yummy is actually giving her body heaps of health-boosting veggies! I serve this with a salad and sometimes another cooked veggie on the side for a super loaded veggie meal when I want to stay in S-mode. Buttered, sprouted bread on the side for Crossover family members is all that is needed.

   Note: If you don't want to do the work of spiralizing zucchini yourself, you can easily find it fresh and already spiralized in the produce department of most grocery stores. I take the extra few minutes to spiralize my own by hand with one of those nifty gadgets (THM has one if you can't find one at the store), but I'm a cheapskate!

---

1 lb. 85% ground beef
8 oz. mushrooms (processed)
3 garlic cloves (crushed)
1 tsp. Italian seasoning
1 tsp. dried rosemary
1 tsp. oregano
½ tsp. black pepper
½ tsp. Mineral Salt

Optional ¼ tsp. chili flakes
1 (25 oz.) jar no-sugar added pasta sauce
⅔ cup Parmesan cheese (divided; the green can is fine)
4 medium zucchinis equaling about 5–6 cups spiralized zucchini
1 cup part-skim mozzarella cheese (grated)

---

1. Preheat oven to 425°F.
2. Brown ground beef in a large saucepan set to medium-high heat. Pour off fat. Add ground mushrooms, crushed garlic, spices, and salt. Let cook for 5–10 minutes then add pasta sauce and ¼ cup of the Parmesan.
3. Squeeze spiralized zucchini to get excess liquid out and then add to the pot. Mix together then transfer to a 9 x 13 baking dish. Sprinkle remaining Parmesan and mozzarella cheese on top. Bake uncovered for 35–40 minutes.

COMPANY CASSEROLE

Makes About 6–8 Servings

Pearl Chimes In You know you can count on me for a Drive Thru Sue-style casserole, right? This is a chicken and broccoli casserole that comes together so easily. It is show-offy enough to serve for company, but easy enough to just throw together for your own family any night of the week. I get lots of requests for this recipe any time I take it to a potluck or any get-together. I opt for the cream cheese-version when making this for company and I also use diced rotisserie chicken and add a little extra cheddar than what is called for as it tastes extra spectacular that way. The first time you make it, you may want to try it the cream cheese way with a little extra cheddar and you'll get everyone on board. For basic family meals, I go lighter and nix the cream cheese and just stick to cottage cheese…Sometimes I even use canned chicken as I am that much of a Drive Thru Sue. This turns out great either way. Here ya' go!

2 (10 ounce) bags frozen broccoli
3–4 cups pre-cooked, diced, or shredded chicken (if using canned, use 2–3 (12 ounce) cans; drained)
1 cup liquid egg whites
¾ cup unsweetened almond or cashew milk
12 ounces cottage cheese (or, 8 ounces cottage cheese plus 4 ounces ⅓ less

fat cream cheese for an extra creamy, company-worthy result)
2½ tsp. creole seasoning (you can sprinkle in added garlic powder if you like that)
½ tsp. black pepper
⅓ cup green can Parmesan cheese (divided)
1 Tbs. dried onion flakes
8 ounces grated cheddar cheese (divided)
Optional coconut or olive oil cooking spray

1. Heat oven to 400°F and lightly spray a 9 x 13 casserole dish with coconut or olive oil cooking spray.

2. Put chicken in casserole dish and set aside.

3. Lightly steam broccoli until just under done (10 minutes on high heat from start to finish).

4. While broccoli is steaming, blend all other ingredients together (except for cheddar cheese and onion flakes) and use only ¼ cup of the Parmesan on this part.

5. Put the broccoli in dish with chicken then pour blended ingredients over top. Add dried onions and half of the grated cheese (use a bit more cheese here if making for company). Stir well so everything is coated with the cream sauce.

6. Top with remaining cheddar then sprinkle remaining Parmesan over the top and bake, uncovered for 40–45 minutes.

MAN WORTHY LENTIL LOAF

Makes About 6–8 Large Servings (leftovers—freeze well or halve recipe since this makes a huge amount)

Serene Chimes In Ever heard of a man getting excited over lentils for dinner? Well, my man is loving this loaf and his health is thriving on it! But, hey … if there is no man in your home (or you can't drag him onto the Trim Healthy train yet), but you like to eat as hearty as a dude, then this plant-focused protein loaf will be a game changer for you. While meat is celebrated on the Trim Healthy Plan, plant food needn't always take second stage on the dinner plate. Fill up tonight with gut-healing fiber, all-important folate, and a fresh idea for anchoring with protein. (If you're the only one eating this … divide it into individual portions and freeze for future easy meals.)

So, here I am in in the middle of writing this intro, all revved up excited and telling my husband about the name I've chosen and what I'm writing, etc. He just told me not to give the impression that it tastes like regular meat loaf. "You don't want men to think it tastes all meaty, Serene" he is saying.

Me to husband … "But you told me you really enjoy it."

Husband … "I do, but you'll never fool men into thinking it is meat!"

Okay … okay … so this doesn't exactly taste like a greasy pork 'n chili casserole. But it is by jingoes a hearty meal and with not even a trace of dairy. Honestly … we all need a break from heavy dairy sometimes and most bakes and casseroles are piled with it. There's a place for those cheesy sorts of casseroles that my sister Pearl is so famous for giving you … but she doesn't eat them every night! They are only a now-and-then meal for her. So, let's find some balance! It is too easy to get into a rut of piling almost every meal with cheese and meats and end up overdoing them. This over-cheesing thing was an issue with my husband and while he still enjoys some heavier meals now-and-then, his health is doing much better with more lean E meals and less heavy dairy and red meat.

This loaf is actually loaded full with everything most of us tend to underdo … like secret high-fiber veggies, disguised mushrooms, superfoods, soluble fiber, resistant starch, ultra-lean protein, and of course plenty of lentils. So, yeah … my hubby is right … don't expect it to taste like Cheeseburger Pie because you'll be disappointed. But it shines with its own confident yummy vibe, all moist, soothing, and succulent and it will keep your waistline from getting bogged down with constant Heavy S dinners. Remember, it's the juggle of fuels that is at the heart of the Trim Healthy Plan.

Notes to Read Before Making: The carrots, mushrooms, and beets are processed so picky kids or adults won't detect them as much. You can grate them if you are a veggie lover … up to you.

- 4 cups pre-cooked or canned brown lentils (well drained)
- 16 oz. mushrooms (I use portabellas, but any will work; processed or grated)
- 4 medium-sized carrots (processed or grated)
- Approx. 2 small beets (to make 1 packed cup of processed or grated)
- 2 stalks celery (processed or finely diced)
- 6 cloves garlic (crushed)
- 1 large red onion (finely diced; or you can process, if preferred)
- 2 Tbs. mellow miso
- 3 Tbs. Baobab Boost Powder
- 3 Tbs. Nutritional Yeast
- 2 Tbs. Integral Collagen
- 2 cups egg whites
- 3 Tbs. Whole Husk Psyllium Flakes
- 4 Tbs. Baking Blend
- 1 cup old fashioned rolled oats
- 2½ tsp. Mineral Salt
- 1 tsp. black pepper
- 2–2½ Tbs. Bragg Liquid Aminos or soy sauce
- 1 Tbs. dried parsley

TANGY TOM TOPPING:

- 1 (6 oz.) can tomato paste
- 1 Tbs. Gentle Sweet
- ½ Tbs. apple cider vinegar
- ½ tsp. Mineral Salt
- 2½ Tbs. water
- 1 Tbs. Baobab Boost Powder
- ⅛ tsp. black pepper

1. Preheat oven to 350°F degrees. Lightly spray a 9 x 13 baking dish with coconut or olive oil then get out your food processor and line up all your veggies.

2. Pulse the mushrooms in the food processor one pack at a time, until nicely broken down into tiny pieces (but not puréed). Place them in a large mixing bowl. Quickly rough cut the beets and carrots and process them by pulsing, just like you did with the mushrooms, and add them to the bowl. Process onion in the same way (or finely dice) and add to the bowl along with the crushed garlic and all other ingredients, except egg whites and psyllium.

3. In a smaller mixing bowl, whisk the egg whites and psyllium until free of clumps. Add this to the big bowl of ingredients and combine everything really well with a wooden spoon.

4. Put the loaf mixture into the baking dish then flatten it down. Spread the Tangy Tom Topping on top and bake for 1 hour and 15 minutes.

Note: Best served with Pearl's Go To Gravy (page 376) drizzled generously on top and a side salad spritzed with balsamic and Braggs.

LEMON PEPPERY CHICKEN

Makes About 4–6 Servings (add another 2–4 pounds of drumsticks and increase seasonings if you have a larger family or want to enjoy leftovers for other meals)

Any bone-in chicken pieces work here, but my family prefers drumsticks. I pair with cauliflower mash and steamed green beans for a perfectly satisfying S meal. Simply add a healthy carb such as sliced, sprouted bread with butter or a piece of fruit to make a Crossover for family members needing that.

4 lb. chicken drumsticks
2 Tbs. melted unflavored coconut oil (or I use MCT oil sometimes as it doesn't clump like coconut oil does)
2 Tbs. baking powder
1 Tbs. garlic powder
½ tsp. ground coriander
½ Tbs. sage

½ Tbs. black pepper
½ Tbs. oregano
1 Tbs. lemon zest
1 tsp. Mineral Salt
1 tsp. citric acid
1 tsp. marjoram
Juice of 1 lemon

1. Preheat oven to 425°F.
2. Place drumsticks, coconut oil, and lemon zest in a clean bag or large bowl and mix together. Combine all remaining ingredients minus the lemon in a small bowl then sprinkle it all over the chicken.
3. Place drumsticks on an extra large, shallow baking tray (you can line it with parchment paper for easy clean up) and bake for 1 hour and 25 minutes. When you take them out of the oven, squeeze lemon juice all over them.

JOLLY JACK CHICKEN

S

Makes About 4–6 Servings (add another 2–4 pounds drumsticks if you have a larger family or want to enjoy leftovers for other meals)

My Aunty Pearl gave us all Hubby Lovin' Chicken in the Trim Healthy Table book . . . Well, I agree that is delicious, but this here is my husband's all-time favorite chicken! To use a Down Under word from my mom . . . it makes him so jolly happy! Jack literally raves about this crispy-style chicken every time I make it. I get to feel like an amazing cook, but with hardly any effort because it is so super simple . . . win-win! Jack used to work as an EMT on the ambulance so sometimes his partners would all take turns cooking dinners since they had crazy long shifts. I would make this chicken for him to take as his contribution. His co-workers would all devour it, then endlessly harass him because he never actually cooked anything! When making this for home, I like eating a drumstick or two with a big salad and green beans to stay in S-mode. If you're wanting to serve as a Crossover, perhaps have some buttered corn on the cob on the side . . . . yum!

BTW—Forgive me for my non-exact measurements for hot sauce and cheese here . . . you really can't mess this up . . . just put on how much you want!

Pearl Chimes In While Hubby Lovin' is still a fave chicken meal around my home, my sons devour the Jolly Jack now! They ask for it often and I don't mind making it because this dish is not only so jolly tasty, it is so jolly easy! I'm a literal sucker for easy and for that reason, it has become one of my go-to Sweat Pants Meals to feed my hungry teenagers and their many cousins and friends who are always hanging around here (I make a double batch and hope for leftovers, but that doesn't always happen). It doesn't hurt that chicken drumsticks are one of the most inexpensive protein sources out there either.

---

4 lb. chicken drumsticks
Hot sauce (I use Louisiana brand, but you can
   use your own favorite.)

Grated cheddar cheese

---

1. Preheat oven to 375°F. Cover 1 very large (or 2 medium) baking sheet with parchment paper.
2. Place drumsticks on parchment paper, making two lines. (Be sure they each have space to crisp; don't shove them too close together so they are touching one another.)

3. Douse hot sauce all over drumsticks, literally go to town with it, and then sprinkle cheese all over them.

4. Bake uncovered for 1 hour and 25 minutes or until the cheese has nicely "crispatized" on the chicken.

ROSEMARY CHICKEN ROAST

Makes 4–6 Servings

This roast is a great dinner if you're busy. It only takes a few minutes to prepare, then all you do is stick it in the oven and set a timer. We all need more E dinner ideas and this one never fails me. The chicken comes out tender and tasty and the root veggies get lovely and seasoned while cooking along with the tasty juices from the chicken. Pair with a fresh side salad with a low-fat dressing and you have the perfect E meal. To make a Crossover, you can put grated cheese and creamy dressing on your salad.

2½ lb. boneless, skinless chicken breasts	1½ tsp. Mineral Salt
4 medium sweet potatoes (cut into fours)	1 tsp. ground sage
2 (16 oz.) bags fresh radishes (cut in halves)	½ tsp. crushed dried rosemary
2–3 cups of water	2–3 sprigs fresh rosemary (or 2 tsp. non-crushed dried rosemary)
1 tsp. black pepper	

1. Preheat oven to 375°F.
2. Put chicken in a large baking dish, add sweet potatoes, and radishes.
3. Mix water with salt and dried spices in a jar then pour over chicken and veggies, sprinkle on fresh rosemary. Cover dish with lid (or foil) and bake for one hour.

BEST BUFFALO WINGS

Makes About 4 Servings

These wings go great with a big salad or cut celery and some cooked non-starchy veggies on the side to keep it in S-mode. Add a serving of brown rice or another healthy carb for a Crossover.

4 lb. chicken wings	2 cups Creamy Buffalo Sauce from page 375
¼ tsp. Mineral Salt	

1. Preheat oven to 425°F.
2. Place chicken wings on an extra-large cookie sheet (or a couple of smaller ones). Sprinkle salt over them and bake uncovered for 1 hour and 15 minutes.
3. Once baked, turn oven to high broil and broil for 2 minutes or until the tops look slightly crispy. Remove from heat, flip wings, and then place back in the oven for another 2 minutes to broil to crisp up the other side. Remove from oven, pour the sauce all over them, reduce heat to a low broil, and then put back in the oven to broil on low for 5–7 minutes. (Be careful they don't burn under the broiler.)

FRIENDLY

ADDICTIVE BAKED FISH

Makes 6–8 Servings (leftovers make great lunches and can be used for any fuel type)

If you are not a fish lover, give this a try and maybe it'll change your mind. The seasonings used here take over any fishiness and offer pure fun to your mouth! I am a curry spice lover so this is inspired with the spices of India, but don't worry, this is not too spicy ... even my little girls enjoy. I serve with sautéed or steamed string green beans or cauli rice to stay in FP or S (with added butter) or brown rice for E or a Crossover (with added butter).

2 lb. tilapia fillets (or other white fish)

3 Tbs. Nutritional Yeast

1 Tbs. curry powder

1 Tbs. ground coriander

1 tsp. black pepper

1 tsp. garlic powder

½ tsp. Mineral Salt

Coconut or olive oil cooking spray

Optional 1 lemon or 2 limes

Optional cilantro for garnishing

1. Preheat oven to 375°F and line a large baking tray with parchment paper.

2. Set fillets on baking tray and lightly spray tops with coconut or olive oil.

3. Mix the nutritional yeast and the other seasonings in a small bowl, and then sprinkle half the seasoning mixture onto the fish. Flip the fish over and repeat the process by spraying and sprinkling on the remaining spice mixture.

4. Spray the tops of the fish lightly one last time then put in oven and bake uncovered for 35 minutes. Once baked, squeeze lemon or lime on top (if you like citrus on your fish, otherwise leave it off and garnish with cilantro . . . if you want to).

10

SEXY SOUPS

R's Gumbo (S)

Millennial Split Pea Soup (E)

Green Bean Chili (S) or (FP)

Greek Chicken Soup (E)

Flexible Fajita Soup (E), (FP), or (S)

Corn Chowder (XO)

Navy Seal Soup (S)

Taco Chicken Chili (E)

Dream of Mushroom Soup (S)

R's Indian Curry (S)

Creamy Dreamy Limas (E)

Why the name? Well, Jack was actually the one who came up with this title for my soup chapter . . . typical of a husband's thought process, right? I left the title in when I sent my first rough copy of this book to Aunty Pearl to edit. I never meant for it to stay . . . just kept it in thinking my aunty would get a laugh out of it, but we'd of course change it before the book was published. But my aunt was all like . . . "No . . . we should keep it! Why can't soups be the new sexy?"

Here's how the conversation pretty much continued . . .

Me: "But what if they eat one of these soups and get a little gassy . . . not that my soups are very gassy, but I can't promise zero gas when it comes to veggies. . . . gas is not so sexy right?"

Aunty Pearl: "Oh, a bit of gas is a part of life . . . a part of every marriage . . . so a natural part of being sexy."

Me: "Right . . . and soups are so slimming and so healthy . . . and those are definitely sexy."

Aunty Pearl: "For sure . . . so it's official . . . soups are totally the new sexy now. Jack's a genius."

I'm here to tell you, sexy or not, I love a good soup, no . . . you're not hearing me . . . I mean I LOOOVE soup. For me, eating yummy soup is like being wrapped in a nice, warm blanket on a chilly day. As my mom would say, "It warms the cockles of your heart!" I make these soups all year around, not just when it's a bit nippy out. Since they're so easy and oh, so healthy . . . why would I not???

All of these are full-sized family meals, but you can throw whatever you're not going to eat into the freezer for a later date. (Pro Tip: Don't literally throw the soup into your freezer because that would end up being quite messy, but instead place the soup into a container or a zippy or if you are a purist . . . a glass jar with room for air before you put the lid on.) Also, don't miss out . . . I have a few more single-serve soup recipes in the Speedy Chapter, along with Aunty Serene's new soup recipe . . . so be sure to go check those out, too.

R'S GUMBO

Makes About 6–8 Servings (freezer friendly)

The flavors of this gumbo are absolutely scrumptious! I like to eat it plain to keep in S-mode. If I'm wanting a Crossover, it's great to have over brown rice. I don't like eating shrimp, but if that's what you like, throw some in.

3 Tbs. unflavored coconut oil (divided)
4 cups chicken broth or stock (divided)
5 garlic cloves (crushed)
½ cup Baking Blend
3 Tbs. Nutritional Yeast
2 Tbs. smoked paprika
1 tsp. black pepper
1½ tsp. creole seasoning
2 lb. chicken sausage links (sliced)
1 onion (chopped)

1 (12 oz.) bag cut frozen okra
1 (12 oz.) bag frozen cauliflower
½ a small cabbage (chopped; or a bag of coleslaw)
2 celery stalks or ribs (chopped)
1½ bell peppers (any color; chopped)
1 (14.5 oz.) can diced tomatoes
1 (10 oz.) can Rotel-style diced tomatoes with chilies

1. Put 1½ tablespoons of the oil and 2 cups of the chicken broth into a large soup pot set to medium-high heat along with garlic, nutritional yeast, Baking Blend, and spices. Cook for five minutes, uncovered, stirring a few times.

2. While those ingredients are cooking, put chicken sausage slices in a skillet with remaining 1½ tablespoons of the oil until they have a crisped edge to them. Then add chopped onion to the same skillet and let it crisp up for a few minutes.

3. Now add everything (remember the last 2 cups of broth) to the big pot and cook covered on medium heat for 30 minutes. Give it a good stir every 5–10 minutes so it doesn't all sink to the bottom of the pot and burn. Reduce heat to medium-low and let simmer for another 15–30 minutes or so.

MILLENNIAL SPLIT PEA SOUP

Makes 6–8 Servings (freezer friendly)

It may come as a shock, but millennials are good for something, actually lots of things! Many consider Split Pea Soup to be something your grandma might make … well that's because our grandmas knew what was awesome in life. As a millennial, I want to bring a new love and respect for Split Pea Soup back to my generation.… but with a modern twist. This soup is totally one of my top favorites; it's so comforting, delish, and so inexpensive … and thanks to the okra and spinach it has even more amazing, health-giving ingredients than the old-fashioned type. Split peas are high in vitamins, minerals, fiber, and folate. They have resistant starch that creates a healthier gut biome and they also help you stay full for longer. As an E, this is great topped with a little 0% Greek yogurt or just a small garnish of cheese, if you can do dairy … if not, just eat it as is. For a Crossover, I like to have it with more sharp cheddar cheese on top and extra turkey bacon.

1 lb. split peas	½–1 tsp. black pepper
2 quarts water	Optional 1 chamomile tea bag*
12 oz. frozen cut okra	2 Tbs. apple cider vinegar
½ onion (cut into fourths)	3 Tbs. fresh or 1 Tbs. dried parsley
4 garlic cloves	2 heaped cups tightly packed spinach
2 tsp. dried ground sage	3–4 cups chicken broth or stock
1½–2 tsp. creole seasoning	8 pieces cooked turkey bacon (diced or
3 Tbs. Nutritional Yeast	crumbled)

1. Put peas, water, frozen okra, onion, and garlic in a large soup pot set to high. Cover until it starts to boil then reduce heat to medium. Cut open tea bag, if using, and sprinkle contents into pot, then add everything but the parsley, spinach, and chicken broth.

2. Cook until split peas are all mushy and then put half of it in a blender with the parsley and spinach and blend until smooth. Pour that into a bowl or another pot and then blend the rest. Add all of it back to the pot and stir in chicken broth. Let simmer for a few more minutes. Serve with turkey bacon on top of each bowl.

*Note: Why the chamomile tea? Apparently, it can help with indigestion, and abdominal gas that some people get with legumes like split peas. It does have other awesome benefits, too! It doesn't really change the flavor so if you don't have it on hand—you're all good. You may just have an extra POOT! Kidding . . . but, not really!

GREEN BEAN CHILI

Makes About 4–6 Servings (freezer friendly)

Okay, so this is one of my favorite chilis and it is a true to the core S ... or you can even have it as a FP. There are ZERO beans in it ... well, except for green beans, but those are totally S-friendly so yay! Seriously, if someone else would make this for me I wouldn't even notice it has no pinto beans in it. The green beans give it a great texture. If I'm staying in S-mode, I like to have this with some sharp cheddar cheese on top along with some roasted, salted sunflower seeds for crunch

action... absolutely divine! I know sunflower seeds on chili sounds crazy, but to me it is almost like having crunched up chips on top. If you want to have this as a FP, top with a little 0% Greek yogurt and just a few crunched up Shameless Crackers-Classic Toppers. Of course, when I'm having it as a Crossover, I'll have it with cheese and blue corn chips.

1 lb. lean ground beef (*Use 96–99% lean if you do not want to drain/rinse the fat in FP-mode.)	2 tsp. onion powder
	2 tsp. garlic powder
	Optional 2 bay leaves
8 oz. mushrooms (processed)	Optional ¼ tsp. chili flakes
3 Tbs. chili powder	5 cups water
3 Tbs. Nutritional Yeast	1 (14.5 oz.) can diced tomatoes
1 Tbs. ground cumin	1 (14.5 oz.) can petite diced tomatoes
1 Tbs. paprika	1 (8 oz.) can tomato sauce
1 tsp. black pepper	1 (12 oz.) bag frozen cut green beans
1 tsp. Mineral Salt (or more to taste if needed)	

1. Brown the meat in a large soup pot. While beef is cooking, process those mushrooms if you didn't do that already. Once meat is cooked, drain off most of the extra fat for S (you can leave some in if you like) but, if you want it FP, *put it in a colander and run very hot water over it to get rid of all the fat.
2. Add the meat back to the pot along with the mushrooms, all the spices, and 1 cup of water. Cover, and cook on medium-high heat for 5 minutes.
3. Throw in the rest of the ingredients and cook for 15 minutes with the lid left on. Give it a good stir here and there, so it doesn't all go to the bottom of the pot and burn.

GREEK CHICKEN SOUP

Makes About 6–8 Servings (freezer friendly)

This soup is such a fun, refreshing way to use up that healthy quinoa that might be sitting in your cupboard all alone and forgotten. I love Greek food so this is a great meal for me since it's so easy. If you want to turn this into a Crossover, just drizzle some olive oil into your bowl of soup and don't worry about making sure your feta is low-fat. You could always make my Home Run Hummus from page: 347 to have on the side with some sliced veggies or homemade pita chips made from a low-carb Joseph's pita too.

2½ lb. boneless, skinless chicken breasts (chopped or snipped into small pieces)
1 Tbs. plus 1 tsp. dried oregano
1 tsp. Mineral Salt
1¼ tsp. black pepper
5–6 garlic cloves (crushed)
3 large lemons
4 cups chicken stock or broth
1 purple onion (chopped)

1¼ cups uncooked quinoa
6–8 cups water (your preference on brothiness)
12–15 Kalamata olives (sliced)
½–¾ cup Kalamata olive brine (yep, the juice from the olive jar)
2 (14.5 oz.) cans diced tomatoes
1 bunch fresh parsley (chopped)
Optional low-fat feta cheese for sprinkling

1. Put chicken, salt, spices, crushed garlic, the juice from one lemon, and one cup of the chicken stock into a large soup pot. Cover and cook on high for 10 minutes.

2. Add onion and another cup of the chicken stock and cook for 10 more minutes on high.

3. Add quinoa, remaining chicken stock, and water. Cook covered on medium heat for 15–20 minutes.

4. Add the olives, olive brine, diced tomatoes, and squeeze remaining lemons into the pot. BOOM . . . you're done! Now just add parsley to the pot right before serving, or garnish each bowl with it, and the low-fat feta if desired.

FLEXIBLE FAJITA SOUP   , , OR —WHOA!

Makes About 6–8 Servings (freezer friendly)

I love recipes that are flexible enough to be easily converted to any fuel type with just a quick switcharoo of an ingredient. If you want this as an E, use all ingredients in the list. If wanting this as a FP, just don't add the rice or corn and use only one of the cans of black beans. You can add a bag of frozen cauliflower rice to give it a little extra volume. For S, use the FP-version and just top with some grated cheese and sour cream (or some chopped up avocado if you have a dairy intolerance). For a Crossover, just make the soup the normal E way and have it with cheese, sour cream, and some blue corn chips if desired . . . that's my fave!

1½ lbs. boneless, skinless chicken breasts (chopped or snipped into small pieces)
Juice of 3 limes
5 garlic cloves, crushed
3 bay leaves
1 tsp. dried parsley flakes
1 tsp. onion powder
1 tsp. Mineral Salt

2 tsp. creole seasoning
7 cups water (divided)
2 (12 oz.) bags frozen pepper & onion blend
2 (15 oz.) cans black beans (drained)
1 cup quick cook brown rice (the 10-minute kind)
1 cup frozen corn kernels
1 (28 oz.) can petite diced tomatoes

1. Add chicken, lime juice, crushed garlic, seasonings, and 2 cups of the water to a large soup pot set to high heat. Cover, bring to a boil, and then reduce temperature to allow soup to strongly simmer for 15 minutes.

2. Now add brown rice, if you're doing the E version. Cook covered for another 10 minutes. Now add everything else to the pot including the rest of the water and cook for another 10–15 minutes on medium heat.

CORN CHOWDER

Makes About 8 Servings (freezer friendly)

I have always loved Corn Chowder; to me, it's like one of those All-American comfort soups. You can never go wrong with making this for a Light Crossover (Light Crossovers, ones that are just over fat limits for E meals are awesome for us pregnant women, those at goal weight, and even for a change up while you are still in weight-loss mode). I enjoy this hidden veggie packed chowder topped with cooked turkey bacon and some blue corn chips on the side . . . oh, so yummy!

1 large onion (chopped)
1½ lb. radishes (peeled and diced)
3 small-medium yellow squash (chopped)
2–3 bay leaves
2 tsp. black pepper
2 tsp. garlic powder
2 tsp. paprika
2 tsp. parsley flakes
1½–2 tsp. Mineral Salt
½ tsp. dried thyme
½ tsp. dried ground sage
½ tsp. chili flakes
6 cups chicken broth
⅓ cup oats (ground)
4½ cups (which is 1½ [24 oz.] containers) low-fat cottage cheese
2 tsp. Gluccie or xanthan gum
2½ cups water
1 (8 oz.) package reduced fat cream cheese
1½ (16 oz.) bags frozen corn kernels

1. Add onion, radishes, squash, seasonings, chicken broth, and ground oats to a large soup pot. Cook on high heat with a lid unit it comes to a rapid boil. Give it a good stir and then reduce heat to medium-low to let it simmer until all the veggies have cooked.

2. Blend the cottage cheese in a blender until smooth and then add to the pot. Give it a nice stir.

3. Now pour 2 cups of the hot liquid from the pot into the blender along with the water and Gluccie or xanthan gum. Blend and then pour into the pot. Give it another good ol' stir!

4. Finally, add cream cheese and frozen corn. Let simmer for a few more minutes.

NAVY SEAL SOUP

S

Makes About 6–8 Servings

Serene Chimes In: You've heard about superfoods, right? Those incredible foods with special powers to heal disease, boost your immune system, and rejuvenate your body? We're all about those on the THM plan because they are the "special forces" of foods, the ones that actually have the muscle to change things around ... to turn lackluster health into surging vitality. Well, this soup brings together the toughest and most exceptional of superfoods ... think of it as a soup full of Navy Seal fighters. It is brimming with antioxidants and teeming with vitamin C from the ample supply of colorful peppers. I've said it before, but I'll put it on repeat ... peppers are a vitamin C powerhouse ... they contain even more than other high in vitamin C foods like oranges and leafy greens. And why do we need vitamin C? Well, of course, for our immune system ... but also for a trim waistline. People lacking in vitamin C have trouble losing weight as their livers have trouble filtering fat out of the body. Peppers help your

weight in another powerful way, too…they contain capsaicin and this chemical promotes the release of your fat from storage—a process called lipolysis. Baobab joins in here as another of the highest vitamin C foods on the planet. There's so much vitamin C in this soup I was actually originally thinking of calling it Ultra C, but I changed my mind last minute. The awesome thing is that unlike a supplement…you can't overdo vitamin C in natural whole food form like this! Navy Seal Soup also packs a powerful punch of immune stimulating nutrition through nutritional yeast but also through virus-busting lauric acid from the coconut milk.

I guess I should talk more about the taste here rather than just all the health benefits. I am a soup maker by trade …haha … by that I just mean that soup is my specialty and I make more soup than anything else in my house. The Allison house equals soup house! But this soup has now become the king of the castle in my home and the most requested of all the many varieties I've made over the years. Basically, this just means it is yummy. Navy Seal Soup is bound for victory, for health, and for mouthwatering pleasure…not one family member left behind!

---

2 (8 ounce) packets mini rainbow peppers (roughly chopped to fill the 8-cup mark on your blender—you may have a few left over; or you can use large, colorful bell peppers)
8 cups (2-quarts) just off the boil water
5 Tbs. Baobab Boost Powder
5 Tbs. Nutritional Yeast
1 Tbs. onion powder
1½ tsp. black pepper
1½ Tbs. Mineral Salt

2 tsp. cumin powder
2 Tbs. dried parsley flakes
Optional 3 Tbs. Integral Collagen
2 (13–15 oz.) cans coconut milk

PROTEIN OPTIONS:

2 (14.75 ounce) cans wild salmon (this is our usual go-to for this soup)
2–4 cups diced pre-cooked chicken
2–3 cups cooked ground turkey or beef

---

1. If you have a large blender, squish in all the chopped peppers and 4 cups of the boiled water (you'll need to do a couple blending batches if your blender is smaller). Blend well (with a vented lid so the steam can escape) until the peppers and water become a totally smooth purée.
2. Place the blended mixture in a large sized soup pot set to high.
3. In the same blender (don't worry about washing it) place all other ingredients except for coconut milk with the remaining four cups of water and blend until smooth. Add to the pot along with the coconut milk. Bring to a boil while stirring and then turn off the heat.
4. Add your protein of choice and serve along with a side salad for an S or with brown or black rice for a Crossover.

TACO CHICKEN CHILI

Makes About 6–8 Servings (freezer friendly)

This chili is a breath of fresh air when you don't have any ground beef in your fridge or freezer but still want a yummy, heart and soul warming chili. Okay, even if you do have ground beef in your house, this is worth making. It is so easy and wonderfully tasty. If you want to keep this in E-mode, top it with non-fat Greek yogurt and have a few blue corn chips or Shameless Crackers-Classic Toppers on the side. To have this as a Crossover, top with some grated cheese and/or some sliced avocado and enjoy some blue corn chips or buttered, sprouted bread or toast on the side.

2½ lb. boneless, skinless chicken breasts (chopped or snipped into small pieces)
1 onion (chopped)
4½–5 cups water
4 Tbs. chili powder
2 Tbs. ground cumin
1 tsp. black pepper

1½ tsp. Mineral Salt
1 tsp. garlic powder
1 (15 oz.) can black beans
1 (15 oz.) can red kidney beans
2 (15 oz.) cans diced tomatoes
1 cup frozen corn kernels

---

1. Put chicken and onion into a large soup pot with a cup of water, cover and cook for 15 minutes on high heat.
2. Add remaining ingredients and simmer until flavors have melded and all is cooked through.

DREAM OF MUSHROOM SOUP

S

Makes About 8–10 Servings (freezer friendly)

This is my biggest soup. When you make it, you'll have enough to use for the Cream of Chicken & Rice Skillet Meal on page 124 and plenty left over for a full family meal or to freeze. Two meals for one ... yay! I know, this ingredient list looks crazy long but please don't let it scare you from making this. It's delish and very creamy, if I say so myself! Most of those ingredients are seasonings ... so phew! This soup pairs perfectly with a big side salad topped with grilled or baked chicken–the perfect soup and salad combo. If you're not having some sort of meat on the side for protein ... just add some collagen as it doesn't have much protein in itself. If you want to Crossover, have some buttered, sprouted bread or toast for dipping.

1 large onion (finely diced)
6 garlic cloves (crushed)
2 Tbs. butter or unflavored coconut oil
3 cups water
2 tsp. Mineral Salt
2 tsp. black pepper
1½ tsp. crushed dried rosemary
½ tsp. dried oregano
1 tsp. garlic powder
1 tsp. ground sage

1 tsp. thyme
6 cups chicken broth or stock (divided)
½ cup Baking Blend
⅓ cup ground oats
1 lb. mushrooms (finely sliced)
12 oz. ⅓ less fat cream cheese
2½–3 tsp. Gluccie
3 cups unsweetened almond milk
1 Tbs. dried parsley (or a sprinkle of fresh for garnishing)

1. Put the onion, garlic, butter, 1 cup of the water, salt, and all seasonings (minus the parsley) into a large soup pot set to high heat. Cover and let all ingredients bubble and caramelize for a few minutes.

2. Add 1 cup of the chicken broth to the pot then whisk in the baking blend and ground oatmeal. Let simmer for a few minutes.

3. Add the remaining 5 cups chicken broth and sliced mushrooms, reduce heat to medium-high and cook for 10–15 minutes.

4. Turn the heat down to medium-low and whisk in the Gluccie, cream cheese, almond milk, 2 cups of water and parsley flakes. Let the soup simmer for another 10 or so minutes before serving.

R'S INDIAN CURRY

S

Makes About 6–8 Servings (freezer friendly)

So, while this is not an actual soup … more of a stew'ish consistency … it is going here in this chapter. I love Indian Curries so much. I'm pretty sure it runs in my family as we grew up eating tons of it and so I perfected this recipe early in my life. Thankfully, my husband and little girls love it too. Actually, the first time I went on a picnic with my husband Jack after we had started dating, I told him I would make the food to bring. I made Indian Curry. What??? I know, definitely not picnic food, but he loved it so much that he's been hooked ever since that point. It might have even been what made him marry me! Haha!

To keep this in S-mode, I'll have it over a big bowl of chopped cabbage or sautéed up cauliflower rice. I serve it to my family as a Crossover with brown rice … BUT … the next time I make this curry, I'm totally having it with my new Handy Naan Bread recipe from page: 262.

2½ lb. boneless, skinless chicken breasts (chopped or snipped into small pieces)	1 tsp. ground fennel
	3 Tbs. paprika
5 garlic cloves (crushed)	1 cup water
1 Tbs. ground cumin	1 (13.5 oz.) can coconut milk (I use the Imperial Dragon brand.)
2 Tbs. ground coriander	
2 Tbs. curry powder	2 (15 oz.) cans tomato sauce
1 tsp. black pepper	1 mint tea bag
2 tsp. ground ginger	1 cup 0% Greek yogurt
1 tsp. Mineral Salt	8 oz. ⅓ less fat cream cheese

1. Put chicken and garlic into a large soup pot set to high heat. Add all the spices, water, and coconut milk. Cover and cook for 10 minutes.

2. Reduce heat to medium-high and add in tomato sauce, dried mint from inside the teabag, Greek yogurt, and cream cheese. Cook for 15 minutes and then reduce heat to low and let it simmer for 10–15 minutes or longer. Best garnished with cilantro.

Note: If you like your curry spicy, then add cayenne pepper or red pepper flakes.

CREAMY DREAMY LIMAS

Makes About 6–8 Servings

Serene Chimes In Pearl and I created this dish together when I was still a teenager and that is the name we gave it way back in the early 90's. This is more of a stew consistency than a soup … it is so creamy that it is totally dreamy, without even a split of fat. It has been one of my comfort meals for decades now so I don't know why we've never included it in one of our recipe books, but it is about jolly time!

If you're in need of some E-nergy (yeah, that was a pun for an overdue E meal) but your mouth and belly is really wanting one of those heavy, creamy, fatty S meals…. don't fret … this meal has ya' covered! It stars the large variety of lima beans which have the nickname of "butter beans" because of their absolutely buttery texture. They trick your brain into believing you're eating fat!

This makes a super hearty bowl of gentle energy that will rev your metabolism, soothe your thyroid, and nurture your adrenals. Limas boast lots of soluble fiber and allow a very slow and stable delivery of their energy. These buttery beans also contain pectin which studies show reduces post-meal blood sugar spikes. They are also rich in manganese which is important for energy production. Folate and magnesium are abundant in limas and are important to everyone, but especially those who have MTHFR mutations and are at risk for lack of folate through compromised methylation pathways. Both of these nutrients are also well known to keep your heart healthy.

As a Trim Healthy Mama, we're always encouraging you to not get stuck in a rut so let me do it again … Change things up and enjoy protein from varied sources. Don't just constantly eat red meat and chicken. Lima beans are a lovely source of plant protein that will allow you to save your budget by having a meatless meal, and let your body thrive through partaking of all God's wonderful protein sources. The protein in the beans here should be plenty for a plant-based meal now and then, but if you need more … feel free to include the collagen option or put a nice piece of baked or air fried white fish on the side. (Both the baobab and collagen options here are not needed for taste … they're just there if you desire boosted nutrition.)

Note Before Making: The success of this recipe is dependent on soaking the limas the night before or for at least 7-hours during the day. A quick soak method is not sufficient to set the beans up to reach their full, creamy potential. Also, it is important that your beans have not been hiding in your bean cupboard for a year. Old limas will not be as dreamy or creamy.

2 pounds dry, large lima beans (otherwise known as butter beans)
2 quarts plus 1 cup water
6–8 cloves fresh garlic (sliced, not crushed)
2–3 large onions (diced)
1 Tbs. Mineral Salt

1 Tbs. Madras Mild Curry Powder
1 tsp. black pepper
3–4 Tbs. Bragg Liquid Aminos
Optional ¼ cup Baobab Boost Powder
Optional 2 Tbs. Integral Collagen

1. To soak, place beans in a large bowl with plenty of water covering them by ample inches. (Remember, 7-hours minimum on soaking.)

2. Once ready to cook (they'll take a couple hours cooking time to get creamy dreamy) drain beans and put them in a large soup pot with the water set to high.

3. Cover and bring beans to a boil then reduce heat to a gentle simmer. Let them become super tender and release their creamy fiber into the water . . . over an hour or more. . . . slow and long is the ticket. (This is hardly any hands-on work. Time is the only one working hard.)

4. After over an hour has passed and the beans are becoming super creamy, throw in the onions and garlic and all the seasonings (just start with 3 tablespoons of the Braggs). Let the flavors meld with the beans and the onions become translucent through some slower simmering. If you opt to add the boosted additions, do this at the end when the heat is turned off, having first whisked them with a little of the soup in a smaller bowl.

5. Taste and adjust flavors, owning the soup and perfecting it to your own taste bud love fest. You might need that extra tablespoons of Braggs if you love a salty flavor. Serve with a side salad topped with generous balsamic vinegar, just a spritz of virgin olive oil spray, your favorite herbs, black cracked pepper, and that extra protein source we talked about earlier . . . only if you feel you need it.

11

FIVE MINUTE MEALS

Tuna Melt **E**

Cabbage Face **S** or **FP**

The Pizza Omelet **S**

Pesto Pizza **S**

Drive-Thru Sue's Fancy Pizza **S**

Mashed Potatoes & Gravy **E**

Golden Stir Fry **E**

Avocado Bacon Pasta Salad **S**

Sunshine Salad **E**

Speedy Cuke Salad **FP**

R's #1 Salad **S**

Hawaiian Salad **E**

Nut Smart Salad **S**

Red Revival Salad **S**

Black Is Beautiful Salad **E**

Chicken & Broccoli Thai Soup **S**

Chicken Zoodle Soup **FP**

Thai-rific Soup **FP**

Cream of Tomato Basil **FP** or **S**

Rescue Soup **FP**

This chapter consists of delicious, super-speedy, single-serve meals. Okay, so maybe a few don't take exactly five minutes (please don't sue me), but they're close enough. I think of these as my messy bun, AKA "Sweat Pant Meals" as my Aunty Pearl calls them. Most are single serve with just a few making a double serving that you can share with someone or put in the fridge for the next day. . . . perfect for lunches, dinners, or yes . . . even breakfast, if that's your thing! Oh, and if you love this quick meal jive . . .please don't miss the Air Fried Goodness chapter . . . I have a bunch of speedy single-serve recipes in that chapter, too.

BTW . . . If you enjoy ("love" was used in the previous statement . . .) these five-minute meals, it only takes a minute or two more to add extra ingredients to make enough for your family.

TUNA MELT

Makes a Single Serve

My family and I love these Tuna Melt sandwiches so much. They're definitely a major "Sweat Pants Meal" in my home. I make them for lunches and even for dinners, especially when I forget to take meat out of the freezer or if I don't have a lot of time to cook. My intense phobia of mayonnaise is part of the reason I came up with this recipe . . . I wanted to be able to eat a mayo-free, yet still all kinds of creamy, hot and toasty tuna melt! I love sliced, crispy veggies on the side such as cucumbers or peppers for added crunch to the meal and perhaps a glass of chocolate milk . . . made the THM way of course. If you want to make this a Crossover, you can replace 1 of the tablespoons of yogurt with mayo . . . just don't tell me you did it. Another way to Crossover is to increase cheese amounts, which is what I do for my husband and little girls.

---

2 pieces sprouted bread
1 (2.5–3 oz.) pouch tuna
3 Tbs. 0% Greek yogurt
⅛ tsp. black pepper

⅛ tsp. Mineral Salt
Optional ⅛ tsp. crushed red pepper
3 Tbs. part-skim mozzarella cheese (grated)

---

1. Preheat the oven to 400°F. Set a piece of parchment paper on a small baking sheet and mix tuna in a small bowl with yogurt, salt, and spices.

2. Spread half the tuna mixture on each piece of bread followed by half of the cheese. Bake for 10–12 minutes.

Air fryer Option: Instead of cooking in the oven, place in the air fryer at 390°F for five minutes.

CABBAGE FACE

 OR

Makes a Single Serve

Can I just say that I am obsessed with this meal?! In fact, it used to be a problem. When I was a teenager, I went through a stage where I would literally have this for every meal with two eggs scrambled up in it. Call me weird, but for days on end, cabbage was in my face for every, single meal. That was until my Dad convinced me that while, yes…cabbage is super healthy…I needed more variety. Ha! Then I changed it to just once or twice a day.

You can have this with eggs for breakky or with precooked chicken, fish, or diced smoked sausage for lunch or dinner…add more cabbage if you want to have an even bigger meal…you can't overdo it…stuff your cabbage face!

1 Tbs. unflavored coconut oil for S (use just 1 tsp. for FP)
3 cups shredded cabbage (from bag; or shred or slice thinly yourself)
⅛ tsp. black pepper

2 pinches Mineral Salt
Optional 2 pinches cayenne pepper
1 Tbs. Nutritional Yeast
Protein of choice—eggs or any precooked or canned meat (keep it lean for FP)

1. Heat oil up in a skillet set to high then add all the ingredients and cook for 3 minutes. Add your protein and cook for another minute or two. Boom!

198

THE PIZZA OMELET

Makes a Single Serve

This is anytime . . . breakfast, lunch, dinner, or even midnight FILL YOUR FACE food!!! You get all the taste of pizza without having to bother making a crust here. If I can't think of what to eat and I want quick and tasty . . . just imagine me sitting down and indulging in this pizza-fied deliciousness . . . because that's probably exactly what I'm doing. This is literally so fast to make; it used to be one of my go-to meals to take to work. I would make it the night before and just heat it up at work. Delicious! When I make this for my hubby and girls, I'll leave a few yolks in to up calorie amounts for them . . . with sprouted toast it is the perfect Crossover.

Note . . . I used to make this without the nutritional yeast (and you still can do that), but while delicious, it still looked more like an egg white omelet. My Aunty Pearl's trick of putting the nutritional yeast in the pan before cooking omelets takes this over the top!!!!

3–4 egg whites (or about ½ cup liquid egg whites . . . more if you are hungry)
¼ tsp. Italian seasoning
Optional ¼ tsp. crushed red pepper flakes
2 pinches Mineral Salt
Optional sprinkle of Nutritional Yeast

¼ cup no-sugar added pizza sauce
5–7 slices pepperoni (I use turkey pepperoni)
Optional small handful spinach leaves
1 Tbs. Parmesan cheese (green can)
¼ cup part-skim mozzarella cheese (grated)

---

1. Spray a non-stick pan with coconut or olive oil and set to medium-high heat.
2. Whisk egg whites with salt and seasonings in a small bowl then pour into pan and cover with a lid. Cook for a few minutes or until it starts to turn white and is firm enough to flip the whole thing over. If using the nutritional yeast, right before flipping, spray egg whites with a little bit more oil then sprinkle some nutritional yeast (about a teaspoon or so) over top. Flip, then spread the pizza sauce on top and add remaining ingredients. Fold omelet in half and continue to cook with the lid on until everything has melted.

PESTO PIZZA

Makes a Single Serve

This is so easy to make as a single serve, but I also like making multiples of these. I wrap each one in plastic wrap and keep in the freezer for any time a craving hits.

1 low-carb Joseph's pita (or 1 THM Truly Trim Pizza Crust)
1½ Tbs. Pesto (I use store-bought if I haven't made any "For the Love of Pesto" from page 355.)
⅓ cup part-skim mozzarella cheese (grated)

½ Roma tomato (thinly sliced)
5–7 pepperoni slices (I use turkey pepperoni)
⅛ tsp. garlic powder
⅛ tsp. Italian seasoning
2 pinches Mineral Salt

1. Preheat oven to 425°F. If using a Joseph's pita, line a small cooking sheet with parchment paper.
2. Spread pesto onto the pita or Truly Trim Pizza Crust. Top with cheese and then add sliced tomato and pepperoni. Sprinkle spices and salt on top.
3. Bake for 12 minutes. (Truly Trim Pizza Crust should be baked directly on the middle oven rack while the pita needs to be baked on the lined cooking sheet.)

DRIVE-THRU SUE'S FANCY PIZZA

Makes Two Servings (halve ingredients if you want just one, but handy to freeze the other)

I love this pizza! It feels super fancy but only takes a minute or three to throw together. I was not even planning to put this pizza recipe in this book; I would just make it for us to enjoy. Then one of our neighbors (Melissa) stopped by after dinner; I still had some of the pizza left out. I offered her some and then she kept going on about how good it was and insisted on the recipe. After that I decided to add it in here so you all can enjoy it too.

1 Joseph's low-carb lavash flatbread (or 2 THM Truly Trim Pizza Crusts)
⅓ cup sugar-free pizza sauce
½ cup part-skim mozzarella cheese (grated)
15 pepperoni slices
1–1½ Tbs. sundried tomatoes

1½ Tbs. goat cheese crumbles
1 Tbs. Parmesan cheese
⅛ tsp. black pepper
¼ tsp. garlic powder
Optional red pepper flakes

1. Preheat oven to 425°F. Line a cookie sheet with parchment paper.
2. Set lavash or Truly Trim Pizza Crusts on parchment paper; Spread pizza sauce and then sprinkle cheese . . . and remaining ingredients. Bake for 10–12 minutes. (If using Truly Trim Pizza Crusts, top then put directly on the middle oven rack and bake at 425 for 12 minutes.)

MASHED POTATOES & GRAVY

Makes a Single Serve

Pearl Chimes In Real mashed potatoes and gravy are back in your life! And no skimping on portion sizes... here's a way to eat a huge bowl of mashed potatoes as your meal and lose weight. What the ????? Yup. Trust the experience.

Excuse this long intro, but I have some 'splaining to do. I know many of you have learned to do a cauliflower mash to replace the real thing, but do you notice cauliflower needs fats with it to be good as a mash? If you don't include a bunch of dairy fats like butter and cream cheese it tastes... well... extremely cauliflowerish... so it always has to be in S-mode and that makes it hard for dairy-free people and those with metabolism challenges to get to enjoy it. In this recipe, the combination of golden potato, golden squash, and cauliflower means no need for added fat or dairy for succulence. So, you get to finally enjoy real mashed potatoes as an E fuel! Wahoo! If you listen to our Poddies, you'll know I'm now at menopause stage... adding in more E meals like this and more plant-based meals overall has been my ticket to staying slim during this interesting time. I still love my fish meals and some other meat here and there, but a stronger focus on plants is what has helped me through.

How on earth does a potato and gravy meal slim you? Golden potatoes are easier on your blood sugar than regular white potatoes due to their waxy interiors. They are healing to your adrenals and this is important because healthy adrenals boost thyroid health which in turn boosts metabolism. If you don't mind an odd color for your mash, go ahead and use purple or red potatoes, they have even more anthocyanins (potent, health boosting flavonoids) than golden.

The added veggies bulk this mash up. You'd have to use far more potatoes to get this amount of mash if not including the yellow squash and cauliflower. That would be potato excessive and take you well over the recommended 45-gram limit for E meals. Here... you are safely under that limit, but you get a generous amount of mash! Wahoo!

So, here's my challenge. If you miss the fat in this meal... go on the main THM Facebook group (where I hang out sometimes) and let me know I'm crazy. But I don't think I'm crazy. I honestly don't miss the gobs of butter in this mash. And the gravy is totally fat-free so pour it on good and heavy!

I love this as a filling meal all on its own—for lunch or sometimes even for dinner... boy, do I feel like the luckiest lady in the world sitting down to a big bowlful of this. Sometimes I'll include some New Way Sautéed Broccoli (page 254) on the side... all of it smothered with heaps of gravy. You can add some collagen to a drink for some protein or just put some in the gravy if you want. If you'd rather have this mash as a side item . . . it will give two generous side servings. Or you can double or triple amounts to serve more people or to have as leftovers for future meals throughout the week. To be honest, this recipe does take more than five minutes to make, but not really much more than 10–15 if you already have the gravy made and sitting in the fridge (I always have some made up as I use it for a lot of things). And since this is a single serve meal . . . I didn't know where else to put this recipe. Sorry, Rashida!

Notes to Read Before Making: I don't ever weigh my food, but I want this to turn out right for you so you may want to weigh your potato at first to get the right amount . . . you might need to use 2 small or several baby golden ones if you don't have a medium/large one. Try to get squash amounts close to what I've said here . . . too much squash and your mash will be too liquidy.

---

1 medium/large golden potato (approx. 190–220g or 7–8 oz; chopped)

1 heaped cup frozen or fresh cauliflower florets (I use frozen because I hate chopping raw cauliflower.)

1 very small yellow squash or half a medium, (about 100 grams or 3½–4 oz.; cut into fourths)

3 pinches Mineral Salt

Sprinkle of black pepper

Braggs Liquid Aminos to taste (couple good squirts)

2 tsp. Nutritional Yeast

---

1. Put all three vegetables into a small saucepan and set to high heat with enough water to cover. Put lid on and bring to a quick boil. Turn heat to medium and simmer until veggies are tender.

2. Pour cooked veggies into a large colander to drain and press down firmly on cauliflower and squash with the back of a spoon to help get rid of their excess water . . . doesn't matter if they squish a little because they'll end up mashed anyway. Transfer veggies to a medium bowl, add seasonings and Nutritional Yeast and using a hand-held blender, blend until super smooth. Taste to see if you need any more salt or Braggs. Enjoy with my Go To Gravy page 376.

GOLDEN STIR FRY

E

Makes a Single Serve

Pearl Chimes In Me again. And I have more potatoes and squash here for you because they're a big deal in my life right now and one recipe is just not enough! This is a quick, (just 5-minutes … I promise) recipe as long as you have some steamed yellow squash and golden potatoes sitting in the fridge. I always do these days. I steam up a big batch once a week and I urge you to do the same as together they can be a sublime and slimming addition to

your food world. You get creamy, gentle carbs in the golden potatoes and non-starchy filling goodness in the squash . . . by themselves, either is not really enough and leads to lack of volume on your plate, in my opinion. I keep 'em married and end up with a huge plate of food!

I often have this for dinner or a quick lunch. You'll never believe it is an E . . . it feels like a jolly big indulgent Crossover, but nope, this slims you down. I've got my husband loving it now, too and even Serene's husband is on board with it and asks for "Pearl's stir-fry thingy". Well . . . what man doesn't love potatoes? I shouldn't be too surprised.

The idea here is to really focus in on the carbs and veggies . . . I include just a little bit of canned chicken as some protein. You put it right on top of the stir-fry at the end and you or your man will never know the stir-fry isn't full of it. Nothing wrong with chicken, but we're going for the max 45 grams of carbs of potatoes in this recipe, so we don't want to overdo chicken at the same time. If you feel you need more protein, add a couple teaspoons of collagen to a drink. But of course, we are all in different seasons. If you or your man are at goal weight and needs more calories to maintain your weight, or if you are pregnant or nursing and need plenty of crossovers . . . go with a whole single serve can of chicken or use leftover diced chicken and also don't forget to use more than a teaspoon of the Tahini to Crossover.

---

2 Tbs. water
1½–2 cups pre-steamed golden potatoes—
or enough to equal about 8–10 oz. (large
diced)
2–3 cups pre-steamed yellow squash—have
as much as you want, no limits to fill up
(large diced)
Several super large handfuls fresh spinach

2 pinches Mineral Salt
Braggs Liquid Aminos to taste (several
generous squirts)
Little sprinkle cayenne pepper
1 tsp. Tahini (sesame butter) or almond butter
½ single-serve can chicken
Creole seasoning (to taste)

---

1. Put water, potatoes, and squash in a skillet set to medium-high heat. Allow veggies to heat up for a minute or two and then add spinach and let it wilt (tossing all ingredients periodically).

2. Add Bragg Liquid Aminos and any other seasonings of choice. Taste stir-fry to see if seasonings are to your liking yet or if you have to add more. Once you've seasoned completely to your liking, add the teaspoon of Tahini and allow it to melt into the stir-fry and then transfer everything to a plate.

3. While the pan is still hot, add your half single-serve can of chicken and season it with just a little sprinkle of creole seasoning . . . heat it for just half a minute or so (or until hot), then sprinkle it over top of stir-fry. That's it!

AVOCADO BACON PASTA SALAD

Makes a Single Serve

I think Aunty Serene will be so proud of me for this creamy and fresh pasta that tastes super yummy but only has ever-so-puristy ingredients. The "pasta" here is in the form of spiralized zucchini, but as I've mentioned in a few of my other recipes that call for spiralized zucchini, don't be put off by this. These days you can find pre-spiralized zucchini in most produce departments. It is delightful in this creamy, yet dairy-free, health-boosting salad.

1 medium zucchini (spiralized)
1 mini avocado (or half a large)
⅛ tsp. garlic powder
⅛ tsp. black pepper
¼ tsp. plus 2 pinches Mineral Salt

2–3 pieces cooked bacon (ripped up or diced;
   I use uncured turkey bacon.)
1 small tomato (chopped)
⅓ cup cilantro (chopped)
1 chive (thinly sliced)
Optional juice from ½–1 lime

1. Mash avocado with all the spices (except for the extra 2 pinches of salt) in a personal-sized salad bowl.
2. Squeeze excess water out of the zucchini noodles and then add to the bowl. Mix the mashed avocado very well with the noodles. Go down the ingredient list and top with all the remaining ingredients, including the last two pinches of salt.

DF FRIENDLY

SUNSHINE SALAD

Makes a Single Serve

This salad is gorgeous and light. It pairs well with half of any of the FP shakes or smoothies found in the *Simply Splendid Shakes and Smoothies* chapter . . . if you need to fill up further, but stay in E-mode. If you'd rather Crossover, have it with half an S smoothie.

2–3 heaping cups spring mix or chopped kale (more if you want)

1 tangerine (peeled and segmented)

¼ cup Dried Cranberries from page: 243 (or ½ cup fresh cranberries; halved and tossed with 1½ tsp. Gentle Sweet)

For protein: choose between 1 single-serve can or pouch of tuna or chicken, a few oz. sliced lean deli meat, or any lean precooked meat you have around.

2 tsp. sliced almonds

Optional few slices purple onion

Raspberry Vinaigrette from page 363

---

1. Go down the list and throw everything on a plate. Top with dressing.

SPEEDY CUKE SALAD

Makes a Single Serve

I feel so healthy and energized when I eat this salad. It's one of my "alone meals"... you know the ones you eat by yourself. I like having it for lunch, since that is when I am most often not sharing with my family. I just make my little girls a sprouted bread sandwich, or some yogurt and fruit and

then put them down for their nap. While they're down, I am finally able to get the most stuff done that needs doing so I can't spend a lot of time preparing lunch. I whip this up, fast-as-a-snap, take a little down time to relax and enjoy it, and then get back with renewed energy to all that has to get done! Perhaps stretch yourself and try a change up from constant S and E meals by having this as written. As written, it's a very slimming FP. To fill up further, you can have with Creamy Piña Colada (page 45) or some THM Chocolate Milk—make it just by mixing unsweetened almond milk with Pristine Chocolate Whey Protein Powder, or if you don't

have that, mix it with 1 tsp. each cocoa powder and Super Sweet Blend with a pinch of salt. If you'd rather have this salad as an E, that's fine too. All you'll need to do is add another ¼–⅓ cup of black beans. To make it as an S, simply add ½ avocado or ¼ cup sharp cheddar cheese.

---

1 medium cucumber (sliced; I prefer the seedless kind.)
1 (2.5–3 oz.) tuna pouch (or precooked or canned chicken)
¼ cup black beans

¼ cup cilantro (finely chopped)
2 pinches Mineral Salt
2–3 tsp. hot sauce
Juice from 1 lime

---

1. Chop the cucumber into small pieces and place on your plate or bowl along with everything else. Stir and enjoy!

R'S #1 SALAD

Makes a Single Serve

I know this is crazy simple, but please don't doubt it. Just go make it. This is my go-to lunch . . . super simple, super inexpensive, and super amazing. Most of the time I just make it the fast and simple way with none of the extras listed here.

- 2–3 heaped cups chopped lettuce (more if you want; or whatever greens you have)
- 1 (2.5–3 oz.) tuna pouch (or precooked or canned chicken)
- 2 Tbs. roasted/salted sunflower seeds
- 1–1½ Tbs. olive oil
- 1½–2 Tbs. hot sauce
- Optional Extras: ½ an avocado, ¼ cup cheddar cheese, chopped cilantro, sliced and pickled jalapeños, salsa, and green onions.

1. Go down the list and throw everything onto your plate. Done.

HAWAIIAN SALAD

Makes a Single Serve

I made this for Jack the other day and I honestly was not expecting him to love it. It was more . . . "Here you go . . . just eat it because it's healthy." To my surprise, he loved it just as much as I did, if not more!

1½–2 cups chopped tightly packed kale (or use spinach or romaine)
1 large carrot (grated)
½ cup fresh or canned pineapple (diced)
1 (2.5–3 oz.) tuna pouch (or precooked or canned chicken)

12 raisins (you heard me . . . 12!)
1 Tbs. unsweetened coconut flakes
3–4 Tbs. Orange Sesame Dressing from page: 360

---

1. Go down the list and throw everything onto your plate ending with the dressing. Enjoy!

NUT SMART SALAD

Makes a Single Serve

Pearl Chimes In You've probably heard me describe this salad quite frequently, if you listen to our Poddy, but this is its debut in official print form. I love the crunch of nuts on salad and Nut Smart delivers that without overdoing fats. In my new season of life, AKA menopause, I have created lots of lighter recipes that are still chock-full of flavor and enjoyment but don't pile my body with needless fat fuel. Nut Smart fits this category and comes to my rescue over and over again as a wise version of an S meal for this time of my life. It includes both nut butter and sprinkles of nuts, but they are in smart amounts with no other fat added...so no calorie abuse—yay! It is fun to match nut butters with your sprinkled nuts here. For instance, if I do almond butter for my dressing...I sprinkle on slivered almonds. If I do peanut butter for my dressing, I sprinkle on dry roasted peanuts, etc. But if you'd rather be a rebel and do different nuts from your nut butter, feel free to express your bad, sassy self!

Lots of leafy greens to fill a big dinner plate (chopped)
Optional cucumbers and/or tomatoes (chopped)
Generous drizzle balsamic vinegar
Squirt or 2 Braggs Liquid Aminos

Single-serve size pouch tuna (drained; you can use chicken if you don't love tuna)
1 rounded Tbs. nut butter of any kind
2 Tbs. chopped nuts of any kind
Optional sprinkle of cayenne pepper

---

1. Drizzle veggies with vinegar and Braggs and toss them in this simple dressing (you can add on plan sweetener here if you like a sweeter dressing).

2. Dollop little amounts of the nut butter all over salad so it is not in just one clump. Now do the same thing with the tuna. Finally sprinkle with nuts and cayenne pepper if using.

RED REVIVAL SALAD

S

Makes a Single Serve

Serene Chimes In In a food world of whites, a few browns, and a smattering of green … it's time to treat your plate to a revival of red. Come and dine on a ruby bowl that pushes you past former health boundaries. Experience over-the-top goodness … far beyond mediocre same olds as you drown your palette in red phytonutrients that revive and restore ravaged health. Deeply pigmented plant foods, like the ones in this salad, are a tell-tale sign of brimming antioxidants, vitamins, and minerals. A good tip to remember in the plant food world is that green is fantastic, but red and purple are even more spectacular! This salad is simply bursting (like nine months pregnant) with the three super phytonutrients lycopene, betalain, and anthocyanin. To list all their disease-busting and health-boosting benefits would take an entire chapter of this book, but you can experience their powerful rewards for yourself by digging your fork into a Red Revival of deliciousness!

1 cup red cabbage (grated or shredded)

¾ cup raw red beet (grated or shredded)

½ red onion (sliced ultra-thin in half rings)

½ cup frozen raspberries

2–3 Tbs. crumbled goats chèvre cheese (or use an on-plan, creamy-style nut cheese for dairy-free)

4 pinches Mineral Salt

4 dashes black pepper

Optional smattering (2–3 ounces) canned red sockeye salmon (if not using the collagen in the dressing)

RED REVIVAL DRESSING:

1 Tbs. balsamic vinegar

1½ tsp. Tahini (sesame butter)

4 Tbs. water

1 Tbs. Baobab Boost Powder

¼ tsp. Mineral Salt

½ Tbs. soy sauce (or a squirt of Bragg Liquid Aminos)

1 doonk Pure Stevia Extract Powder

2 generous Tbs. raw beet (grated on the finest option)

Optional 1 Tbs. Integral Collagen for protein (if not using the canned sockeye salmon)

1. Make the Red Revival Dressing first by putting all ingredients in a mug that fits hand held blender blades and blend until smooth. Set aside.

2. On a large dinner plate, lay a first foundation of the red grated cabbage then top that with the layer of grated beet.

3. Lightly spray a sauté pan set to medium-high heat with coconut or olive oil and sauté the thin sliced red onion halves with the salt and pepper for a minute or two. Turn heat to low, cover with lid, and let cook another few minutes to caramelize.

4. Lay the hot and steamy onions on top of the first two red layers. While the pan is still hot, throw in the frozen raspberries and let them quickly thaw and warm and then sprinkle those hot tangy bursts of goodness all over the yummy red mess.

5. To top it all off, sprinkle the soft goat's cheese on top, little bits will start to melt and soften into yummy pinkish creamy pot holes.

6. Now for the finale . . . drizzle all the Red Revival dressing over the splendid mass of red vividness and dive into health in full color.

BLACK IS BEAUTIFUL SALAD

Makes a Single Serve

Serene Chimes In Meet the vivacious cousin to my Red Revival Salad on the previous page. Let's celebrate another of God's glorious colors, shall we? While all colors may be equal when it comes to people, black has definite superiority when it comes to the plant kingdom. The deep pigments that God weaved into their matrix make them even more health-promoting and skin-beautifying than most other plant colors. The antioxidant anthocyanin is responsible for this black/purplish hue and it fights cardiovascular disease, improves brain function, reduces inflammation, detoxifies the liver, and a host of other benefits.

The forbidden black rice you'll get to enjoy here is one of the most potent in this antioxidant. It was forbidden in ancient China for common people and commandeered for only the nobles because of how esteemed in nutrition this rice was held. Well, that might be centuries

ago, but they knew a thing or two about nutrition because modern science reveals how right they were. Black rice is nutty and yummy in flavor, but its nutrition profile is through the roof! It is significantly higher in fiber and gentler on blood sugar than brown rice and is much higher in antioxidants. Now, with the click on the internet, or a toss into a grocery cart, we can experience it for ourselves.

The other food star here you are probably more familiar with is black beans. But perhaps you didn't know just how healthy they are for you. Their black color says it all. Black beans are also brimming with anthocyanins so you'll get a double dose in this salad. They are more packed with antioxidants than other varieties of beans and studies show they reduce the risk of type 2 diabetes through their high amounts of resistant starch fiber.

Note to Read Before Making: Black beans and black rice do contain some protein so you don't have to add meat or collagen for further protein, but you can if desired.

Generous handfuls fresh baby spring mix
½ a bunch fresh cilantro (chopped)
½ cup cooked black rice
¼–½ cup cooked or canned black beans
½ Tbs. soy sauce
½ Tbs. water
1 tsp. mild chili powder

Extra Protein Options:
Small amount leftover cooked or canned chicken breast, canned or pouch tuna, or 1 Tbs. Collagen in your dressing
Optional, but spectacular, topping of fresh or frozen blackberries

TANGY LIME DRESSING:

1 tsp. Tahini (sesame butter)
2 Tbs. water
1 Tbs. Baobab Boost Powder
Juice of 1 lime
¼ tsp. Mineral Salt
⅛ tsp. red pepper flakes
½ Tbs. balsamic vinegar
1 Tbs. soy sauce (or a squirt of Bragg Liquid Aminos)
1 doonk Pure Stevia Extract Powder
Optional 1 Tbs. Integral Collagen (if not using meat protein)

---

1. Make the Tangy Lime Dressing first by putting all ingredients in a mug that fits hand held blender blades and blend until smooth. Set aside.
2. Spread the spring mix and cilantro on a large dinner plate.
3. Sauté black beans, black rice, and optional protein for just a couple minutes in a pan with the water, soy sauce, and chili powder. Plate these yummy and hot beautiful, black, gentle carbs in the center of your green canvas. (If berries are frozen, you can thaw them quickly in the hot pan.)
4. Drizzle dressing in luscious lines all over your food/art then top with blackberries, if using. Eat with a fork or take your chopsticks out for a date.

CHICKEN & BROCCOLI THAI SOUP

Makes a Single Serve

Thai Soup is one of my favorites, but it is often time consuming to make. This soup has all the flavors of Thai, but you go from start to finish within several minutes. Oh, yeah!

½ cup canned coconut milk*
4–6 oz. raw chicken (very thinly sliced; or single-serve amounts of canned or pre-cooked chicken)
2 garlic cloves (crushed)
⅛ tsp. black pepper
⅛ tsp. chili flakes

½ tsp. onion powder
Optional 2 bay leaves
Juice of 1 lime
¼ tsp. sesame oil
1–2 cups frozen or fresh broccoli florets
1 Tbs. low sodium soy sauce
½–¾ cup chicken broth

1. If using raw chicken, place everything but the last three ingredients into a small saucepan set to high heat and bring to a boil. Cook chicken until the chicken is all white and has no pink left in it . . . takes only a few minutes, if sliced thinly . . . no food poisoning happening here!

2. Add broccoli, soy sauce, and chicken broth. Allow to come back to boil and then reduce heat to low and let simmer for a few minutes until broccoli is just done . . . no mushy broccoli allowed! (If using precooked or canned chicken, put everything in the pot at the same time and simmer until broccoli is just done . . . again, I repeat . . . don't get it mushy!)

Note: I use Imperial Dragon coconut milk which I find at Walmart. If you use another brand (such as Thai Kitchen) it may be much higher in calories and fat, so best to stick to ⅓ cup for that brand.

CHICKEN ZOODLE SOUP

Makes a Single Serve

I love this soup on cold days or whenever I feel like a good ol' comfort soup. It's super-fast to make and it's so healthy. The zucchini noodles aka "Zoodles" give it a nice bit of oomph.

2 garlic cloves (crushed)	⅛ tsp. black pepper
3 cups chicken stock or broth (divided)	⅛ tsp. Mineral Salt
3 baby carrots (chopped)	⅛ tsp. dried parsley flakes
½ a celery stalk (chopped)	Optional ⅛ tsp. cayenne pepper
1 (5 oz.) can chicken breast (drained)	1 small zucchini—or ½ a medium (spiralized)

1. Add half of the chicken stock plus everything but the spiralized zucchini to a small pot. Cover and cook on high heat for 7 minutes.
2. Add zucchini and remaining chicken stock to the pot and cook for another couple minutes.

THAI-RIFIC SOUP

 (WITH & OPTIONS)

(GET IT . . . LIKE TERRIFIC? I CAN'T STOP EXPLAINING MY TITLES!!!)

Makes a Single Serve

What in the world . . . Fuel Pull Thai Soup? Yep! I know I already gave you a Thai Soup in this chapter, but I love the flavors of Thai so much I had to give you this extra super-speedy recipe that I make repeatedly. It is great just as a FP, but if you want to make this an E, add in ½ cup of cooked brown rice or quinoa. For an S-version, add in 2–3 teaspoons heavy cream or 1–2 tablespoons coconut cream and a few roasted peanuts.

½ tsp. ground ginger
½ tsp. garlic powder
1 cup unsweetened almond (or cashew milk)
4 oz. chopped raw chicken breasts (or single-serve amount of canned or precooked chicken breast)
1–1½ cups shredded cabbage (or coleslaw mix from the bag, or string green beans, or a mix of your favorite non-starchy veggies)
⅛ tsp. chili flakes (or ½ jalapeño peppers; diced)
1½ tsp. soy sauce (or good squirt of two of Bragg Liquid Aminos)
⅛ tsp. black pepper
¼ tsp. ground cumin
½ tsp. Coconut Natural Burst Extract
Juice from ½ a small lemon or lime

1. Put ginger, garlic, almond milk, and chicken in a small saucepan set to high heat. Cover and allow to come to a gentle boil. (If you're using raw chicken, let it fully cook . . . go from pink to white before moving onto this next step.)

2. Add everything else but the lemon. Reduce heat and cook for another 5–7 minutes uncovered. Squeeze in juice from lemon before serving.

CREAM OF TOMATO BASIL

 OR

Makes 2 Servings

I have always been a big fan of flavorful Tomato Soup. So much so that when I was a late teenager, still living at home and my parents would go out-of-town, I would make a massive pot for all of my siblings and myself. Here's how weird I am ... I would have it every meal of the day, including breakfast! While I've tamed my ways and don't do this for breakfast anymore, I sure love it for lunch or dinner.

Why the double serving here? If it were only a single-serve, you'd have to put half a can of tomato sauce back in the fridge with good intentions to use it for something. Don't know about you, but despite any good intentions I have, I always waste halves of cans. They sit in my fridge and get nasty! Trust me ... you'll want the other serving of this tomorrow if you eat this today.

I love how quick and versatile this soup is. If staying in FP-mode, I just add a light sprinkle of Parmesan cheese on top and crumble in a few Shameless Crackers-Classic Toppers or a few low-carb Joseph's Pita Crisps. For S-mode, I like to top with extra sharp cheddar cheese and also have some on-plan crackers mentioned above for dipping. If you don't have THM's Shameless Crackers, to make Joseph's Pita Crisps, all you do is preheat your oven to 425°F and then lightly spray both sides of a Joseph's pita with coconut oil and sprinkle a few spices on both sides. Then cut the pita into triangles and cook for a few minutes until they become hard like pita chips. Or you can microwave the cut triangles on a paper plate for a minute. For a Crossover... Have some blue corn chips or a sprouted grilled cheese on the side of your soup.

1 cup low-fat cottage cheese	1 tsp. Italian seasoning
1–1½ cups water	¾–1 tsp. Gluccie or xanthan gum
1½ tsp. garlic powder	2–3 Tbs. fresh basil (chopped)
¾ tsp. Mineral Salt	1 (15 oz.) can tomato sauce
½ tsp. black pepper	S-Option: ¼ cup heavy cream

1. Add cottage cheese, water, and spices to a small saucepan set to high heat. Bring to a boil, then reduce heat to medium-high. Give it some good whisks to help break up the cottage cheese and help the melting process. Continue to cook until all the cottage cheese has melted.
2. Whisk in Gluccie or xanthan gum then add remaining ingredients and let simmer for a few more minutes. Taste and see if you would like more spices or a little more salt . . . up to you!

RESCUE SOUP

 FP

Makes a Single Serve

Serene Chimes In You're in a hurry with no time for crazy prep. You're hangry and almost ready to make an unwise, but easy food choice … but then you remember browsing through this book and looking at this page … yep, there's a rescue. This soup rescues time-deprived, idea-deprived, and health-deprived mamas. It rescues your waistline and it sure rescues your taste buds. You don't even need to use your stovetop … all you need is a blender. I'm on a roll with the sales pitch here so let's just keep going … It is sassy and scrumptious and goes down easy, leaving you satisfied but dreaming of a next time. Designed around some of the richest sources of vitamin C in the world (basically a baby version of my Navy Seal Soup on (page 184), this soup targets stubborn weight and sends fat running scared. (Low levels of vitamin C are known to hinder fat release and Rescue Soup takes action to remedy this situation.) It is teeming with antioxidants, polyphenols, carotenoids, soluble prebiotic fiber, certain neglected amino acids, immune enhancing beta glucans, and blood sugar-stabilizing chromium.

The foundation of this recipe is an FP, which can be enjoyed as a simple broth on its own for a snack or as a meal enhancement. I love enjoying it as a simple broth; I'll have it as a super-slimming snack or on the side of a salad that contains a protein source for my meal. But it can easily be amped up into hearty soup-mode by adding lean protein, leftover cooked veggies, and/or the S or E add-ins I listed below the recipe (added directly to the blender after blending). Leftover cooked cauli rice or pre-cooked diced or spiralized zucchini are wonderful, quick veggie additions (if you start with raw veggies, you'd need to pour the soup into a small pot and simmer them for a few minutes). This soup is also a real shiner when it comes to being dressed up into an S or an E meal and gladly plays along with either fuel.

1 Tbs. Baobab Boost Powder
1 Tbs. Nutritional Yeast
1 Tbs. Integral Collagen
1 flat tsp. Mineral Salt
⅛ tsp. black pepper

½ tsp. onion powder
3 fresh good sized baby red or orange peppers (rainbow peppers)
1 tsp. coconut oil
1½ cups just-off-the-boil water

1. Put all ingredients in a blender and blend until completely smooth (venting your lid for safety). Add in your extra protein of choice if desired, or any other S or E add-ins; then pour into your bowl and enjoy!

NOW FOR ALL THE ADD-INS AND TWEAKS:

As written, this is delicious, vibrant, and brothy. If you prefer to make a little creamier soup, then blend in a generous ⅛ tsp. of Gluccie.

Extra Protein Ideas:

- Single-sized serving left over diced chicken or clean-labeled, canned chicken
- Single-sized serving left over crumbled beef or turkey (S only; or make sure it was well-rinsed under hot water after browning)
- Single-sized serving canned or pouch salmon (S for canned; pouched salmon is usually FP, so can go in E-version)
- ½ cup of low-fat cottage cheese (blended in)
- 1 Tbs. Integral Collagen (blended in)

E Add-in Ideas:

- Pre-steamed and cubed baby yellow or purple waxy potatoes (my husband's favorite way)
- Precooked or pouch style black or regular brown rice (pouch-style, precooked grains are now available at most grocery stores and are so handy)
- Canned or pre-cooked black beans, or any favorite bean
- Precooked or pouch-style quinoa
- Baked corn chips on the side (nice with a smattering of black beans and chicken for a tortilla-style soup)

S Add-in Ideas:

- Grated cheese
- Diced avocado
- Sour cream
- Black olives

12

AIR FRIED GOODNESS

The Air Fried Meal **E**

The Air Fried Apple **E**

Street Quesadilla **FP**, **E**, or **S**

Crispy Fried Sandwich **E**

Golden French Fries **E**

Air Fried Sausage Balls **S**

Fried Pickles **S**

Cinnamon Sweet Potato Fries **E**

Purple Sweet Potato Chips **E**

Dried Cranberries **FP**

Nana's Delicious Brussels **S**

My journey into the air fried world actually began with the writing of this book, and boy, what a fun time it has been! Aunty Pearl thought it would be great to have an air fried chapter, and knowing we were on a strict budget while my hubby was finishing up his medical training, she scooped me one up to experiment with and gave me this command … "Go, create!"

Since that time (a couple years ago now), I have seriously become addicted to my air fryer, and I use it almost daily. I even heat my left-overs up in it! So much better than a microwave, how groovy … Aunty Serene should be proud! Now I can make French fries that taste like the real good junky kind, but they don't end up messing with my waistline! Most of these recipes have an alternative cooking option, but they definitely cook faster with an air fryer. Hope you enjoy using one as much as I do!

IMPORTANT NOTE: The kind of air fryer I have is a Ninja 4-Quart Air Fryer and it is awesome (not even being paid to say that). I can't promise that the cooking times I mention in this chapter will work perfectly if you are using a different brand of air fryer, but they're probably close.

THE AIR FRIED MEAL

Makes a Single Serve

Entire meal in the air fryer … not to mention … an E! Taking my bow to all my imagined applause!

1 medium sweet potato (diced—I used purple sweet potato in this image)	¼ tsp. garlic powder
½ tsp. creole seasoning (divided)	2 pinches Mineral Salt
¼ tsp. black pepper (divided)	Quick Cook Veggie of choice e.g. 1 cup (or more) frozen cauliflower rice, or green beans, or diced okra, or fresh or frozen kale.
1 tsp. coconut oil (divided)	
4–6 oz. chicken breast (chopped small)	

1. Remove all oven racks and add chopped sweet potato sprinkled with ¼ tsp. creole seasoning, ⅛ tsp. black pepper, and half a tsp. coconut oil to the bottom of the air-fryer. Mix well then cook for 10 minutes on 390°F. During cooking time, pull the cooking tray out and give it a few good shakes a couple times.

2. Add the chicken, remaining spices, and rest of the coconut oil. Cook for five more minutes giving it a few good shakes. Add non-starchy veggies to the air-fryer and then cook for a few more minutes until tender (larger veggies take longer that is why I often use cauliflower rice or kale). Top with hot sauce if desired.

THE AIR FRIED APPLE

Makes a Single Serve

You can turn an apple into a lovely whole meal or a wonderful snack. For extra protein, I like to top this with some 0% Greek yogurt mixed with ground cinnamon and Gentle Sweet. That way, it can be breakfast, lunch, or a lovely snack. If you can't do yogurt due to dairy issues, no worries. It goes perfectly with a Collagen Coffee or Collagen Tea. Such a great way to start the day. If you want to Crossover, feel free to add more nuts!

---

1 apple
3 Tbs. old fashioned rolled oats
1½ Tbs. Gentle Sweet
2 pinches Mineral Salt
½ tsp. ground cinnamon
Optional ¼ tsp. blackstrap molasses

¼ tsp. Vanilla Natural Burst Extract
¼ tsp. Butter Natural Burst Extract
1 egg white
2–3 tsp. sliced almonds (just enough to stay within E fat guidelines)

1. Cut the apple in half and scoop out the seeds with a knife creating a nice hole so you can fill later.
2. Remove all oven racks, lightly spray bottom of air fryer with coconut or olive oil, place apple halves in air fryer and then lightly spray both halves with the oil spray. Cook for 10 minutes at 390°F.
3. While that's cooking, add everything else to a small bowl and mix up. Once the 10 minutes is up, place half the mixture in each apple hole then cook for another 5 minutes.

STREET QUESADILLA

Makes a Single Serve

When I'm eating this open face quesadilla, I feel like I just ordered it off the streets of Mexico. No, I have never been there (dream vacay) but I feel like I have a good imagination of what the street food would taste like. I could be totally wrong! Go ahead and make this (your choice of FP, E or S... but try this all ways at some point) and let me know.

Note: I like to use Extreme Wellness Low Carb Tortillas.

- 1 single-serve can (about 4–5 oz.) chicken breast (drained)
- ½ a bell pepper (sliced)
- Juice of ½ a lime
- ¼ tsp. garlic powder
- ¼ tsp. ground cumin
- ¼ tsp. creole seasoning
- ¼ tsp. black pepper
- ¼ cup non-fat refried beans (use ½ cup for E)
- 1 low-carb tortilla (for FP or S) or sprouted tortilla (for E)
- 1 Roma tomato (sliced)
- 3 Tbs. low-fat cottage cheese
- 2 Tbs. shredded low-fat, part-skim mozzarella cheese for FP or E (you can use more for S)

1. Remove all racks from the air fryer. Dump the chicken into the bottom of the air fryer along with the bell pepper slices, the lime juice, and spices. Stir and then cook for 7 minutes at 390°F.

2. While that's frying, spread the refried beans onto the tortilla. Once chicken and peppers are cooked, put them onto the tortilla along with everything else ending with the cheese. Put the bottom rack back in and spray the rack with coconut or olive oil and then gently set the quesadilla on top and cook for another 3–5 minutes. Garnish with cilantro and hot sauce if desired. Fill up further with half a FP shake, smoothie, or a chocolate milk the THM way.

CRISPY FRIED SANDWICH

Makes a Single Serve

Sandwiches are the stuff of LIFE!!!! I go through stages of making this crispy, flavorful sanga (as they call sandwiches down under where my Mom is from) for my husband and me multiple times a week since it is so quick as a lunch or even a light dinner with a side salad. Depending on my mood, or my body's needs, I sometimes like to enjoy the Crossover-version of this (which I always make for my high metabolism husband), which includes a slice or two of cheddar or other favorite cheese, but it still tastes wonderful without.

2 pieces sprouted bread
1 Light Laughing Cow Cheese wedge (use Cheesy Wow-Spread page 370 for DF)
Optional 2 tsp. mustard
3–4 oz. deli meat

2 baby dill pickles, (sliced)
Optional 3–5 slices pickled jalapeño peppers
⅓ of a small onion (thinly sliced)
2 pinches Mineral Salt

1. Spread the Light Laughing Cow Cheese onto both slices of bread, along with mustard if using. Add everything else onto the sandwich, but the onions.
2. Leave the bottom rack in the air fryer. Spray it lightly with coconut or olive oil. Place the sandwich in the air fryer along with sliced onions and then spray them with the oil and sprinkle the salt on them.
3. Cook at 390°F for 7 minutes, then flip both the sandwich and the onions. Cook for another 4 minutes, then take the crisped onions and place them into your sandwich. DONE!

GOLDEN FRENCH FRIES

Makes About 3–4 Servings

---

4 medium/large golden potatoes (or smaller ones to equal amount)

1–2 tsp. unflavored coconut oil (or use coconut or olive oil spray)

1 tsp. plus ⅓ tsp. Mineral Salt

½ tsp. black pepper

---

1. Slice potatoes into French-fry slices and add them to the air fryer on the bottom rack. Drizzle coconut oil on them and sprinkle 1 tsp. of the salt and black pepper on them. Mix them up well so they have an even coat of everything on them.

2. Turn your air fryer to 390°F and cook for 20 minutes. (While cooking, take the air fryer drawer out and give the fries a few good shakes or flip them with tongs every few minutes.)

3. When they're done, sprinkle on the remaining salt.

Note: If you like dipping your fries into honey mustard, make the Real Thing Honey Mustard recipe from page: 358.

AIR FRIED SAUSAGE BALLS

Makes About 8–10 servings (freezer-friendly)

Sausage Balls have always been a big hit with Jack. His mom and grandmother have always had the family tradition to make them around the holidays. Well, as delicious as they are, let's just say they're not the healthy way at all! I decided to try to "healthify" them up with an air fried-version without all the empty starches that regular Sausage Balls often include, and yay…it worked! Husband-approved! I took them to a Christmas party this past year and my mom kept going on about how much she loved them. Since she loved them so much, I took them to my parent's house for our Christmas brunch. They were definitely a hit with my whole family.

8 Light Rye Wasa crackers (or 1½ bags Shameless Crackers-Classic Toppers)
1 tsp. black pepper
½ tsp. ground fennel
½ tsp. chili flakes
2 tsp. Italian seasoning

1–1½ tsp. creole seasoning
2 lb. ground turkey sausage
8 oz. sharp cheddar cheese (grated)
5 egg whites or ½ cup plus 2 Tbs. liquid egg whites

1. Put Wasa or Shameless Crackers into a gallon Ziploc. Smash with a jar until they're a nice course flour. Mix in everything else (yes, I just use the Ziploc bag as my bowl).

2. Make balls out of ⅓–½ of the mixture. Stick balls onto the bottom rack in the air fryer (lightly sprayed) and let cook on 390°F for 12–15 minutes. After the first 4 minutes, take the air fryer drawer out and shake it. Do that every few minutes.

3. While the first batch is cooking, make balls out of the rest of the mixture. Set cooked sausage balls onto a paper towel, cover, and then proceed to cook the remaining balls.

Note: For a Skillet Option: Put 1 layer of sausage balls into a large nonstick skillet set to medium-high heat. Cook until they have a nice, crisped edge and then flip and do the same.

FRIED PICKLES

Makes About 6–8 Servings (freezer-friendly)

Jack absolutely loves Fried Pickles. Whenever we go out on a date to a place that has them, he's sure to order them. I have been working on perfecting a healthy version of them for a while and finally succeeded. Now they're totally "Jack-approved." He loves them so much that I caught him eating them frozen! No kidding, right out of the freezer where I store batches of them!

3½ cups whole dill pickles (slice into rounds)	1 tsp. onion powder
6 Light Rye Wasa crackers (or 1 bag Shameless Crackers-Classic Toppers)	1 tsp. parsley flakes
½ cup Parmesan cheese (from the green can)	½ tsp. black pepper
⅓ cup Baking Blend	2 pinches Mineral Salt
	1 egg

1. Add Wasa or Shameless Crackers to a large Ziploc, then smash with a jar until broken up into a coarse flour. Add everything but the egg to the Ziploc bag then give it a good shake. Dump it onto a baking sheet.

2. Crack the egg in a bowl and whisk it with a fork. Dip a sliced pickle into the egg and then flip into the batter. Keep going until you have enough covered in the batter to cook the first batch (about ½ of the batch).

3. Liberally spray half of the battered pickles with coconut or olive oil. Gently set them into the air fryer (with the bottom rack left in) and cook for 10–12 minutes on 390°F. Pull out the air fryer drawer and flip pickles with tongs a few times after the first 3 minutes of cooking have passed. After the second time of flipping them, you may want to spray them again. Set Fried Pickles on a tray or plate when done and then do the same thing with the remaining half batch. Freeze any leftovers in a Ziploc bag.

Note: For a Skillet Option: Put a tablespoon or so of unflavored coconut oil into a non-stick skillet set to medium-high heat. Put 1 layer of battered pickles into the skillet and cook until slightly crispy. Flip to the remaining side and crisp again. Remove pickles from skillet and then continue process with remaining pickles. (You'll probably need to do this 2–3 times depending on how big your skillet is, but thankfully they don't take long to cook.)

CINNAMON SWEET POTATO FRIES

Makes About 2 Servings

I love sweet potato fries. I decided to make these in the cinnamon sugar style since that's how a lot of people like them at restaurants.

2 medium sweet potatoes	**½ Tbs. plus ½ tsp. ground cinnamon**
½ tsp. plus 2 pinches Mineral Salt	**2½ Tbs. Gentle Sweet***

1. Cut sweet potatoes into French-fry sized slices. Spray with coconut oil; and then put them on the bottom rack in the air fryer and cook for 9–10 minutes at 390°F. Take the air fryer drawer out and give the fries a few good shakes or flip them with tongs every few minutes.

2. Mix ½ teaspoon of the salt with 1½ tablespoons of the Gentle Sweet and ½ tablespoon of cinnamon, sprinkle onto the fries and cook for 2–3 more minutes. Dump fries onto a plate or tray and then mix up the remaining 2 pinches of salt, ½ teaspoon cinnamon, and 1 tablespoon Gentle Sweet to sprinkle onto the fries.

Note: I use Xylitol-Free Gentle Sweet for these fries. The recipe works using regular Gentle Sweet, but the xylitol-free version is less sticky.

PURPLE SWEET POTATO CHIPS

Makes a Single Serve

My mom loves this crispy, savory snack so much! I'll probably be making her some for her birthday along with some R's Granola from page: 96. She's crazy about super crunchy food! These purple sweet potatoes are so much fun in my opinion and they have even more health benefits than regular sweet potatoes. Anything purple is chockfull of healing flavonoids... not only great for skin, but for the entire body. Try to eat purple lettuce, purple onions, and purple potatoes whenever you

can. I buy my purple sweet potatoes from Sprouts. They can have great sales on their produce. When I eat purple veggies, I always think to myself, "*I'm doing wonders for my skin,*" and that makes me glow (pun intended, hehe!).

---

1 medium purple sweet potato*	**1¼ tsp. Mineral Salt (divided)**
1 Tbs. apple cider vinegar	

---

1. Fill a medium sized bowl halfway up with water. Add the vinegar and ½ teaspoon salt.
2. Take one of those heavy-duty, extra-wide peelers and start peeling the potato using good pressure to get thick peels. Put the thick peels into the water mixture. Continue until you have made peels out of the whole potato . . . not just the skin.
3. Take all the peelings out of the water and dry them off with a clean, dry dishtowel. Leave the rack in the bottom of the air fryer and place the peels on it. Spray them with coconut or olive oil and sprinkle with the remaining ¼ to ½ teaspoon salt (depending on your salt preference) and mix them well into the salt.
4. Cook at 375° for 10–11 minutes. After the first 3 minutes, pull out air fryer drawer and give a few good shakes. Continue shaking every few minutes until they're done.

Oven Option: Do everything the same, but mix up in bowl once you have dried them off. Add the salt and spray them with coconut oil. Set parchment paper on a large cookie sheet and then set your peels on it. Don't layer them, they all need to have a single layer so they cook evenly, but it's okay to have them touching each other. Bake at 325°F for 20–24 minutes.

Note*: You can use regular sweet potatoes for this recipe, too, but you'll need to press down harder when you're doing the peeling so the peels aren't too thin. Also, the cooking time may vary a little so you may need to take a few out early.

DRIED CRANBERRIES

Makes Multiple Servings

I absolutely love dried, sweetened cranberries on salads and in desserts and snacks but they're impossible to find without sugar! Here is my solution to sweetened, dried cranberries on plan. (Make sure during cranberry season that you load up so you can use them all year. I put them in the freezer, then when I need them for recipes . . . I just place on counter at room temperature and they thaw out pretty quickly.)

Pearl Chimes In These are life I tell you! I even love to snack on a handful as my dessert after a meal. Perfect accompaniment to ⅓ of a Trim Healthy Bar for my dessert or even just alone. These pops of tangy tartness have a way of helping me close my meal and leave me feeling blessed with taste bud glory.

1 (12 oz.) bag cranberries (thawed if frozen)
⅓ cup Gentle Sweet

Optional 1 tsp. Super Sweet Blend (if you like things sweeter)
1 tsp. unflavored coconut oil

1. Place the cranberries into a food processor. Give 6–8 quick pulses and then add Gentle Sweet and coconut oil. Stir.

2. Remove bottom rack from air fryer and place cranberries into the very bottom of the air fryer and spread around. Turn on the dehydrator setting and the temperature to 150° (and low bake for 4 hours.

Note: To make these in an oven, place a piece of parchment paper on a large cookie sheet then bake at 170°F for 6 hours.

NANA'S DELICIOUS BRUSSELS

Makes About 6 Servings

My Nana (Aunty Serene and Aunty Pearl's mom) is such a wonderful cook! I do not say this lightly, but I actually think she is one of the best in the world. She has this amazing talent to make incredible, yet healthy meals without having hardly anything in her fridge and it literally seems like no effort for her. Perhaps I get some of my love for having company over from her, as she loves to put on a meal for a houseful of family plus new friends and/or old friends. This is just one of the hundreds of yummy things she makes that everyone raves about.

2 (12 oz.) bags frozen Brussel sprouts
1 Tbs. unflavored coconut oil
½ tsp. black pepper
½ tsp. Mineral Salt

Optional ⅛–¼ tsp. cayenne pepper
¼ cup heavy cream
¼ cup Nutritional Yeast

1. Take all of the racks out of the air fryer and then go down the list throwing (well, I guess you don't have to throw) everything into the bottom of the air fryer. Mix well.
2. Turn temp to 390° and then let cook for 15–17 minutes, pulling the air fryer drawer out and giving a few shakes here and there.

Oven Option: Preheat the oven to 425°F. Go down the list mixing everything on a shallow oven tray/cookie sheet. Or if you want to make more dishes you can mix in a bowl and place onto the tray. Bake for 25 minutes and then take out of the oven to flip. Place back in the oven for 10–12 minutes.

13
SMART SIDES

3-Minute Shred (S) or (FP)

Orange Sesame String Beans (FP) or (S)

Stuffed Jalapeños (S)

Rad Kebabs (S)

New Way Veggies (FP)

Pickled Beets (FP)

Toasted Corn & Pepper Salad (E)

Spiced-Up Mexican Cauli-Rice (FP)

Italian Cucumber Side Salad (FP) or (S)

Handy Naan Bread (E)

Mac & Cheese Cups (S)

Here you go . . . my favorite side recipes. This chapter has some super simple and easy sides to go alongside a protein or whatever you're serving. I've included these in this cookbook just because they are my special ones, but here's the truth . . . you don't actually need recipes for sides. On the THM plan it is as simple as this; when it comes to sides to accompany your protein, just pick any non-starchy veggie like broccoli or green beans or sliced cabbage and cook it however you like . . . steam, sauté, bake, or broil. Add lots of yummy seasonings and butter, or coconut oil or cheese for S. Use just a tiny bit of oil or butter for FP or E . . . or melt some Light Laughing Cow Cheese (or Cheesy Wow-Spread from page 370) over it or pour on Aunty Pearl's Instant Cheese Sauce (page 380) or Go To Gravy (page 376).

I've included a few of my own favorite side salads here, too . . . but again, that doesn't mean you really need a recipe for a basic side salad. You do you! Your salad can be as simple as plonking down a bunch of ripped lettuce on your plate, drizzling on a little vinegar, and/or a little olive or MCT oil and then putting your protein source on top of it.

I'd be wasting ink here to write down recipes for all the simple, cooked non-starchy veggies or side salads you can create on your own with the abundance of veggies that God made. But if you're stumped for sides or want to try some new ones to pep up your plate . . . give some of my faves here a go. They make my THM life a happy and easy place to live and I hope they do the same for you.

Oh . . . don't forget to check out the previous chapter *Air Fried Goodness,* if you haven't already, for sides, too. There you'll find delicious French fry-style recipes and other crispy veggies.

3-MINUTE SHRED

 OR

Makes Any Amount You Want

This is a spin-off from my Cabbage Face meal in the *Five Minute Meals* chapter, but without the protein. Cabbage is the absolute easiest side veggie to quickly cook up and I turn to it over and over again. Just grab some out of a bag (or shred it yourself)... shove it in a pan with oil and seasonings and you have a delish, healthy side to any protein in under five minutes. I'm not going to give you amounts here, you can use whatever amount you want just for you or shove tons in your pan to feed your whole family... this is just too easy and you can't mess up.

Unflavored coconut oil for cooking (more
    than 1 tsp. for S, but stick to 1 tsp. for FP)
Shredded cabbage
Black pepper

Mineral Salt
Optional cayenne pepper
Nutritional Yeast

---

1. Heat oil up in a skillet on high heat and then add all the ingredients and cook for 3 minutes or so, stirring occasionally.

ORANGE SESAME STRING BEANS

  FP OR S

Makes About 6 Servings

These have a beautiful Asian flavor. Trust me, if you like green beans you can't go wrong with making these. If you want to have a FP meal, they go great with some lean protein like grilled or baked chicken

breast or tilapia (or other white fish if you don't love tilapia). Feel free to add a side salad with low-fat dressing or just some cut up veggies like peppers or cucumbers. If you'd rather have these with an E meal, simply add some brown rice or quinoa. For S, your protein option could be the chicken or fish, or you could have sliced up beef or venison, or dark meat from chicken, if preferred ... and use the higher nut amount. As a Crossover, do the brown rice or quinoa as well as the fattier protein option. Also, you can have a heavier dressing on your side salad.

---

3 Tbs. sliced almonds (⅓ cup for S)
½–1 Tbs. low-sodium soy sauce
2 (16 oz.) bags frozen fine green beans

1 cup Orange Sesame Dressing from page: 360
1 tsp. Mineral Salt

---

1. Put sliced almonds in a non-stick skillet and set to medium-high heat. Cook for 3–4 minutes, tossing occasionally so they're nice and dry roasted.
2. Pour soy sauce over them, then remove and set on a little plate.
3. Add frozen beans to the skillet with the Orange Sesame Dressing and salt. Cover and cook on high for 10 minutes, giving a good stir here and there. Sprinkle almond slices on right before serving.

STUFFED JALAPEÑOS

S

Makes About 6–8 Servings

Whenever I make these, they are devoured!!! I normally serve them as a fun appetizer when we have friends or family over. Got a feeling they'll be a huge hit for you and your family too!

8 medium jalapeño peppers (10, if they're smaller)
4 oz. goat cheese (or ⅓ less fat cream cheese)
¾ cup 0% Greek yogurt
¼ cup sundried tomatoes

⅓ tsp. black pepper
⅓ tsp. Mineral Salt
Optional ⅓ tsp. dried rosemary
5 pieces bacon (any kind; each piece cut into fourths)

1. Preheat oven to 425°F.
2. Slice jalapeños down the middle lengthways. (I like to wear gloves when I'm playing with these peppers because you never know how hot they're going to be; I've burned my hands on jalapeños before, so I'm more careful now.) Remove all seeds and set aside.
3. Mix goat cheese with the yogurt in a medium bowl, then add everything but the bacon; mix until smooth.
4. Stuff peppers with the cheese mixture then wrap each one with two slices of bacon and set them on a baking sheet.
5. Bake for 20 minutes and then broil for 2–3 minutes, if you like them extra crisp.

RAD KEBABS

S

Makes About 6–8 Servings

I served these with dinner the other night and half way through I asked Jack if he thought they tasted a little like potatoes. He abruptly responded, "What? They are not potatoes??? You sabotaged my food … you tricked me!" I was really not expecting him to think they were potatoes, but I was thrilled they tasted like it to him. As I sit here writing this intro, we're heading into warmer weather (finally) so I think these would be awesome to stick on the grill too, although I haven't tried that so tell me how they do. Oh, and these are awesome for parties too . . . see how many people you can fool! Rad Kebabs pair perfectly with any grilled or baked protein source. . . . chicken, salmon, fish, or steak . . . take your pick! Just add a healthy carb like a piece of fruit or buttered, sprouted bread to make an easy Crossover meal for family members.

2 lb. radishes
1½ tsp. Mineral Salt (divided)
5–6 pieces bacon (I use turkey bacon)
1 pint cherry tomatoes
2 Tbs. unflavored coconut oil

1 tsp. dried parsley flakes
1 tsp. crushed rosemary
1 tsp. oregano
¼ cup Parmesan cheese (green can is fine)

1. Preheat oven to 425°F. Soak 12 wooden skewers in water.
2. Cut radishes into thirds and then stick them into a medium-sized saucepan with 1 tsp. of the salt and enough water so that ⅔ of the radishes are covered in the water. Cook covered on high heat for 15 minutes and then drain water from the pot.
3. Slice bacon down the middle lengthways and then six times sideways. Add everything to the pot with the radishes and mix well.
4. Now start loading up your skewers. Just make sure you get at least some of everything on each skewer. Set each one on a large baking sheet (as shown in the picture), then bake for 35 minutes.

NEW WAY VEGGIES

Makes Any Amount You Want

Pearl Chimes In I was determined to include this as one of my twelve recipes because I think it will help many of you who may be in similar seasons to me. I'm currently in the thick of menopause which can often mean a metabolism slow down . . . yikes! What's a girl to do? Or perhaps you have a slower metabolism for reasons other than menopause . . . this recipe can be your saving and slimming grace.

Since entering this season, I have found that I don't burn fats as well or as quickly as I used to. I still enjoy S meals (along with more E meals than I used to), but on the whole, my S meals are lighter now than they used to be. Thankfully, I have come to love them this way. Don't get me wrong, I am not against fats . . . we all just have to know our season. Rashida is young, she's having babies, and breast feeding . . . this means she needs more fats than I do. Serene is not yet in menopause and still has a super high metabolism . . . she also needs more. My season reads differently. Even a teaspoon of oil here or there that I didn't even used to

think about (in veggies or Trimmies, etc.) can affect my weight now as they add up over the day. So, I am more intentional with fats, I use only what is needed for my health and only what really enhances my meals.

But do I feel deprived? Not at all! I used to think veggies were no good without coconut oil or butter and that was a fine approach for my younger THM years, but now I eat many of my veggies without any fats. I have learned they can still be so succulent and flavorful . . . in fact, I've come to crave them this way. You can always steam veggies to cook them without fat (and I do that, too) but when it comes to steaming . . . you have to put flavors on after cooking and they're harder to get succulent and flavor infused that way. This New Way Veggies recipe uses water sautéing which allows you to infuse flavor during the cooking process for more satisfying flavor and texture. Filling up on super large amounts of these water veggies with my meals has been one of my biggest breakthroughs to keeping a trim figure as I enter this new era of my life. I can literally eat pounds of New Way (or steamed) Veggies a day. I often make them the largest part of my meal. I pour my Go To Gravy (page 376) over them for FP or my Instant Cheese Sauce (page 380) for E or FP. At other times, I just eat them in super large amounts with no topping and just have a nice piece of protein on the side or perhaps some plant protein like beans. If you, too, are in a new metabolic season, join me in using this method for cooking many of your veggies. Really load up on them so they are the largest part of your meal and I think you'll love the result.

Broth or water	**Any non-starchy veggie or a few veggies of**
Nutritional Yeast	**choice**
Optional Braggs Liquid Aminos or soy sauce	**seasonings of choice**

1. Put a small amount of water or broth (about ¼ cup) in a large skillet set to high heat. Sprinkle in some nutritional yeast (however much you want) and some squirts of Braggs or soy sauce. Let the pan heat for a short while until the water starts to steam.

2. If you want to include onions and/or garlic, put them in skillet first. Cover skillet with a lid and let cook for a couple minutes. Now add more veggies starting with firmer veggies like broccoli, green beans, or Brussel sprouts. Cook those a little and then add other softer veggies like zucchini or yellow squash, since those take less time. Add more seasonings of choice, if you want, and more water or broth as needed to keep veggies from sticking as they cook. Toss them here and there.

3. Taste at the end to see if they need more flavor or saltiness and then tweak to own it! Now, don't worry about portion size for them on your plate, load your plate sky high and enjoy!

PICKLED BEETS

Makes Multiple Servings—Makes enough to fill a pint jar (double amounts for a quart jar, if desired)

Serene Chime In Vibrantly red, simple, yet sensational. The soft baked flesh of beets married with this gently sweetened tangy brine brings to life so many meals in my home. There is no such thing as mediocre meals with pickled beets, they make any plate a culinary masterpiece and powerfully boost health at the same time.

2–3 medium to large beets (cut into fourths)

SIMPLE BRINE:
2 Tbs. apple cider vinegar
1 Tbs. Gentle Sweet
6 pinches Mineral Salt
6 pinches black pepper

---

1. Preheat oven to 350°F.
2. Put beets on a large baking tray and bake about 30 minutes . . . or until you can easily pierce their flesh with a fork.
3. Let them cool enough to touch and then cube into ½-inch squares or slice into your own desired shapes. Place the cubed beets into a wide-mouth pint jar (or quart jar if doubling the recipe). Pour the brine mixture over beets and cover the jar. Shake well and store in the fridge.

TOASTED CORN & PEPPER SALAD

Makes About 4–6 Servings

This is an awesomely, zesty, and refreshing side to any lean meat such as grilled chicken or perhaps try my Cancun Chicken from page 117. Just add some sautéed cauliflower rice to fill up further, if you feel like you'll need it. Take this to any cookout and watch it get demolished! You can even make lettuce wraps by placing this onto some big lettuce leaves along with some chicken, or tuna, and R's Fresh Salsa from page: 353.

1 cup frozen corn kernels
1 small onion (chopped)
3 bell peppers (chopped; I use 3 different colored ones)
1 bunch cilantro
1 (15.5 oz.) can black beans (drained and rinsed)

1 tsp. Mineral Salt
1 tsp. ground cumin
½ tsp. black pepper
Optional ¼ tsp. chili flakes
Juice of 2 limes

1. Add frozen corn to a skillet and cook on high heat for 3–4 minutes so the edges get roasted, just a touch.
2. Put onion, peppers, and cilantro into a medium bowl and then add the black beans, roasted corn, salt, spices, and lime juice. Toss well.

SPICED-UP MEXICAN CAULI-RICE

Makes About 4–6 Servings (you can halve ingredients if you want to make less, but left-overs are great for other meals . . . say with eggs in the morning)

This is so fast to whip up . . . perfect as a side to your favorite Mexican dish or any dish! Enjoy with some grilled chicken or fish or other protein of your choice with some chopped cilantro, tomatoes, and cucumbers for a lovely, fresh FP meal. Or add some beans for an E meal. Yummo!!!

2 (10–12 oz.) bags frozen cauliflower rice	1 tsp. garlic powder
⅓ cup water	1 tsp. onion powder
2–3 tsp. unflavored coconut oil	1 tsp. creole seasoning
1 Tbs. ground cumin	¼–½ tsp. black pepper
1½ Tbs. chili powder	

1. Add the frozen cauliflower rice and water to a large non-stick skillet set to high heat. Cover with lid and let cook for 10 minutes.
2. Remove lid, add coconut oil, and stir in all the spices. Let cook for another 5 minutes (no need to adjust the heat).

ITALIAN CUCUMBER SIDE SALAD

Makes About 6–8 Servings

I would say I'm the cucumber's biggest fan! I can literally eat them like they're candy. So, of course, I have to have a salad with them as the main ingredient in my food world. I eat a very large portion of this as the only side to many of my meals … simply pairing it with whatever protein I'm craving. As written, this recipe makes a lot, but I love having leftovers after our dinner for the next day to eat with my lunch or sometimes I even enjoy it as an afternoon snack. But, I get it … if you're not sure you love cucumbers as much as I do … just make a half serving of this at first.

- 4 medium seedless cucumbers (those long ones wrapped in plastic; or 6 medium standard cucumbers, seeds removed and diced; peel if you want … up to you)
- 1 pint cherry tomatoes (halved)
- ½ cup fresh basil (finely chopped)
- 3 Tbs. Parmesan cheese for FP or ⅓ cup for S (green can is fine)
- Optional ½ an onion (diced)
- ¾ tsp. black pepper
- 1 tsp. Mineral Salt
- Juice of 1 lemon
- 1 Tbs. extra virgin olive oil

1. Add everything to a bowl and mix well.

HANDY NAAN BREAD

Makes 6 Servings

These Naan bread rounds are so simple to make and they're delightful as a side to your meal or even as pizza crusts if you want . . . they make amazing pizza! Once you've soaked the grain, they only take 10 minutes to bake! They're such a healthy bread item for your children who will love their soft and buttery texture. As written, these are plain; so they can be versatile for any meal, but you can add whatever spices you want to them. You could rub garlic and butter on top before baking and enjoy on the side of a creamy curry for a yummy XO. Aunty Pearl loves this bread with the Apricot Wow-Spread from page: 366 and my girls love it with peanut butter and honey for a great XO snack. The sky's the limit on what you can use them for.

Pearl Chimes In Rashida is not lying . . . I am head over heels in love with this soft and lovely bread. Rashida used regular einkorn flour shown here in the image. While whole grain einkorn is more optimum and works just as well, regular einkorn gets soaked overnight to make it more blood sugar-friendly, so it still kinda-sorta fits on-plan. Jessica, one of our editors for this book, made this recipe and loved it so much she has tried lots of different flours with it. She even had great success using whole grain dark rye flour in the overnight soak. She also tried it using sprouted whole wheat flour and didn't soak overnight. Here's what she messaged me: "Hey, so I wanted to report about Rashida's Naan bread . . . love it so much! I just made it with sprouted flour and no overnight soaking. I literally mixed the dough while the oven was preheating, baked for 10 minutes, and then ate the most delicious bread ever!! It's like a 15-minute from start to finish legit, on-plan, real-tasting bread! I've always considered myself a THM bread failure when it comes to E bread. Mine always turn out like a brick . . . this is a total game changer."

1½ cups einkorn flour (or other on-plan flour)
1¼ cups low-fat kefir

1 tsp. baking powder
1 tsp. baking soda
¾ tsp. Mineral Salt

1. Soak the flour in a medium bowl with the kefir, covered with a clean towel, on your countertop for 10–14 hours.

2. Preheat oven to 375°F. Line 2 large baking sheets with parchment paper, then lightly spray with unflavored coconut oil.

3. Add all ingredients to the bowl of soaked flour and mix well. Scoop out 3 even mounds of the dough onto each cookie tray (to make a total of 6 Handy Naan Bread pieces). Wet your hands with water then spread each mound out about the size of a pita or store-bought naan bread (which will work as individual pizza crusts) or spread out into 2 larger pizza crust sizes, each one covering the majority of a tray. (The water will help you spread the dough out without it sticking to your hands.)

4. Bake for 10 minutes (a little longer if making big pizza crusts).

MAC & CHEESE CUPS

⬡ S

Makes About 8–10 Servings (about 21 Mac & Cheese Cups that are freezer friendly . . . just plastic wrap each one before freezing in a big Ziploc bag)

Growing up on the Hilltop, my cousin Meadow (Aunty Pearl's oldest daughter) would make these for parties and picnics or any fun event. She's always been so good at making scrumptious finger food. I asked her if I could put her special recipe in the book and of course she gave the go ahead. I decided to make a purist version, too (using zucchini instead of Dreamfield's noodles).

   Both versions of these are so great for children. My girls are pros at getting their food everywhere when they eat, so I love making these for them because they don't get as messy as eating regular mac & cheese. Speaking of that . . . here's a tip . . . when I do make regular mac & cheese for them with Dreamfield's elbow pasta, I add a few scoops of Integral Collagen to it for protein. My girls can be picky sometimes and don't always eat meat, so that's a great way to get healthy protein in them.

FOR THE MAC & CHEESE:
1 box Dreamfield's elbow pasta (or for the purist version use 4–5 medium zucchini spiralized into noodles—about 6 cups)*
1½ cups sharp cheddar cheese (grated)
2 Tbs. unflavored coconut oil
½ cup Greek yogurt
½ cup unsweetened almond or cashew milk (omit if making the purist version)
1 cup sour cream
½ tsp. black pepper
½ tsp. onion powder

½ tsp. parsley flakes
1 tsp. paprika
1½ tsp. creole seasoning
2 eggs

FOR THE CRUNCH TOPPING:
4–6 Light Rye Wasa crackers (or 1 bag Shameless Crackers-Classic Toppers)
½ tsp. dried parsley flakes
¼ tsp. creole seasoning
½ cup Parmesan cheese (green can)
2 Tbs. unflavored coconut oil

1. Preheat oven to 375°F. Spray muffin trays (enough trays to make 21 muffins) with coconut oil (or you can use muffin liners if you want).

2. Start cooking the Dreamfield's noodles in a medium-large saucepan. While they're cooking, place everything but the coconut oil from the Crunch Topping into a large Ziploc. Smash the crackers until they're broken up into a gritty flour and then add the coconut oil and mix around. Set aside for later.

3. Once cooked, drain noodles and then go down the list adding everything to the saucepan ending with the eggs. Mix ingredients well, then place into 21 of the muffin holes. Sprinkle the Crunch Topping on them and bake for 25–30 minutes.

Note: If making the purist version, no need to cook the spiralized zucchini. Just squeeze out some of the excess zucchini water then everything else is the same (but remember not to add almond milk).

14

BAD GIRL BAKERY

Coconut Macaroons (S)

Banana Choc Chip Muffins (XO)

Pumpkin Muffins (S)

Peanut Butter Chocolate Chip Cookies (S)

Aunty Pearl's Muffins (E) or (XO)

Chocolate Mint Cupcakes (FP)

Deep Dark Decadent Cupcakes (E)

R's Carrot Cake (S)

Mocha Layer Cake (S)

Brownie Cheesecake (S)

Oat Bakes (E)

Pistachio Chocolate Chip Biscotti (S)

Oatmeal Raisin Cookies (XO)

Ginger Snaps (S)

Date Night Choc Chip Cookie (S)

Orange Scones (S)

Yup, that's right! You read it correctly. Welcome to my bakery! Get ready to feel like a bad girl while eating these delicious baked muffins, cakes, and cookies. Your taste buds will think you are being oh, so naughty . . . but your waistline will know you are being oh, so healthy! I wanted to make my baked goods taste and feel like the sugar-filled nonsense-type, but without all the fluff . . . literally . . . without the belly fluff! Hope you enjoy your BAD self in the very best sense of that word!

COCONUT MACAROONS

Makes Multiple Servings

4 egg whites (from whole eggs)
½ tsp. xanthan gum
½ tsp. Vanilla Natural Burst Extract
½ tsp. Maple Natural Burst Extract
½ cup Gentle Sweet
¼ tsp. Mineral Salt
5 cups shredded unsweetened coconut flakes
Coconut oil cooking spray

FOR THE CHOCOLATE DRIZZLE:

3 oz. Trim Healthy Chocolate Chips or 85%
   dark chocolate
¼ cup Gentle Sweet
½ tsp. Vanilla Natural Burst Extract
2 Tbs. coconut oil

1. Preheat oven to 350°F. Line 1 large baking sheet with parchment paper and lightly spray with coconut oil.

2. Separate whites from yokes, add whites to a big bowl and then begin beating them with an electric mixer. Once they start to get poofy, slowly add the xanthan gum. Continue to beat until stiff peaks form. Gently fold in remaining ingredients.

3. Place mounds of about 2 tablespoons each onto the baking sheet. Bake for 14–16 minutes. Remove from oven and allow to cool off while you make the Chocolate Drizzle by melting everything in a small pot on medium-low heat.

4. Drizzle the Chocolate Drizzle over the macaroons and chill in the refrigerator (or freezer for a faster chilling process). Keep refrigerated.

BANANA CHOC CHIP MUFFINS

Makes 12 Muffins

For me, the best part about having ripe, or overripe, bananas is being able to make these scrumptious muffins. They taste so unhealthy (like they're made with white flour and sugar). I love having one or maybe two as an afternoon snack with a coffee! I promise you it is not just me who adores them. Whenever I share them with friends and family they all love them and often ask for the recipe.

Pearl Chimes In I first tasted these when I was over at Rashida's house for one of her amazing lunches. Sometimes she'll just invite me over and you bet I'll show up because hey … great food and great company … her little girls always have me in hysterics with the funny things they say. Rashida had just made these muffins and was unsure if we should put them in the book. They are a Light Crossover, but she wondered if she was putting too many "Crossies" in the book. After just one bite, I insisted these had to be included … Crossovers are a wonderful part of the THM plan … no, they might not be quite as weight-loss friendly, but they're still healthy, great for growing children, pregnant and nursing women, and some-times they just keep the rest of us sane!!! Time of the month? These are 1,000 times better than most other sweet treats you might want to grab. Let these save you.

2 ripe bananas	1 cup Baking Blend
2 eggs	¾–1 cup Gentle Sweet (depending upon
½ tsp. Mineral Salt	sweet tooth)
2 tsp. baking soda*	⅓–½ cup Trim Healthy Chocolate Chips or
1 cup regular or Greek yogurt (any fat %)	85% dark chocolate (chopped)
1½ tsp. Vanilla Natural Burst Extract	

1. Preheat oven to 375°F and set muffin liners in 12 muffin holes. Spray with coconut or olive oil.
2. Mash the bananas with a fork in a medium mixing bowl, then mix in all other ingredients.
3. Scoop the mixture into holes and bake for 20–25 minutes.

*Note: Be sure you have fresh baking soda for this recipe as old baking soda can cause the muffins to fall too much, if preferred you can use 1½ tsp. baking powder and ½ tsp. baking soda.

PUMPKIN MUFFINS

Makes 12 Muffins

I worked at a local certified kitchen before I got married and one of things we made were pumpkin muffins ... the sugar-laden kind, of course, but people went nuts over them! Sometimes, I would bring Jack some as a treat when we were dating and he loved them so much (I do think that gave me extra girlfriend points!). Anyway, I decided to "THM-ify" them for us all to enjoy now.

1½ cups canned pumpkin puree
2 eggs
1 tsp. blackstrap molasses
1 tsp. Vanilla Natural Burst Extract
½ tsp. nutmeg
2 tsp. ground cinnamon

2 tsp. baking soda
1 Tbs. Super Sweet Blend
1 cup Baking Blend
¾ cup Gentle Sweet
½ cup flax meal

1. Preheat oven to 350°F. Line muffin trays with paper liners and then spray them with coconut or olive oil.

2. Go down the list and throw everything into a large bowl, mix well. Scoop mixture into muffin holes, then bake for 20–25 minutes. If you can tolerate dairy, let muffins cool off and top with my Cream Cheese Icing from page 372.

PEANUT BUTTER CHOCOLATE CHIP COOKIES

Makes About 15–25 Cookies (depending upon how big you make them)

If you like peanut butter and chocolate … get these in the oven!

---

1 cup Pressed Peanut Flour
1 cup Gentle Sweet
½ tsp. Mineral Salt
1 cup Baking Blend
1 tsp. baking soda
1 tsp. baking powder

3 doonks Pure Stevia Extract Powder
1 stick (½ cup) butter
1 egg
⅔ cup Greek yogurt (any fat %)
⅔ cup Trim Healthy Chocolate Chips or
    chopped 85% chocolate

---

1. Preheat oven to 350°F and lightly coat a large cookie sheet with coconut oil spray.
2. Add all dry ingredients into a big bowl and put the yogurt and egg into a smaller bowl and whisk well.
3. Melt one stick of butter in a small saucepan or microwave in a bowl (make sure you don't get it too hot!).
4. Combine wet ingredients with the dry mix until you have some yummy looking cookie dough then mix in the chocolate chips. Form into cookie sizes and bake for 10–12 minutes. Don't overcook, please!

AUNTY PEARL'S MUFFINS

 OR

Makes 12 Muffins

If you love cinnamon, raisin, and apple muffins . . . get baking! As Aunty Pearl was editing this book she mentioned we needed another E muffin for this chapter. She'd been craving a good cinnamon-raisin muffin so gave me the idea to create one (I think basically so she could be the taste tester and get her fix! Haha) I started working on it, but I honestly had no success each time I tried making them. I eventually told Aunty Pearl I was done trying. My pregnancy tastes buds just couldn't stand tasting them a 5th time. Well, the next day she texted me and said she had nailed it. I guess she couldn't handle going one more day without one. I had to photograph them for this book and after all my failures I was nervous about making them again. But I did them Aunty Pearl's way and they came out wonderful. Way to go, Aunty! I like having them as a XO with a smear of butter. Oh . . . and they also make your house smell like a wonderful cozy candle.

Pearl Chimes In Raisins in muffins are my total weakness so I'm glad I got off my behind and created these as now I no longer feel deprived. I can just whip these up any time as they're so easy! I also love making them for new moms who are nursing as they are excellent for milk supply (I made several batches for my daughter Meadow who recently had a baby). My blood sugar is pretty stable so I can handle these well, even though they include an apple, oats, and a few raisins … but they still fit into E … just a jolly good and packed one! Haha! If they raise your blood sugar too much, try having a baobab drink with them to help slow the rise of your blood sugar. (One of Serene's "Baobab Milk" versions would be good.)

2 cups old fashioned rolled oats (ground in a blender)
½ cup whole old fashioned rolled oats
⅓ cup Gentle Sweet
1 heaped Tbs. cinnamon
¼ tsp. Mineral Salt
1½ tsp. baking powder
½ tsp. baking soda
⅓ cup liquid egg whites
1 cup unsweetened apple sauce

½ cup unsweetened almond or cashew milk
1 apple (diced)
⅓ cup raisins
2 Tbs. finely diced pecans or walnuts for E (¼–⅓ cup for XO)

FOR THE GLAZE:
1 Tbs. unsweetened almond or cashew milk
¼ cup Gentle Sweet
¼ tsp. Vanilla Natural Burst Extract

1. Preheat oven to 350°F and lightly spray 12 muffin holes or use parchment muffin liners.
2. Mix dry ingredients together in a medium bowl and then add wet ingredients, followed by diced apple, raisins, and nuts. Mix well.
3. Scoop mixture into muffin holes and bake for 25 minutes. Once cooked, remove from muffin tin and put on a plate. While still hot, spoon the glaze over top of the muffins. This glaze keeps them moist and adds a nice extra hint of sweetness.

CHOCOLATE MINT CUPCAKES

Makes 12 Big Cupcakes

I had a dream to create a Chocolate Mint Cupcake, not just any cupcake … I wanted it to not only be both a FP and delicious (two challenging things for a baked good), but also to secretly contain hidden healthy veggies. In my head, this cupcake would be a decadent delight and nobody would detect anything else in it but sweet treat goodness. Well, often in reality my recipe dreams become abysmal failures but occasionally dreams do come true! These babies are not only FP, they're crazy easy to make and they have two cups of spinach in them but you'd never know … WAY TO GO, ME! Just don't tell whoever you're sharing them with that they have spinach in them. … well maybe you can after they've eaten one and are reaching for another—wink!

FOR THE CUPCAKES:

8 egg whites or 1 cup liquid egg whites

1 cup low-fat cottage cheese

2 cups frozen spinach (loose leaf kind)

1 tsp. baking soda

1 tsp. baking powder

½ tsp. Mineral Salt

1 tsp. Vanilla Natural Burst Extract

½ tsp. peppermint extract

2 Tbs. Super Sweet Blend

1 cup cocoa powder (I use Special Dark, which really makes it spectacular.)

1 cup Baking Blend

1 cup Gentle Sweet

¼ cup Oat Fiber

FOR THE CHOCOLATE ICING:

3 Tbs. cocoa powder

3 Tbs. Unflavored Pristine Whey Protein Powder

2 pinches of Mineral Salt

4 Tbs. egg white powder*

4 Tbs. Gentle Sweet

4 Tbs. hot water

1. Preheat oven to 350°F. Spray muffin holes with coconut or olive oil. Place everything down to the cocoa powder in the blender and then blend until smooth.

2. Add remaining ingredients, then blend well. Pour into muffin tins and bake for 30 minutes.

3. Let the cupcakes cool and then make the icing by placing all of the ingredients into a ceramic bowl and beat with a hand mixer for 5 minutes.

*Note: I get egg white powder, Anthony's brand, online from Amazon . . . but you could get any brand you like. This ingredient is important for this icing recipe. I have a feeling you will make these muffins (and the Deep Dark Decadent Cupcakes next page over, plus my Date Night Choc Chip Cookies, page 292) frequently enough to justify the purchase of egg white powder.

DEEP DARK DECADENT CUPCAKES

Makes 12 Cupcakes

I love coffee and I LOOOVE chocolate, so I just **had** to make a coffee chocolate cupcake. These are the cousin to my FP Chocolate Mint Cupcakes on the previous page, but these are a lovely E fuel. You would think they have loads of butter in them, but no … it is the okra (yes, I just said okra) and the spinach that make them so moist. Again, a warning not to tell your friends or family what they have in them. Case in point … the other day there was a painting crew in my home, redoing my walls. During their break I gave them some of these cupcakes (not mentioning a word about the okra) and they all loved them. Okay … full disclosure … my painting crew did consist of my mom, sisters, and my cousin Autumn (Aunty Pearl's daughter) But, hey … they're all very honest food critics (sometimes a little too honest). You don't have to put berries on these, but I think it helps balance out the intense chocolate and coffee flavors and gives a lovely refreshing note.

FOR THE CUPCAKES:
1½ cups old fashioned rolled oats or quick oats
1 cup low fat cottage-cheese
1 cup egg whites
½ cup chopped frozen okra
1½ cups chopped frozen spinach
1 cup cocoa powder (I use Special Dark for this which works best here, in my opinion.)
1 cup Gentle Sweet
½ tsp. Mineral Salt
1 tsp. baking soda
1 tsp. baking powder
1 tsp. Vanilla Natural Burst Extract

4 Tbs. instant decaf coffee*
1½–2 Tbs. Super Sweet Blend (for added sweetness)

FOR THE MOCHA ICING:
4 Tbs. egg white powder*
4 Tbs. Gentle Sweet
3 Tbs. Unflavored Pristine Whey Protein Powder
2 Tbs. instant decaf coffee
2 Tbs. cocoa powder (I use Special Dark.)
2 pinches of Mineral Salt
½ tsp. Vanilla Natural Burst Extract
¼ cup hot water
Optional berries (for topping)

1. Preheat oven to 350°F. Lightly spray muffin holes with coconut or olive oil . . . or use parchment muffin liners.
2. Blend oats in blender until they are a flour-like consistency. Then add everything in the cupcake ingredient list down to the cocoa powder. Blend until smooth (no okra or spinach pieces, please).

3. Add the remaining ingredients and blend once more until it's all blended up well. Pour into muffin tins and bake for 30 minutes.

4. Once the cupcakes are out and cooling, throw . . . I mean put . . . all icing ingredients into a bowl and mix with an electric hand mixer for 5 minutes. Top the cupcakes and let some of the icing drip down and get the cupcakes all messy, gooey, and perfectly lovely! Top with optional berries.

*Note: I buy egg white powder online . . . Anthony's brand from Amazon. You'll use it in the Chocolate Mint Cupcakes page 276, too. I think it is a worthy purchase. I use decaf instant coffee powder here because if you use regular you might get too wired from the caffeine.

R'S CARROT CAKE

Makes 1 Large Cake or 12 Cupcakes

I know there are a few THM-approved carrot cakes floating around. My aunties even have one in their Trim Healthy Table book, but we all like different versions and so I thought I'd put my own here for you. My husband is my biggest cheerleader for this cake. Almost every time he's done with his month rotation at the hospital or clinic, he'll ask me to make it as a thank you gift for the preceptor and staff. These are not usually sugar-free people, but they have all loved it so much. I have even received notes back! But now I'm just bragging, so I better stop! I had to make a deal with my husband that he's washing the dishes and cleaning up the mess whenever I make it for him to take.

- 1½ cups carrots (shredded)
- ¾ cup Baking Blend
- ¾ Gentle Sweet
- ¼ cup flax meal
- ⅓ cup Oat Fiber
- Optional 2 Tbs. Simply Sunflower Lecithin
- ½ tsp. ground cloves
- 2 tsp. ground cinnamon
- 1 tsp. allspice or nutmeg
- ½ tsp. Mineral Salt
- 2 tsp. baking soda
- 1 tsp. baking powder
- 5 doonks Pure Stevia Extract Powder
- 1 cup Greek yogurt (any fat %)
- 1 tsp. extract of choice (I like pure orange extract here or either Vanilla or Maple Natural Burst Extract—a ½ tsp. almond extract is nice, too!)
- 4 Tbs. melted butter
- ¼ cup water
- 3 eggs

1. Preheat oven to 350°F and spray a 9-inch cake pan or a muffin tray with coconut oil.
2. Put shredded carrots in a big bowl and literally go down the list putting everything into the same bowl and then mix well.
3. Pour the mixture into the cake pan and cook for 35–40 minutes. Muffins only need 25–30 minutes. Let the cake or cupcakes completely cool off before you ice them with my Cream Cheese Icing from page 372.

MOCHA LAYER CAKE

Makes Multiple Servings (Makes 1 Cake)

I like to keep this chocolaty/coffee-ish/creamy treat in the freezer wrapped in parchment paper. It tastes so amazing frozen. I slice a piece off 5–10 minutes before I eat it just to thaw it the tiniest bit and YUMM . . . perfect with coffee for an afternoon treat! Keeping it in the freezer means you don't need to feel like you have to eat the whole thing in a week, like you would if you kept it in the fridge. It can stay in the freezer for a good while and still taste fresh!

FOR THE COFFEE FLUFF LAYER:

8 fresh egg whites

½ tsp. xanthan gum

2 packets or 2 tsp. instant decaf or regular coffee

½ cup Gentle Sweet

½ cup Unflavored Pristine Whey Protein Powder (or use the Vanilla Bean Pristine Whey Protein Powder and reduce sweetener in this first section of the ingredients by half)

¼ cup cocoa powder

1 Tbs. Super Sweet Blend

2 pinches Mineral Salt

FOR THE CHOCOLATE LAYER:

3 oz. 100% baker's chocolate

1½ Tbs. coconut oil

1 Tbs. Super Sweet Blend

½ cup chopped walnuts

FOR THE CREAM LAYER:

1½ cups heavy cream

½ cup Gentle Sweet

2 packets or 2 tsp. instant decaf or regular coffee

1 tsp. extract of choice: Vanilla, Maple, or Caramel Natural Burst Extract

1. Preheat the oven to 350°F and very lightly spray 2 parchment lined baking sheets with coconut or olive oil.

2. Whip egg whites and xanthan gum in a large bowl with an electric beater until stiff peaks form. Mix up remaining ingredients from the Coffee Fluff Layer in a small bowl, then slowly pour into the bowl with the egg whites while gently stirring together.

3. Divide half the mixture onto each baking sheet, spreading them both out to about the same size as you'll be cutting and stacking them (you want each one to be about a ½ inch thick.) Place in the oven and bake for 12 minutes.

4. Melt all the ingredients in the Chocolate Layer in a small saucepan on medium-low heat. Pour this onto the baked Coffee Fluff Layers, spread it out, and then sprinkle on chopped walnuts. Refrigerate or freeze so the chocolate can set.

5. Whip the Cream Layer with the instant coffee and then add Gentle Sweet and extract of your choice. Take trays out of the freezer and cut each layer in half (you'll end up with 4 pieces). Spread the cream on each layer while stacking them into a cake.

BROWNIE CHEESECAKE

Makes Multiple Servings

This is ridiculously easy to whip up! I like making this when friends or family come over for an evening. I can make it in the afternoon or morning then stick it in the fridge and serve it as an after-dinner dessert. Then, if I have leftovers, I can have a leftover piece for breakfast with my coffee or as an afternoon snack with a coffee or tea. HEAVENLY! OH ... BTW ... I used to add the butter in the brownie part all the time, but one time I left it out by mistake and we all still loved it. Maybe try the butter in this the first time you make it but after that if you want to lighten up this dessert even further ... just leave it out and see what you think.

Serene Chimes In You know me ... I'm not one for rich desserts. My desserts are usually far from normal, wacky creations that always seem to involve secret, zany ingredients ... and I rarely eat cream cheese. But let me tell ya' ... when Rashida brings this to our family gatherings I enjoy it! I have learned that there's a time and place for just throwing away my food wackiness and indulging in "normal." So, my friends ... if you're longing for normal ... well, this is it! Cheesecake, I believe is one of the Seven Wonders of the World and Rashida has nailed this dessert, which is actually two desserts in one. Yes, it does have some cream cheese, but it is not over the top heavy. Even though it tastes super rich, it is actually lighter than many S desserts.

FOR THE BROWNIE BATTER:
¼ cup Baking Blend
¼ cup Integral Collagen
½ cup cocoa powder (I use Special Dark.)
½ cup Gentle Sweet
2 pinches Mineral Salt
½ tsp. baking soda
½ tsp. baking powder
2 doonks Pure Stevia Extract Powder
4 Tbs. softened butter (leave out if you want)
¼ cup unsweetened almond or cashew milk
1 egg

FOR THE CHEESECAKE BATTER:
½ cup Gentle Sweet
¼ tsp. Gluccie
1 egg
8 oz. ⅓ less fat cream cheese (room temp; softened)
½ tsp. Caramel Natural Burst Extract
¼ cup unsweetened almond or cashew milk

1. Preheat oven to 375°F and spray a standard pie dish with coconut or olive oil.

2. Get two medium bowls out. Put everything from the Brownie Batter list in a bowl, then stir well by hand. Do the same with the Cheesecake Batter, you can whisk or use use an electric hand mixer to make the batter smooth.

3. Smooth the Brownie Batter out in the bottom of the pie plate and pour on the Cheesecake Batter mixture. You can swirl them a little together, if you want, but you don't have to. Keep them one layer each if you want . . . no rules . . . it all turns out fine. Bake for 30–40 minutes then allow to cool on the counter before putting in the refrigerator for a while to set up fully.

Note: Best served chilled with fresh strawberries and a little spray of fat-free Reddi Wip.

OAT BAKES

Makes 7 Oat Bakes (enjoy 2–3 at a serving; double recipe and freeze, if preferred)

Serene Chimes In   I love oats! It is hard to choose my favorite E fuel as that's almost like trying to choose my favorite child, but oats must be in my top three. It must be the Scots in me. (My maiden name is Campbell, so I have a ton of Scottish blood … just take a look at my super Scottish "noza" (our down under term for nose.) I love oats for breakie, for lunch, and would even have 'em for dinner if no one else was around. I'll take them sweet, but I also love them all savoried up. They're humble, I know. They're also inexpensive and under assuming, but I also know of their incredible goodness. They are nurturing and nourishing with more protein than most grains and a nutrient composition of vitamins, minerals, and antioxidants that I'm sure made Mr. Quaker so proud. Did you know that the world's oldest living family according to the Guinness Book of World Records attribute their longevity to the humble oat? Yup. You can Google this Irish family of 13 siblings, all of whom are still in good health. The youngest sibling is 72, the oldest is 93 … with a combined age of 1,075 years. They all eat oats on a daily basis … even before bed!

Oats contain a powerful, soluble fiber called beta-glucan that lowers cholesterol, reduces post meal blood sugar and insulin response, and helps you feel full to the gills for a good while (in other words, it satiates without excess calories). This special fiber in oats is not digested, but rather fermented by bacteria in the colon and restores and maintains a thriving gut microbiome.

But I understand not everyone loves a bowl of porridge like us Scotts, so here is a different way of enjoying the multi-talented oat that is super simple, yet super delicious, savory or sweet … your choice or try both! Sometimes we'll enjoy these for breakfast, but they also make great snacks, lunches, or put the savory one on the side of soup or salad.

P.S. While humble due to the oats, this recipe is actually an overachiever and features other star players like baobab, nutritional yeast, collagen and in the sweet version, green banana flour. Mr. Quaker ain't got nothin' on these bad boys … they are oat bakes on steroids.

SAVORY OAT BAKES

1 cup old fashioned rolled oats
2½ Tbs. Nutritional Yeast
2 Tbs. Baobab Boost Powder
1 Tbs. Integral Collagen
¼ tsp. black pepper
¾ tsp. Mineral Salt
½ tsp. onion powder
¼ tsp. baking powder

2–3 mini rainbow peppers (diced fine)
1 cup egg whites
Optional, but delicious, ½ tsp. Tajin or 1 Tbs. lemon juice and an extra ¼ tsp. Mineral Salt
Optional, but delicious, ¼ tsp. dried chili flakes or a sprinkle diced jalapeño pepper (fresh or pickled)

SIMPLE SWEET OAT BAKES

E

1 cup old fashioned rolled oats
1 cup egg whites
2 Tbs. green banana flour*
2 Tbs. Baobab Boost
1 Tbs. Integral Collagen
3 Tbs. Gentle Sweet

3 doonks Pure Stevia Extract Powder
¼ tsp. baking powder
½ tsp. Vanilla Natural Burst Extract
½ tsp. Banana Natural Burst Extract
1 fresh or frozen green banana (finely diced)

1. Preheat oven to 350°F.
2. Mix everything together in a mixing bowl and then spoon into 7 lightly sprayed muffin holes in a muffin tin or use a brownie tin for square Oat Bakes (you can use paper liners if your baking tins cause baked goods to stick).
3. Bake for 15 minutes. When ready to eat, remove from pans, slice cakes open, and drizzle each side with an E appropriate (small amount) of the Boosted Savory-version or one of the Sweet-versions of the Tazincy Dipping and Smothering Sauce page 382.

Notes: I buy Superfoods by MRM brand of green banana flour online. It has only 3 net carbs for a tablespoon of the powder. You will use this in a couple other of my recipes here, too. For the Simple Sweet-version you can sub the green banana for a diced apple and then leave out the banana extract and add 1 tsp. of cinnamon.

PISTACHIO CHOCOLATE CHIP BISCOTTI

Makes Multiple Servings

To be honest with you, I have never liked biscotti…it is a texture thing. I have always felt it resembles slightly sweet, very stale bread. But I know a lot of people like it, so don't let my description of it put you off. I decided to make a healthy version for all of you who enjoy it. I tasted this right out of the oven (before it had time to dry out) and it is delish! I tried this on my biscotti-loving neighbor and got huge approval. Now you have biscotti for your coffee!

1 cup Baking Blend
¾ cup Gentle Sweet (Xylitol-Free)*
1 tsp. baking powder
⅓ tsp. Mineral Salt
1 stick (½ cup) softened butter (for DF use unflavored coconut oil and a couple extra pinches salt)

1 egg plus 1 egg white
1 tsp. Butter Natural Burst Extract
1 tsp. Vanilla Natural Burst Extract
½ cup pistachios (chopped)
½ cup Trim Healthy Chocolate Chips or chopped 85% dark chocolate

1. Preheat oven to 375°F. Place parchment paper on a large cookie sheet.
2. Add everything to a bowl and mix it up. Then, place onto the parchment paper and shape into one big rectangle (about ½ to ¾-inches high).
3. Slice dough into biscotti-sized pieces with a knife (dip the knife into water to have clean edges). Set the slices all around the parchment paper so each piece of biscotti has its own space. Bake for 20 minutes and then let completely cool until room temperature. Store in a Ziploc bag.

*Note: If all you have is regular Gentle Sweet, you can still try these cookies, but they won't get as hard and biscotti-ish.

OATMEAL RAISIN COOKIES

Makes Multiple Servings (makes about 18 cookies)

I have always loved oatmeal raisin cookies and now I can enjoy them as a Crossover treat. I made this recipe up the other day and had them as a dessert when we had some of my family over the other night. I put whipped cream in between two cookies and stuck them in the freezer to make little ice cream sandwiches, and they all loved them. At the time of writing this, I'm pregnant with my third baby and I'm excited to have these on hand for when my baby comes since they freeze great. Oats are great for getting a rocking milk supply so I'll be considering these as a wonderful lactation cookie.

¾ cup Baking Blend
¾ cup Gentle Sweet*
1½ cups old fashioned rolled oats
⅓–½ cup raisins (depending upon how well your blood sugar handles dried fruit)
½ tsp. Mineral Salt
1½ tsp. ground cinnamon
1–2 tsp. Super Sweet Blend (if desired for added sweetness)

½ tsp. baking soda
1 stick (½ cup) butter (melted; for DF swap in coconut oil and add 2 pinches more salt)
1 egg
2 tsp. blackstrap molasses
1 tsp. Vanilla Natural Burst Extract
2 tsp. Maple Natural Burst Extract
¼ cup water

1. Preheat oven to 350°F. Line 2 cookie sheets with parchment paper and set aside.
2. Go down the list adding everything into a medium-large bowl. Stir and then shape into cookie sizes and set on sheets. Bake for 12–15 minutes.

***Note:** Xylitol-Free Gentle Sweet gives a better (less brittle) texture than regular Gentle Sweet for these, but if you have regular they'll still be good.

GINGER SNAPS

S

Makes Multiple Servings

I wanted to create a healthy ginger snap that tasted like the ones of my childhood. When I was growing up, every Christmas we would all make homemade ginger snaps as a family (huge family, so a lot of people in the kitchen at once … but such wonderful memories). My mom had a designated night for it on the calendar every year. It was such a fun tradition and when our children get a little bigger, I definitely want to start doing it with them. In the meantime, I'll just make them and we all can enjoy them as a family.

1 cup Baking Blend	½ tsp. Mineral Salt
½ –¾ cup Xylitol-Free Gentle Sweet*	½ tsp. Gluccie
2 Tbs. Oat Fiber	1 tsp. baking soda
1–1½ Tbs. ginger powder	1 egg
½ tsp. ground cloves	2 tsp. blackstrap molasses
1 tsp. ground cinnamon	⅓ cup unflavored coconut oil or butter
¼ tsp. black pepper	⅓ cup water

1. Preheat the oven to 350°F. Spray 1 large cookie sheet or two medium ones with coconut oil.
2. Mix everything up and then spoon cookie-sized shapes onto the tray(s) and let bake for 8–10 minutes. Let them completely cool off and they'll start to harden up.

*Note: These homemade Ginger Snaps don't actually snap but we still called them that growing up as they do have all that delightful ginger flavor. Xylitol-Free Gentle Sweet gives a bit more of a crisped ginger snap texture. If you use the regular one, it will still work, they just won't harden up as much

DATE NIGHT CHOC CHIP COOKIE

Makes 1 Skillet Cookie to Share (or 4 Regular-sized Cookies)

When my husband and I were dating, I remember sitting together on his parent's wraparound porch when he suddenly disappeared inside for a moment. He returned moments later with a hot, chocolate chip cookie that was topped with ice cream in a mini cast-iron skillet for us to share. It was, of course, full of sugar and I was a crazy health zealot back then. But, it was such a sweet gesture that I could not help but enjoy it with him. Almost five years later, I decided to create a healthy version for us, and let me tell you we still enjoy eating this together as much as that first time.

2 tsp. egg white powder (or 1 Tbs. liquid egg whites)*

2 Tbs. Baking Blend

2 Tbs. Gentle Sweet (or 2 Tbs. Erythritol + ¼ tsp. Super Sweet Blend)*

⅛ tsp. baking soda

1½ Tbs. Trim Healthy Chocolate Chips or chopped 85% dark chocolate

1 pinch Mineral Salt

1½ Tbs. softened butter (or use unflavored coconut oil with a couple pinches more salt)

1 Tbs. water (optional; may not be needed if using liquid egg whites)

Optional little splash Vanilla Natural Burst or other extract of choice

1. Preheat oven to 375°F. Spray a mini cast iron skillet or very small cookie sheet with coconut or olive oil or grease with butter.

2. Place mixture into a small bowl, mix well then put into skillet. Bake for 10–12 minutes.

*Egg Note: I like to make this with egg white powder-vs-liquid egg whites because I make lots of these at a time (I go down the list putting everything but the water and butter into snack-sized "zippies"). When my husband and I want one, all we need to do is add butter and water. I buy Anthony's brand of egg white powder from Amazon. You'll use this in my Chocolate Mint Cupcakes and Deep Dark Decadent Cupcakes on pages 278, so it is worth getting some.

*Sweetener Note: When I first was creating this, I made it like 6 times straight. If you do the regular Gentle Sweet, you'll have a moister and slightly cake textured cookie. It's still wonderful, but if you do the erythritol and Super Sweet Blend, it will be more of that standard, hard outside, moist inside-type cookie. Jack and I enjoy the one made with erythritol topped with healthy ice cream best. If you're not having anything with it, I would make the other one.

ORANGE SCONES

Makes Multiple Servings

Guess what? This was the first recipe I actually typed up to start this book with. Most of my recipes before this were just in my head or lying around on pieces of paper. My nature is to rarely even measure anything when I'm cooking. I'm more of a dash, dump, pour, and throw; kind of cook. This recipe started off the self-discipline it has taken to measure correctly and try to explain myself in a somewhat understandable way. That has been my greatest challenge! Aunty Pearl has called me so many times throughout the editing process saying … "Nobody will know what the heck you mean by that!!!"

Back to these scones . . . every year on the Hilltop my cousin Breeze (Serene's daughter) has her big Princess Birthday Ball. We all have a blast! Everyone on the Hilltop, both family and friends, come all dressed up in formalwear and we dance the night away. We all bring homemade scones and have them with jam and fresh whipped cream. Delicious! I made up these scones to bring to the ball a couple years ago and everyone loved them. Aunties Pearl and Serene both said I have to put them in a book . . . a THM book! The idea for Trim Healthy Future was born and so here they are! I hope you love them and that they make you want to dance! Remember, they are best served with jam and cream.

---

2 cups Baking Blend
½ cup Whole Husk Psyllium Flakes
Orange peel from one large orange (finely chopped or grated; or 1 Tbs. dried orange peel)
½ cup Gentle Sweet
¾ tsp. Mineral Salt
3–4 doonks Pure Stevia Extract Powder
2 tsp. baking powder
1 tsp. baking soda
1 stick (½ cup) softened butter
8 oz. ⅓ less fat cream cheese (room temp; softened)

½ Tbs. pure orange extract (or Apricot Natural Burst Extract)
1 Tbs. apple cider vinegar
1 cup water

FOR THE ORANGE SCONES TOPPING:
¼ cup Gentle Sweet
1 tsp. pure orange extract (or Apricot Natural Burst Extract)
¼ tsp. citric acid

---

1. Preheat oven to 350°F. Line 2 baking sheets with parchment paper and lightly spray them with coconut or olive oil.
2. Put all the dry ingredients in a large bowl and stir them up. Set aside.
3. Add the softened cream cheese and butter together in a medium bowl. Stir until smooth and then add the remaining wet ingredients. Mix well.
4. Add the wet mixture to the dry mix. Stir everything together and then start shaping your scones . . . how I have them in the image, or however you want. Put them on the sprayed parchment trays.
5. Cover the scones with another piece of parchment paper and bake for 15 minutes. While they're cooking, mix up the topping in a small bowl. Then, sprinkle it on the scones as soon as they come out of the oven. Cool off and enjoy!

15

SWEET TREATS & DESSERTS

Deny Me Not Toffee **S**

Strawberry Gummy Worms **FP**

Peanut Brittle **S**

Super Woman Trail Mix **S**

Sweet & Salty Popcorn **E**

Spicy Candied Ginger **FP**

R's Candied Pecans **S**

Michelin Star Popcorn
(Large Version) **XO**

Peanut Butter Cookie Dough
Bites **S**

Mint Chocolate Chip Protein
Balls **S**

Greenie Meanies **S**

Chocolate Chia Seed Bites **S**

Cherry Jello **FP**

Nutty Chai Cups **S**

Chocolate Covered
Strawberries **S**

Berry Boost Roll Ups **FP**

Apple Crumble **XO** (with **E**
Option)

Blueberry Crumble **XO**

Sweet Potato Soufflé **XO**, **S**,
or **S** Helper

Bananas Foster **XO** or **E**

This chapter consists of candies, popcorn, balls, bites, crumbles, and other fun things to deliriously satisfy your cravings. This chapter, along with the *Bad Girl Bakery* and *Simply Splendid Shakes and Smoothies* chapters, are all here to satisfy your sweet tooth and, of course, that of your friends and family . . . that is if you're willing to share!

DENY ME NOT TOFFEE

Makes Multiple Servings

I love the flavor of toffee; it's just so buttery and caramely (if there is such a word). We Trim Healthy Mamas should not have to be denied toffee, so I had to go and make a healthy version.

1 cup unsweetened almond or cashew milk	3 Tbs. butter (or coconut oil for DF, plus 2 more pinches salt)
1 tsp. blackstrap molasses	¼ tsp. Mineral Salt
1 tsp. Vanilla Natural Burst Extract	Optional ⅓ cup almonds (chopped)
1½ tsp. Caramel Natural Burst Extract	Optional ⅓ cup Trim Healthy Chocolate
1 tsp. Butter Natural Burst Extract	Chips or chopped 85% dark chocolate
1 cup Erythritol (ground in a blender)	

1. Put almond milk, molasses, vanilla, caramel extract, and butter extract into a wide bottom saucepan or skillet set to high heat. Cook for five to eight minutes so mixture starts bubbling and reducing. Give lots of good stirs so it won't burn.

2. Reduce heat to medium-high. Add the remaining ingredients and cook for six to ten more minutes, stirring the whole time so it doesn't burn.

3. Pour mixture onto a large parchment paper-lined baking sheet and then sprinkle almonds and chocolate over it and let it set. You can let it set at room temperature or in the refrigerator, if you want the toffee to harden faster.

STRAWBERRY GUMMY WORMS

Makes Multiple Servings

If you like sour candy, please do yourself a favor and make these! I gave some to my Aunty Pearl to try and she literally handed them out to everyone at my grandparent's home church (Hilltop Church). It is mostly family that goes there ... but still ... ha! I heard on the Hilltop grapevine that everyone went crazy for them. The funny thing is ... these are another of my mess-ups gone right. I was trying to create a healthy strawberry marshmallow, but I failed big time and they came out more like gummies. So, I decided to perfect the gummy instead of the marshmallows and thankfully it worked. I think your children will love these and once again, they're another great way to get the three superfoods baobab, collagen, and whey into them! Perfect for building immune health and raising vitamin C and iron levels. Oh, I need to mention ... they're great for parties as well because they can stay out for hours at a time without melting.

¼ cup **Baobab Boost Powder**

¼ cup **Strawberry Pristine Whey Protein Powder**

¼ cup **freeze-dried strawberries (smashed or ground—measure after grinding)**

¼ cup **Xylitol Free Gentle Sweet**

2 tsp. **Super Sweet Blend**

1 tsp. **citric acid**

¼ tsp. **Mineral Salt**

1 cup **water**

3 Tbs. **Just Gelatin**

½ tsp. **xanthan gum**

1½ tsp. **pure strawberry extract (you can use Apricot Natural Burst Extract, if you don't have a strawberry extract)**

Optional red or pink natural food coloring

FOR THE SWEET & SOUR COATING:

3–6 Tbs. **erythritol (use smaller amount for less sweet, more sour gummies)**

½–¾ tsp. **Citric acid (use larger amount for less sweet, more sour gummies)**

1. Place all the dry ingredients, except for the gelatin and xanthan gum, into a bowl. Heat water in a small saucepan and then add in the gelatin and the xanthan gum. Whisk until they both have dissolved. Add in the strawberry extract and a few drops of natural food coloring, if using.

2. Pour the hot liquid into the bowl with the dry ingredients and stir well. Then, lay the mixture out (about gummy worm thickness) on a 13x7 cookie sheet lined with parchment paper. Place in the refrigerator to set for 15–20 minutes.

3. Once set, take a pizza cutter and run down the tray making wormy looking strips. Mix up the coating and then sprinkle onto your gummies. You can store them in a zippy or container out of the refrigerator for a few days ... if they last that long! You can also store them in the fridge so you don't eat them all in one day.

PEANUT BRITTLE

Makes Multiple Servings

Granny (Jack's grandmother), who has a well-developed sweet tooth, tasted this and kept asking me if I made it with brown sugar. I couldn't help but grin ridiculously and mentally pat myself on the back … Wow! Granny approved! I felt so honored.

1 cup unsweetened almond or cashew milk
1 tsp. Vanilla Natural Burst Extract
½ tsp. Caramel Natural Burst Extract
½ tsp. blackstrap molasses
¼ tsp. Mineral Salt

¾ cup Erythritol (preferably ground)
4 Tbs. butter (or unflavored coconut oil for DF, plus 2 more pinches salt)
¾ cup dry-roasted peanuts

1. Preheat oven to 375°F and line a cookie sheet (with raised sides) with parchment paper.

2. Add everything but the peanuts and butter to a large non-stick skillet or saucepan (you want to make it in something that has high sides so it doesn't overflow while it's cooking). Then, cook for 4–5 minutes on high heat.

3. Add peanuts and butter and cook for another 8–9 minutes on medium-high, stirring every so often. Towards the end, when it starts to seriously bubble, stir constantly. Don't burn it!

4. Pour mixture onto the lined cookie sheet and cook for 6 minutes in the oven. Then, take it out of the oven and let it cool down to room temperature to allow it to harden.

Note: If you want a faster hardening process, let it cool off enough so no steam is coming off and then place a piece of plastic wrap over it and stick it in the fridge. I don't keep mine in the fridge, but if you want it a little cold (and maybe even a little harder) go ahead.

SUPER WOMAN TRAIL MIX

Makes Multiple Servings

Most trail mix is loaded with sugar, but thankfully not this one! I like to put ¼–⅓ cup portions into "zippies" to have them for on the go for snacks when I'm running out the door into fast-paced life.

1 cup walnuts (or any nut you prefer)
1 cup Dried Cranberries from page 243
1 cup Trim Healthy Chocolate Chips or chopped 85% chocolate (For this image, I used ½ cup stevia-sweetened white chocolate chips that I found at the grocery store for extra fun.)
½ cup sliced almonds
½ cup pumpkin seeds
Optional Spicy Candied Ginger from page 306

1. Mix everything together and you're done.

SWEET & SALTY POPCORN

Makes About 6 Servings (4 cups each)

If you want to turn this into a Crossover, just add some Trim Healthy Chocolate Chips—delish!

1¼ cups water
1 cup Gentle Sweet (Xylitol-Free)
1 tsp. blackstrap molasses
1½ tsp. Mineral Salt
1 tsp. Vanilla Natural Burst Extract
1 tsp. Butter Natural Burst Extract
1½ tsp. Caramel Natural Burst Extract
24 cups air popped popcorn (made from ½ cup + 2 Tbs. of popcorn kernels)
Optional Trim Healthy Chocolate Chips

1. Add everything but the popcorn to a wide pan or skillet. Cook for 10 minutes on high, stirring frequently. Once reduced, you should end up with slightly less than a cup of liquid.

2. Spray popped popcorn with coconut oil and sprinkle on the remaining salt. (***NOTE:** I use a big brown paper bag to shake everything together when I'm making a lot of popcorn.)

3. Slowly pour a little of the wet mixture onto the popcorn and then shake the bag really well. Do that a few times until all the sweet mixture is used up. (If you want to add the chocolate chips . . . add a small amount in between each pouring so they actually melt in and stick to the popcorn, rather than just falling to the bottom of the bag or bowl.)

SPICY CANDIED GINGER

FP

Makes Multiple Servings

Ginger raises your metabolism! You'll notice I use it a lot in my drink chapter (Dangerously Delicious Drinks & All-Day Sippers) as it has so many health benefits. A study carried out in China

showed that 4 hours after eating ginger, the metabolic rate in a ginger fed group was elevated over the control group who didn't eat ginger. Another study showed that just half a teaspoon's worth of ginger increased the rate at which people burned fat by 10 percent two hours after eating it (that's similar to what a work out session can do for your body). The way ginger manages this is through its natural spicy heat. It turns on the brown fat in your body (a good type of fat). When your brown fat is activated, you burn more regular body fat. Wahoo!

It seems not many are used to candied ginger here in the USA, although Down Under where my mom's family is from, it is much more popular. The heat and sweet sensations together are a different combination, but for those of us who love it . . . we're that strange group of fans who crave it our whole adult lives through. I gave some of this to my mom and dad and a few of my brothers. My older brother (Zadok) is a HUGE ginger fan and he said it was the best he had ever had and he's a very honest guy. My dad, mom, and husband Jack loved it, too. But please don't think I'm being too proud . . . I do have to admit I noticed one of my younger brothers sneak it into the trash. I think it was just too spicy for him. Haha! You can add it to the Super Woman Trail Mix on page 304 or just eat it plain. But give it a go . . . at least once . . . it might be a learned taste, but you can train yourself to love anything little by little!

10 oz. fresh ginger	2 pinches Mineral Salt
3 cups water	½ cup Erythritol (divided)
¾ cup Gentle Sweet	

1. Using a food processor, slice ginger into ⅛ to ¼ thick slices. (Or slice by hand if you don't have a food processor.)

2. Add water and ginger to a small saucepan and set to high heat. Cover and bring to a boil. Lower the temperature to medium-high and gently boil for 35 minutes. Remove the lid. Ladle out ½ a cup of the ginger water. (I add this ginger water to some fuzzy water aka carbonated water . . . or create a fun drink with it. That way I don't waste it.) Now, add the Gentle Sweet and salt. Stir and let continue to simmer on the same temperature for 20–25 more minutes uncovered.

3. Preheat the oven to 425° F. Lay parchment paper on a large cookie sheet, sprinkle ¼ cup of the erythritol onto the parchment paper. Once the ginger is done cooking, scrape everything from the saucepan onto the parchment paper and spread it out in a single layer. Sprinkle the remaining ¼ cup of erythritol on top of the ginger.

4. Bake for 7 minutes, then take out and let it set (the time to let it set will depend on the humidity of your house). The ginger will get all hard and "candified" when it's fully done. Store in a Ziploc bag or a container that has a good seal to it.

R'S CANDIED PECANS

S

Multiple Servings

Oh, yeah! "I did it, I did it!" That's what ran through my head to the tune of one of the Dora the Explorer theme songs as I fist pumped the air after finally getting this recipe right. I think my girls have been watching too much of that show and that song keeps infiltrating my brain. Seriously, though … this recipe has taken me a while to perfect the cooking time, etc. I'm super happy it's on point now! These pecans are perfect for parties, the holidays, and sneaking into the movie theater. Did I just say that??? Yep, I put them in small Ziploc bags and then stick them in my purse for my husband, friends, and of course myself. Don't call the Police!

Serene Chimes In I feel it is my duty to give you a fair warning here. I tasted these on a road trip and then I just kept on eating! You may not want to even try this recipe at all if you, like me, are a sucker for a good crunch! Yeah, you probably want to quickly turn the page and pretend you didn't see the mouthwatering picture if you love decadent sweet with the warming flare of cinnamon. Final warning ... close the book, dear friend, and take a cold shower because once you taste R's Candied Pecans, you will be making them for life.

4 cups pecan halves	1 Tbs. ground cinnamon
1 egg white	¾ tsp. Mineral Salt
1 cup Gentle Sweet	2 tsp. blackstrap molasses

1. Preheat oven to 275°F and line 2 baking sheets with parchment paper.
2. Add everything into a bowl and mix well. Put half the coated pecans on each tray and spread them out in a single layer. Bake for 20–25 minutes.
3. Remove from the oven and flip the pecans (remember not to layer them), then put back in the oven for another 15–20 minutes. Once baked, allow to sit out for 30 minutes to 3 hours to harden. I know that time range sounds crazy, but depending on the humidity and how hot your house is, the hardening time will vary.

MICHELIN STAR POPCORN (LARGE VERSION)

Makes About 6 Servings (4 Cups Each)

Why is this called "Michelin Star Popcorn"? Let me set the scene. Christmas time . . . a couple years ago . . . I was invited over for a girls' movie night at my Aunty Pearl's house with my best friend/cousin Meadow and her sister Autumn. I made a big bowl of this festive popcorn for all of us to have while we watched *The One Hundred Foot Journey*. If you have not seen it. . . . please do . . . it's all about the art of cooking (the quest for a Michelin Star) and it's my favorite movie.

Anyway, they all loved the popcorn. Aunty Pearl kept blurting out during the film . . . "This is Michelin Star popcorn!" Haha. I was actually going to name this "Stocking Stuffer Popcorn", but Aunty Pearl wouldn't allow it; she said it deserved the Michelin Star. (I got a text from her the next morning saying that she dreamed about the movie all night and in her dream she made curry out of a big cockroach. Let's hope she puts that recipe in her next cookbook, right?)

¼ cup Unflavored Pristine Whey Protein Powder	¾ cup coconut oil (melted)
¼ cup Integral Collagen	½ tsp. Mineral Salt
½ cup cocoa powder	2–3 doonks Pure Stevia Extract Powder
¾ cup Gentle Sweet	24 cups air popped popcorn (made from ½ cup +2 Tbs. popcorn kernels)

1. Add all the ingredients minus the popcorn and coconut oil to a small bowl. Stir until mixture is even and no lumps are remaining.
2. Put popcorn in another very large bowl. Pour coconut oil over popcorn and then start adding the dry mix to the popcorn. Mix it all up, so you have some chocolaty goodness coating each piece of popcorn. (You'll most probably need to use your hands, but if you don't want to get your hands covered in chocolate powder, use a clean paper or plastic bag to shake it all up in or wear some plastic gloves.)

Note: If you want to upgrade to get another "Michelin Star" you could always add either ½–¾ cup Trim Healthy Chocolate Chips, chopped 85% dark chocolate, chopped walnuts, or shredded coconut. If you so desire to take this extra step to get this extra star, make sure you add the chocolate before the coconut oil so it will stick to the popcorn and not just end up at the bottom of the bowl.

Single Serving:

- 4 cups air popped popcorn
- 1½ Tbs. Gentle Sweet
- 1 Tbs. cocoa powder
- ½ Tbs. Unflavored Pristine Whey Protein Powder
- ½ Tbs. Integral Collagen
- 1/6 to 1/8 tsp. Mineral Salt
- Optional 1 doonk Pure Stevia Extract Powder
- 1½ Tbs. coconut oil

(Use the same directions as for the large serving.)

PEANUT BUTTER COOKIE DOUGH BITES ⬡ S

Makes Multiple Servings

Who doesn't like raw cookie dough??? Well, now you have a healthy (salmonella-free—yay!), delish cookie dough bite!

FOR THE COOKIE DOUGH:
- ⅓ cup Baking Blend
- ⅓ cup Unflavored Pristine Whey Protein Powder
- ⅔ cup Pressed Peanut Flour
- ½ tsp. Mineral Salt
- 2 tsp. Super Sweet Blend
- ⅓ cup unsweetened almond milk
- 4 Tbs. melted butter
- 1 tsp. blackstrap molasses
- ½ cup Trim Healthy Chocolate Chips

FOR THE CHOCOLATE COVERING:
- 2 oz. Trim Healthy Chocolate Chips or 85% dark chocolate
- ½ Tbs. unflavored coconut oil
- 2 Tbs. Gentle Sweet

1. Go down the Cookie Dough list and throw everything into a bowl. Mix well.

2. Place parchment paper on a flat plate or baking sheet. Spoon about 1–2 tablespoons of dough into your hand and form ball shapes. Put in freezer to chill.

3. To make the Chocolate Covering . . . put chocolate, coconut oil, and Gentle Sweet into a small pot. Cook on medium-low heat until melted.

4. Take the Cookie Dough Bites out of the freezer and roll each one in the melted chocolate. Place in the fridge to chill or for a faster chill time . . . put back in freezer.

MINT CHOCOLATE CHIP PROTEIN BALLS

Makes Multiple Servings

Once these babies are frozen, I like to put them in a Ziploc bag and store them in the freezer. They taste like mint chocolate chip ice cream in protein ball form. You wouldn't know they are filled with tons of great fiber to support your digestion. They're perfect if you need a snack and are running out the door.

½ cup Baking Blend
½ cup Integral Collagen
½ cup Unflavored Pristine Whey Protein Powder
½ cup Whole Husk Psyllium Husks (ground fine in a coffee grinder)
½ cup Gentle Sweet
2–3 doonks Pure Stevia Extract Powder

½ tsp. Mineral Salt
¼ cup coconut oil
½ cup water
Optional 2 tsp. Dynamic Duo Greens Powder or 1 tsp. liquid chlorophyll
1 tsp. pure peppermint extract
¼–½ cup Trim Healthy Chocolate Chips or chopped 85% dark chocolate

1. Put all dry ingredients into a bowl. Follow with the wet ingredients and then end with the chocolate chips. Mix well.
2. Line a plate with parchment paper and then roll mixture into balls.
3. Chill in the freezer.

GREENIE MEANIES

Serene Chimes In Don't get scared off just cuz these little balls look so dark green and mean yet they're in the Treats chapter. You bet they are green, but green foods can be sweet and delicious, too. And you bet they are mean, but for reasons I'll soon explain. Just be sure to pull up your big girl socks and try them because despite their mean side they're kind to you with how easy they are to throw together.

The mean nature of these balls is how they beat up on bad health. They don't get chewed up and act all insipid . . . lazily floating around in your tummy on a wee hunk of unchewed cracker as a raft. No!!!! They are captains! They get swallowed and mean bidness on badness. Inflammation . . . look out! Disease . . . they're comin' for ya'! LDL cholesterol . . . you're about to take a beating! Anemia . . . you're outta here! High blood sugar . . . you're going down! Toxins and heavy metals . . . get ready to be flushed! Immune system . . . get boosting! Energy . . . get surging! Muscles . . . get building! Skin . . . get firming! Hair . . . get growing! Greenie Meanies are in the house!!

I'll fight the urge to go on and on about the ingredients here and just highlight a couple guns in the arsenal these meanies use for battle. You can either use our THM Dynamic Duo Greens Powder here (which is a combination of spirulina and morninga) for the green part or just use straight spirulina which you can buy online anywhere. Spirulina is gram for gram one of the most nutritious foods on the planet. One single tablespoon provides 4 grams of complete protein and is bountifully laden with a smorgasbord of vitamins and minerals. Spirulina is added to the diets of astronauts in orbit for good reason. While it may look green, it is not a plant, it is actually a health-boosting blue/green bacteria (officially an algae). And on the topic of colors here . . . it may not look orange, but it has 10 times more beta-carotene than carrots! Moringa leaves are also a protein powerhouse with 25% protein by weight which is unusually high for a plant. It is anti-inflammatory, anti-viral, and anti-fungal and is traditionally used to treat diabetes as it helps to normalize blood sugars that are too high. Both spirulina and morninga are excellent if you have MTHFR genetic markers or any methylation issues as they are rich sources of folate and help to cleanse and detox the body.

You have one version for E and two versions for S here. With 3 Greenie Meanie versions there will be no excuses and no one left behind on this Greenie Meanie Boot Camp. I created the tangy version, not only because it is super yum, but also because the citrus helps unleash spirulina's energy power. Lime juice is said to be the best, but I put lemon down as most people have these more readily on hand. But if you have limes, then sub them for sure.

Note: I recommend you grab some green banana flour online or at a health food store somewhere. Its resistant starch is incredible for your gut. I put it in my smoothies and lots of other food creations. I use Superfoods by MRM brand that has 3 net carbs per tablespoon.

TANGY FRUIT GREENIE MEANIES

Makes Multiple Servings

5 Tbs. fresh lemon or lime juice

3 doonks Pure Stevia Extract Powder

1 cup old fashioned rolled oats

¼ cup Unflavored Pristine Whey Protein Powder

¼ cup Integral Collagen

¼ cup Baobab Boost Powder

¼ cup green banana flour* (resistant starch which heals the gut and reverses insulin resistance)

¼ cup Gentle Sweet

2 Tbs. Dynamic Duo Greens Powder or spirulina

¼ cup dried golden berries or goji berries (or 2 Tbs. raisins, if you don't have those)

½–¾ tsp. Apricot Natural Burst Extract

1. Put lemon juice and stevia in a small bowl. Stir to combine and set aside.

2. Put all other ingredients, minus dried berries or raisins, in food processor and process until ingredients break down a little. Add lemon and stevia mixture and process again until mixture forms a ball . . . or you can press the mixture and it holds together with your fingers.

3. Form into balls and put in Ziploc bags and store in fridge for up to a week or store in freezer. They are even yummy straight from the freezer.

ISLAND BOUNTY GREENIE MEANIES

4 Tbs. fresh lemon or lime juice

3 doonks Pure Stevia Extract Powder

1 cup dried coconut flakes (don't stress the size, it all breaks down in the end)

¼ cup Baking Blend

¼ cup plus 1 Tbs. Unflavored Pristine Whey Protein Powder

¼ cup plus 1 Tbs. Integral Collagen

½ cup Baobab Boost Powder

2 Tbs. Dynamic Duo Greens Powder or Spirulina

¼ cup Gentle Sweet

2 Tbs. extra virgin coconut oil

½ tsp. Apricot Natural Burst Extract

Follow the same directions as for the Tangy Fruit Greenie Meanies by dissolving stevia in lemon juice before adding to the food processor.

CHOCO MINT CRUNCH GREENIE MEANIES

Make the Following Changes to Island Bounty Greenie Meanies:

- Replace the ½ cup baobab with ½ cup plus 1 Tbs. cocoa powder
- Replace the 4 Tbs. lemon juice with 3 Tbs. unsweetened almond milk
- Replace the ½ tsp. Apricot Natural Burst Extract with a full tsp. pure peppermint extract
- Add ¼ cup cacao nibs (or if you don't have those, use Trim Healthy Chocolate Chips)

Follow the same directions for Tangy Fruit Greenie Meanies by dissolving stevia in lemon juice before adding to the food processor.

Note: I buy Superfoods by MRM brand of green banana flour online which has only 3 net carbs per tablespoon. I use this flour all the time in my smoothies now and a couple of my other recipes here call for it, too.

CHOCOLATE CHIA SEED BITES

Makes Multiple Servings

These are great to have on hand. I love having one or two as an after lunch sweet treat or paired with a "Collagen Tea" for an afternoon snack. Though I do enjoy them, my mom is the one who goes crazy for these. She loves "CRUNCH" with a passion and the chia brings that for her! She's a very expressive person, so when I say she loves these with a passion, you need to believe me. She'll yell stuff like … "RASHIDA!!! THESE ARE JUST OUT OF THIS WORLD AMAZING!!!" And then she'll go

dancing or jumping around the room to demonstrate her enthusiasm. She can't help it. My mom is a 6 foot tall, feisty, and wild red head who made growing up in our home with my other 9 siblings … well, let's just say … the opposite to dull! I made her these for part of her birthday present last year because she loves them that much. This year she's most probably getting another batch along with some of my new crunch creations.

4 oz. unsweetened baking chocolate
¼ cup coconut oil
2 pinches Mineral Salt
½ cup Gentle Sweet
½ cup chia seeds

¼ cup cocoa powder
1–2 tsp. Super Sweet Blend
2 tsp. pure orange extract or 1 tsp. pure peppermint extract

1. Put chocolate into a small saucepan and set to a medium-low heat. Once chocolate begins melting, add coconut oil and the remaining ingredients. Stir until chocolate has completely melted.
2. Put small spoonfuls into mini muffin liners (no need for muffin tins) and then chill in the refrigerator. To speed up the chilling process, put in the freezer.
3. Once thoroughly chilled, store covered in the fridge. (When I make them, I'll store half the batch in a Ziploc bag in the freezer for another week or so.)

CHERRY JELLO

Makes Multiple Servings

I'm in love with all three of my jello variations, but this cherry one is a great way to get lots of baobab powder in you, your kiddos, or friends. Remember, baobab has more antioxidants than any other food. It's chock full of bio-available vitamin C, calcium, and iron. It heals your gut biome and, in my

opinion, is also super yummy. Any of these jello versions are a great way to end a meal or have for a lovely light snack. They offer glycine-rich protein, which we all need more of for our skin, hair, immune systems, and gut health. If you are not a purist, you could even kick these up a notch and have a squirt of fat-free Reddi Wip on top and it still be in FP-mode. Once you have tried each a few times, you can start getting creative and use new, natural flavors and colors to create your own ultimate jello experience.

5 cups water (divided)
½ cup Erythritol*
5–7 doonks Pure Stevia Extract Powder*
1½ tsp. citric acid
1 tsp. Cherry Natural Burst Extract

½ cup Baobab Boost Powder
3½ Tbs. Just Gelatin
Optional ¼–½ tsp. red natural food coloring

1. Put 2 of the 5 cups of water into a saucepan set to high heat. Add the erythritol, stevia, citric acid, and baobab powder to the pot. Stir it all together and then let it start to boil.

2. Once it has reached a boil, turn to medium-low and whisk in gelatin. Whisk well and cook until all the clumps are out and the gelatin is completely dissolved (about 3–5 minutes).

3. Remove from the heat, then add the 3 cups of remaining water. Pour into whatever molds you want (I like to make them for on the go and put in small jars) and refrigerate until set. (Chilling time will depend on how much mixture you use in a mold, or baking dish—the smaller the faster.)

*Sweetener Note: You can use Super Sweet Blend or Gentle Sweet, if you prefer . . . just taste test to determine the amount you'd want to use.

Orange-version

Sub 1½ tsp. pure orange extract for the cherry and use a natural orange food coloring, or orange flavored fruit tea for two of the cups of water. Baobab powder is optional.

Berry-version

Add 1 ½ cups frozen mixed berries to the pot when you first start the jello. Leave out the baobab powder, extract, and reduce the water by one cup (instead of ending with 3 cups of cold water, just do 2).

NUTTY CHAI CUPS

(S)

Makes Multiple Servings

These actually came from a huge recipe flop. My mother-in-law had chai covered almonds out around Christmas. I had a few, loved them, and decided I had to make a healthy version. This was that attempt ... utterly a failure as chai covered almonds, but actually wonderful as a nutty chai cup thingy. Happy accident. How should I describe these aside from very yummy? The texture is almost chocolaty, but the flavor is chai and they're a great protein-rich snack.

½ cup Integral Collagen	2 tsp. cinnamon
½ cup Unflavored Pristine Whey Protein Powder	½ tsp. black pepper
	⅛ tsp. ground cloves
½ cup Gentle Sweet	¼ tsp. Mineral Salt
1½ cup mixed nuts (or any nut except for peanuts)	4–5 doonks Pure Stevia Extract Powder
	1 cup coconut oil

1. Put all ingredients into a medium bowl, ending with the coconut oil. Whisk well and then put small amounts in mini muffin liners in a mini muffin tin or on a large plate.
2. Chill in the refrigerator or freezer. I love them frozen!

CHOCOLATE COVERED STRAWBERRIES

S

Makes Multiple Servings

I brought these to Aunty Pearl's house for my best friend Meadow's going away party before she moved to Japan for a year. Everyone who got some devoured them. . . . meaning they got snatched up before most people had a chance . . . we have a massive family! Aunty Pearl asked me if I was going to put this recipe in the cookbook, but I said . . . "No, you guys already have a Chocolate Covered Strawberries recipe." That was not a good enough answer for her; she insisted that I put this recipe in the book saying you guys will all love it and that it's better than any other chocolate strawberry they'd created. Well, that's kind coming from you, Aunty Pearl!! You're my favorite Aunty . . . but don't tell Aunty Serene—wink. I guess these are pretty stinking good, if I say so myself . . . while I was photographing these, I ate like 5 of them!

Serene Chimes In Rashida … did you think I wouldn't see what you wrote here? This book is about to go to print, but not without me saying … don't worry … I know I'm your true favorite. You might feel like you have to flatter Pearl because she has done most of this editing and you want to stay on her good side … but in my heart, I know the truth. And, yeah … it was probably me who grabbed most of your chocolate covered strawberries at that party … when something's good … I find little places to hide my stash! One learns tricks growing up as the youngest in a big family. I can teach them to you one day…. since I'm your real favorite and all.

---

2 oz. unsweetened baking chocolate

4 oz. cocoa butter

⅛ tsp. Mineral Salt

½ tsp. Maple Natural Burst Extract

1 tsp. Vanilla Natural Burst Extract

3 Tbs. unsweetened extra dark cocoa powder

⅓ cup Gentle Sweet

2 lb. fresh strawberries (washed and completely dried)

---

1. Put cocoa butter and baking chocolate in a small saucepan set to low heat. While that's melting, add the remaining ingredients and stir frequently until everything is melted and then turn off.

2. Dip washed and completely dried strawberries in chocolate mixture and set on a parchment paper lined tray or plates. Chill in the refrigerator.

BERRY BOOST ROLL UPS

Makes Multiple Servings

Ahhh . . . fruit leather. Remember that stuff? Sadly, it is either high in fruit juice concentrate or sugar, which means not at all kind to your blood sugar or that of your children. These Boosted Roll Ups are super kind to blood sugar and are another awesome way to get vitamin C-rich baobab and protein-rich collagen and gelatin into your family's life to boost their health and immunity! They are perfect for snacks (since they even have protein) or after-dinner treats . . . great for parties, too! This recipe uses cranberries, so I'll repeat here what I said on page 243 for my Dried Cranberries recipe . . . make sure during cranberry season that you load up, so you can use them all year. I put lots of bagged cranberries in the freezer and then when I need them for recipes, I just place them on the counter at room temperature and they thaw out pretty quickly.

2 (12 oz.) bags cranberries (fresh or thawed from frozen)
1 cup Gentle Sweet
3–5 doonks Pure Stevia Extract Powder (or more to taste)
1 cup water

½ tsp. Cherry Natural Burst Extract or 2 tsp. pure strawberry extract (or both)
½ cup Baobab Boost Powder
½ cup Integral Collagen
¼ cup Just Gelatin
1 tsp. Gluccie

1. Preheat oven to 300°F and line 2 large baking sheets with parchment paper.

2. Put cranberries, Gentle Sweet, and water into a medium-sized saucepan set to medium-high heat. Cover and cook for 10 minutes taking lid off periodically to whisk and squish cranberries against the side of the saucepan so they are well broken down. Add the remaining ingredients to the saucepan one by one, stirring each time so no clumps form. Cook on medium-low for another 10 minutes.

3. Pour the berry mixture onto the trays, spreading it out thinly.

4. Bake for 30 minutes. Place in refrigerator and allow to get completely chilled and set thoroughly. Take out and cut into strips and roll up. Store covered in the fridge.

APPLE CRUMBLE

 (WITH E OPTION)

Makes Multiple Servings

This crumble is one of my go-to desserts to take to a potluck or a family gathering because it's so fast and easy-peasy! I almost always make this as a XO, but feel free to try out the E-version if too many Crossovers are not friendly to this particular stage of your THM journey.

FOR THE APPLE FILLING:

4 apples (cored and thinly sliced)

3½ cups water (divided)

1 tsp. Gluccie

½ tsp. pure almond extract

2 Tbs. Super Sweet Blend

1½ tsp. cinnamon

1 Tbs. apple cider vinegar

FOR THE CRUMBLE TOPPING:

⅓ cup (6 Tbs.) butter (for DF, swap in coconut oil and add 2-3 pinches Mineral Salt)*

½ tsp. pure almond extract (or either one of the Maple or Caramel Natural Burst Extracts)

2 tsp. blackstrap molasses

¼ cup water

1 cup quick oats or old fashioned rolled oats (I like to use the quick oats.)

¾ cup Baking Blend

½–¾ cup Gentle Sweet

1. Preheat oven to 375°F.

2. Put the apple slices and 2 cups of the water in a medium saucepan set to high heat. Cover and cook for 7–10 minutes. Reduce the heat to medium-high, take the lid off, and whisk in the Gluccie. (Don't just dump it in, you don't want any clumps to form!)

3. Add remaining water, almond extract (or maple or caramel, if using instead), Super Sweet Blend, cinnamon, and apple cider vinegar to the pot. Stir well and then pour the mixture into baking dish of your choice.

4. Melt the butter or coconut oil in another saucepan or skillet and then stir in the remaining ingredients from the Crumble Topping list and stir well. Sprinkle topping all over the Apple Filling and then bake for 25–30 minutes, or until the top looks just right.

Note: For E, use only 1 tablespoon butter or coconut oil.

BLUEBERRY CRUMBLE (WITH OPTION)

Makes Multiple Servings

This recipe is cousin to the "Apple Crumble" recipe on page 328 . . . As with that one, I prefer the XO-version, but feel free to try the E if too many "Crossies" are not a good fit with this particular stage of your THM journey.

FOR THE BLUEBERRY FILLING:
3 cups blueberries (frozen or fresh)
3½ cups water (divided)
2 Tbs. Super Sweet Blend
½ tsp. citric acid
2 tsp. Gluccie

FOR THE CRUMBLE TOPPING:
¾ cup Baking Blend
1 cup old fashioned rolled oats or quick oats
⅓ cup (6 Tbs.) butter (for DF, swap in coconut
    oil and add 2–3 pinches Mineral Salt)*
1 tsp. Vanilla Natural Burst Extract
½ cup Gentle Sweet

1. Preheat oven to 375°F.
2. Put blueberries, 2 cups of the water, Super Sweet Blend, and citric acid in a medium saucepan set to high heat. Cover and cook for 7 minutes.
3. Slowly whisk in the Gluccie and then the remaining 1 ½ cups of water.
4. Melt butter or coconut oil over low heat in another medium saucepan. Add vanilla, Gentle Sweet, and oats to melted butter or coconut oil and stir well.
5. Pour hot Blueberry Filling into an ungreased baking pan of your choice. Sprinkle the Crumble Topping on top and then bake for 25 minutes, or until top looks just right. Best served hot with stevia-sweetened ice cream or whipped cream on top.

*Note: For E, use only 1 tablespoon butter or coconut oil.

SWEET POTATO SOUFFLÉ

 **XO** , **S** , OR **S** HELPER

Makes Multiple Servings (About 8)

When my husband had his first bite of this, he said he was practically in heaven. He's not the biggest dessert fan, so that's big coming from him. The Crossover-version is my favorite . . . perfect to have on Thanksgiving or for a scrumptious dessert. If you don't want to have an XO, the other options using pumpkin for S or butternut squash for an S Helper are delish as well!

FOR THE SWEET POTATO MASH:
5 medium sweet potatoes (peeled if you want and cut smaller)
½ stick (4 Tbs.) butter
½ cup Gentle Sweet
½ cup unsweetened almond or cashew milk
2 eggs
1 tsp. Mineral Salt
1 tsp. Vanilla or Maple Natural Burst Extract
Optional ½ tsp. Butter Natural Burst Extract

FOR THE SOUFFLÉ TOPPING:
½ stick (4 Tbs.) melted butter or use unflavored coconut oil for DF with a couple extra pinches salt
1 cup pecans (chopped)
½ cup Gentle Sweet
½ cup Baking Blend
2 pinches Mineral Salt
2 tsp. cinnamon
1 egg white

1. Preheat oven to 375°F and spray a 9x13 baking dish with coconut or olive oil.
2. Boil the sweet potatoes until soft and then drain water from the pot. Mash in the remaining ingredients from the Sweet Potato Mash list, then smooth it into your prepared baking dish.
3. Add everything from the Soufflé Topping list into a bowl and mix well. Sprinkle topping onto the mash and then bake for 30–35 minutes.

For the S-version Pumpkin Soufflé:

In place of the cooked, mashed sweet potatoes use . . .

4 cups canned pumpkin
2 tsp. pumpkin pie spice
Only use ½ tsp. of the Mineral Salt
Everything else is the same

For the S Helper-version Butternut Squash Soufflé:

Preheat the oven to 375°F and line a baking sheet with foil or parchment paper. Chop fresh butternut squash up into small pieces, you'll need about 4 cups. Remove the skins and then place them on the baking sheet, cover loosely with foil and bake for 35–40 minutes or until soft. Only do ¼ cup of almond milk instead of ½ cup. Everything else is the same.

BANANAS FOSTER

 OR

Makes About 4–6 Servings

I made this the XO way first and it came out perfect. Then I thought to myself, "I could make an E-option! I could! I could!" It turned out great as well, if I say so myself. When my husband got home, I warmed both types for him to try. I gave him the E-version first and his response was, "Amazing!" Then, when I gave him the XO-version, he said it tasted like "manna from Heaven". Later on, I realized I forgot to put the cinnamon in the E-version, so while I do agree the XO-version is

just slightly better ... that could have had something to do with it. The E-version makes a great breakfast and we love both versions as a snack or dessert topped with on-plan ice cream, but I have the E more frequently. If you're having this as a XO ... add a few chopped walnuts sprinkled on top for the perfect crunch.

3 Tbs. butter*	½ tsp. ground cinnamon
½–¾ cup Gentle Sweet	1½ tsp. Vanilla Natural Burst Extract
½ cup unsweetened almond or cashew milk	1½ tsp. blackstrap molasses
¼ tsp. Mineral Salt	2 big bananas (or 3 small ones)

1. Place everything but the bananas into a skillet. Cook on high heat for 5 minutes. Reduce heat to medium-high and then add sliced bananas and cook for another 3–4 minutes while flipping the bananas in the sauce.

Butter Note for the E-version: Instead of the butter, do 1 tsp. Butter Natural Burst Extract, plus another ¼ tsp. salt. Don't do the ¾ cup of Gentle Sweet, just use ½ a cup. Everything else is the same.

16
SAVORY CRUNCH

Seed Crisps **S**

Nacho Deli Thins **FP**

Sundried Tomato Bread Crisps **S**

R's Late-Night Snack **FP**

Cucumber Sammies **FP** or **S**

Crunch, munch, and prepare your taste buds for a punch! What you have in this chapter are five easy recipes that are nutritious, a load of fun to whip up, and make for great snacks or even as accompaniments to meals. My dips from the *Dips, Dressings, & Spreads* chapter (page 345) go well with anything from this chapter or pair with any non-starchy veggies. BTW . . . if you were wondering . . . I didn't give you an actual "Snacks Chapter" in this book because anything can be a snack . . . leftovers, fruit, nuts, shakes, or any of my baked goods and sweet treats, etc. I didn't want to take your valuable time by giving advice like how to unwrap a cheese stick and insert it into your mouth or how to bite into an apple—Hehe!

SEED CRISPS

Makes Multiple Servings

Due to their crunch factor, my Mom and Nana both absolutely love these Seed Crisps. You can use whatever spices or seasonings you want, I keep them pretty simple, so I can have them with savory or sweet accompaniments.

---

1 cup sunflower seeds
1 cup golden flax seeds (I buy mine toasted but you can use untoasted ones too)
½ cup pumpkin seeds
½ cup Baking Blend

¼ cup sesame seeds
1¼ tsp. Mineral Salt
¼ cup coconut oil
3 cups water

---

1. Preheat oven to 350°F and line a couple large baking sheets with parchment paper.
2. Add everything to a big bowl ending with coconut oil and water. Stir everything together really well and let sit for 35 minutes.
3. Pour the mixture onto trays and spread out as evenly as you can until it is a cracker-sized thickness (about an ⅛ to 1/16th of an inch).
4. Bake for 25 minutes, then take them out and cut into cracker-sized squares while leaving them on the trays (a pizza cutter works wonders for this!). Put them back in the oven for another 10–12 minutes, or until a light golden brown.

NACHO DELI THINS

Makes a Single Serve

These crunch, they're lean protein, and they're full of flavor … triple win! You can have them alone or with any of my dips or even make a fun board with cheese, veggies, dips, and both flavors of these. Don't forget to try out the Italian-version too!

4 oz. natural, lean deli meat of choice	**¼ tsp. paprika**
⅛ tsp. black pepper	**½ tsp. chili powder**
⅛ tsp. garlic powder	**1 Tbs. Nutritional Yeast or Parmesan cheese**

1. Preheat the oven to 425°F and line a cookie sheet with parchment paper. Place deli meat slices on the parchment paper. (Try not to overlap the slices.)
2. Put the seasonings and nutritional yeast into a small bowl and then stir.
3. Lightly spray the deli meat with cooking spray, then sprinkle half the seasoning mixture onto the deli meat. Flip meat slices, then repeat the process by spraying, then sprinkling again. Bake for 12 minutes, then let cool so they crisp.

Italian Deli Thins: Do the same steps as above, but for the seasonings … Use ½ tsp. Italian seasoning, ¼ tsp. garlic powder, same amount black pepper, and nutritional yeast or Parmesan cheese, but leave off the chili and paprika.

SUNDRIED TOMATO BREAD CRISPS

Makes Multiple Servings

These are kind of like crispy, bready crackers. Super yummy! Serve with Home Run Hummus from page 347, or some of my other dips from the *Dips, Dressings, & Spreads* chapter. You could even enjoy with some nice cheese slices, cold cut meats, or whatever you so desire.

---

1 cup Baking Blend
½ cup Oat Fiber
½ cup Whole Husk Psyllium Flakes
8 oz. Gouda cheese (or whatever cheese you have in your fridge; cut into big chunks)
½ tsp. black pepper
¾ tsp. Mineral Salt
½ tsp. creole seasoning

1 tsp. garlic powder
1 tsp. Italian seasoning
1 tsp. paprika
⅓ cup sundried tomatoes
1 stick (½ cup) softened (room temp) butter
¼ cup Nutritional Yeast
8 egg whites (or 1 cup liquid egg whites)

---

1. Preheat oven to 350°F and line a large cookie sheet with parchment paper sprayed with coconut or olive oil.

2. Go down the list throwing everything into a food processor, then process until mixture becomes a nice doughy consistency.

3. Place the dough onto the parchment paper lined sheet and then take another piece of the parchment paper and spray it. Set the sprayed side onto the dough and use a rolling pin, or the sides of a round jar, to spread the dough out.

4. Once the dough is spread out evenly (about ⅛ of an inch), remove the top piece of parchment paper, dip a knife in water, and score to desired sized pieces. Bake for 20–25 minutes.

R'S LATE-NIGHT SNACK

Makes a Single Serve

It's real … sometimes we all get the crazy munchies late at night. Can I see a show of hands? Late nights are not the time to be eating oodles of heavy calories because we'll be just going to bed and unable to burn them off. This is one of my favorite Ultra-FP late evening snacks to have plain, or with hot cocoa or tea with collagen. It's also perfect if you have just had a big meal, but you want to wind down on the couch while watching something and still want to have that hand to mouth thing going on.

Pearl Chimes In I told Rashida this ridiculously simple snack of hers has changed my life! I guess I had to see the idea written out and given a name to start making it so often. I enjoy it not only as a stand-alone snack at night sometimes, but also as an easy, crunchy, and flavorful side to so many of my meals and snacks now.

---

1 seedless cucumber or 2 or 3 mini seedless cukes (you can use a normal, seeded one, if the seeds don't bother you)
1 Tbs. Nutritional Yeast

2 pinches black pepper
2 pinches Mineral Salt
Optional 2 pinches cayenne pepper

---

1. Slice the cucumber, then go down the list and sprinkle everything on them.

Note: You can use Parmesan cheese, if you don't have or like nutritional yeast.

CUCUMBER SAMMIES

 OR

Makes a Single Serve

Perfect snack or you can even make a meal-sized version out of this idea.

½–1 large seedless cucumber
1–2 Light Laughing Cow Cheese wedges
   (use Cheesy Wow-Spread page 370 or a
   spreadable nut cheese such as the Treeline
   brand for DF)

2–3 oz. natural, lean deli meat
2 sprinkles black pepper
Optional 2 sprinkles cayenne pepper
Optional thinly sliced cheddar cheese or
   avocado for an S-option

---

1. Cut cucumber into slices. Spread a thin layer of your chosen cheese spread on one side of each slice. Sprinkle seasonings on half the slices and top those ones with pieces of deli meat. Top with the remaining cucumbers creating cute, little crunchy sandwiches.

17

DIPS, DRESSINGS AND SPREADS

Home Run Hummus (XO) (with (S) Option)

Spinach Artichoke Dip (S)

Crazy Amazing Beet Dip (S)

Light n' Lively Hummus (E)

R's Fresh Salsa (FP) or (E)

Queso Dip (S)

For the Love of Pesto (S)

Hit the Spot Guac (S)

Daddio's Jalapeño Salmon Dip (S)

Real Thing Honey Mustard (E)

R's Tartar Sauce (FP)

Orange Sesame Dressing (FP)

Tangy Wangy Dressing (S)

Raspberry Vinaigrette (FP)

Spunky Ginger Dressing (S)

Sun Basking Basil Dressing (S)

Apricot Wow-Spread (FP)

Berry Wow-Spread (FP)

Cheesy Wow-Spread (FP)

Cream Cheese Icing (S)

Cranberry Pomegranate Sauce (E) or (FP)

Bread Pudding Sauce (FP)

Creamy Buffalo Sauce (FP)

Go To Gravy (FP)

Instant Cheese Sauce (E), (FP), (S), or (XO)

Tazincy Dipping and Smothering Sauce (S)

DIPS

Not kidding . . . I could probably just sit down and eat the dips in this chapter all by the spoon-ful. But mostly I restrain myself from such uncouth behavior and enjoy them with non-starchy veggies, the crackers from the previous chapter, or homemade pita chips made from a Joseph's Low-Carb Pita (just cut ½–1 up and microwave for a minute on a paper plate or crisp in the oven). Oh . . . and if you have any of THM's Shameless Crackers . . . perfect, too! Of course, if you want to enjoy them XO-style, have them with some blue corn chips, Wasa Crackers, or as a nice spread on a sprouted bread sandwich or my Handy Naan Bread from page 262.

DRESSINGS

All these are flavorful, slimming, and super easy to throw together. I never need to make an excuse for why I shouldn't have a salad when I have one of these dressings in my fridge. They're make-you-wanna-eat-your-greens super weapons!! But no excuse . . . even if I don't have one of these speedy dressings whipped up, I just do my other favorite dressing that consists of equal parts hot sauce and olive oil from my R's #1 Salad on page 209. This Mama ain't skipping on her salad!

SPREADS

I've created some jams/jellies that are going to rock your world. They're all FP . . . even the apricot one! While THM makes allowances for store-bought all-fruit spreads, they can only be enjoyed in tiny 1 teaspoon amounts for S and FP meals . . . and since they are made from concentrated fruit juices, they really shouldn't be overdone in E meals either. Well, now . . . with my Wow-Spreads . . . you CAN overdo! Spread my spreads good and high and thick and your blood sugar will stay happy and stable. Oh, yeah! And please don't miss Aunty Pearl's new recipe in this chapter . . . she has taken the basic idea for my sweet spreads and has created a yummy, savory version!

HOME RUN HUMMUS

 **(WITH S OPTION)**

Makes Multiple Servings (you can halve the amounts the first time making this, if you don't have a lot of people to serve it to)

I grew up making hummus all the time for my family and for all the visitors we constantly had over. This was my go-to recipe I made as a child, then as a teenager. Since being married, I've been out of the habit of making this for some reason. I recently made it again for the first time for my own family, and they all enjoyed so much. After photographing it, I left it out to have with dinner and it was quickly devoured.

You can have it with veggies, like I have shown in the image or with any of the other options I mention that go well with dips beginning on page 349.

---

2 (15.5 oz.) cans garbanzo beans (drained)	1 Tbs. plus 1 tsp. Tahini (sesame butter)
½ cup olive oil	1 tsp. smoked paprika
½ cup lemon juice	2 tsp. ground cumin
½ cup water	1 tsp. black pepper
4–5 garlic cloves	1 tsp. Mineral Salt

---

1. Dump all ingredients into a blender and blend until smooth.

Note: For S, if you don't mind having a wee bit of soy in your life now and then, sub the chickpeas for black soybeans as they have barely any carbs.

SPINACH ARTICHOKE DIP

Makes Multiple Servings

Who doesn't like spinach artichoke dip??? Put me in that category . . . but, no more! You see the reason I detested it was because of my aversion to mayonnaise. Spinach artichoke dip is usually loaded with the stuff. Well, this one is mayo-free, which makes me so happy. I don't have to be eating it with fear that I could be ingesting mayonnaise! (I know I must surely have a band of you who don't like mayo either!) But even if you love the normal mayo loaded one, this one will hopefully rock your world, too. It's great for parties, having as an appetizer with any of the options I mention that go well with dips on page 349.

---

12 oz. chopped spinach (fresh or frozen)
3 oz. ⅓ less fat cream cheese
1 cup sour cream
1 cup 0% Greek yogurt
1 (7.5 oz.) jar artichoke hearts (drained and chopped to desired size)
1 cup part-skim mozzarella cheese (grated)
½ tsp. black pepper

1½ tsp. creole seasoning
¼ tsp. red pepper flakes
½ tsp. dried parsley flakes
Optional ⅛ tsp. citric acid
1 tsp. Gluccie or xanthan gum
½ cup unsweetened almond milk
⅓ cup Parmesan cheese (green can works)

1. Add the chopped spinach to a medium saucepan set to medium-high heat. If using fresh spinach, add a tablespoon or so of water to avoid sticking. Cook until spinach has wilted. Remove from heat and if there is any spinach water, discard it.

2. Return pan to the stove and reduce heat to medium. Then, add everything else to the saucepan by whisking each ingredient in one by one. Cook for another 5 minutes or so while stirring constantly.

CRAZY AMAZING BEET DIP

Makes Multiple Servings

I am not usually a beet lover so I thought a beet dip would be a great way to get in all the incredible health benefits. Now that I've made it ... hmmm ... going to be honest ... I'm snacking on some now as I'm typing this out and getting ready to photograph it. Verdicts in ... Oh, yeah! Pretty sure I'll be making a lot more of this. Changing my tune ... I am that beet-loving girl ... this is crazy amazing! Along with the options I list on page 346 to pair with my dip recipes, this will also be great on the side of a salad or salmon.

---

1 lb. fresh beets (chopped)
2–3 tsp. melted butter or unflavored coconut oil
½ tsp. dried rosemary
1 tsp. salt
½ tsp. black pepper
⅔ cup roasted sunflower seeds

¼–⅓ cup olive oil
½ cup plus 2 Tbs. lemon juice
¼ cup apple cider vinegar
3–4 garlic cloves
1 tsp. ground cumin
2 Tbs. Tahini (sesame seed butter)

---

1. Preheat oven to 400°F.
2. Put the beets on a cookie sheet. Add butter or coconut oil and sprinkle with the rosemary, salt, pepper, and butter. Mix together and bake for 45 minutes.
3. Put cooked beets in a food processor and pulse a few times. Then, add the remaining ingredients and process until smooth.

LIGHT N' LIVELY HUMMUS

Makes Multiple Servings

Serene Chimes In Why do we need two hummus recipes in this book? Rashida just gave you one and now I'm pushing mine on you … what's up with this? Well, hummus makes the world a better place. Its tangy zip and hearty creaminess makes life a million times better, I think. Rashida can do lots of Crossovers in her season of pregnancy and nursing periods and also because she naturally has a pretty great metabolism. I do Crossovers, too, but I also love to have an E-option for hummus and I think you will, too. Nobody wants to have to leave a yummy dollop or two of hummus off their plate just because they do better sticking to true S and E in their THM journeys. This is why Light n' Lively Hummus was born. Even in generous portions it is not a Crossover, unless you eat the entire thing by yourself in one sitting. (And even though that is a bit extreme and not really recommended, it is a lot better than other food binges … If the worst you are doing is bingeing on a huge bowl of hummus and crisp veggies … you've come a long way, baby!)

1 (15 ounce) can chickpeas (garbanzo beans) (drained)	1 tsp. plus 2–3 pinches Mineral Salt
5 Tbs. Baobab Boost Powder	¼ tsp. black pepper
2 large cloves garlic (crushed)	1 cup steamed summer squash or zucchini
1 Tbs. Tahini	Optional, but recommended, ¼ tsp. Gluccie
3 Tbs. fresh lemon juice	(makes a thicker, less "light" tasting hummus)

1. Steam up a bunch of summer squash or zucchini, baby-sized ones are best (steam up any amount because you can enjoy leftovers to have with other meals like on the side of fried eggs or with Pearl's Go To Gravy from page 376 or Instant Cheese Sauce from page 380). For this hummus, you only need a cup of the squash/zucchini, so once it is cooked and cooled down a little, take some, squeeze all the excess water out of it with your hands, and pack it down to measure 1 cup.

2. Put squash in a lovely serving bowl with all of the other ingredients and then using a hand blender, blend until completely smooth.

Note: If you choose to use the optional Gluccie (my favorite way), stir the Gluccie into the lemon juice first … before adding to the mix to make sure there are no clumps and that it is dispersed properly in the blend.

R'S FRESH SALSA

 OR

Makes Multiple Servings (you can halve the recipe if desiring a smaller amount)

A good fresh salsa and I are best friends; literally I could drink this stuff! One of my sisters takes after me in that way. I made some to have with our lunch recently and caught her putting some in a bowl and literally drinking it down. That made my heart so happy to see!

½ large onion or 1 regular size (cut into chunks)

9 Roma tomatoes (or any tomatoes your garden grows)

1 bunch cilantro

¼ cup lemon juice (bottled or fresh, but fresh tastes best!)

½ tsp. citric acid

Optional 2–3 tsp. Gentle Sweet (or a doonk of Pure Stevia Extract Powder, or 1 tsp. Super Sweet Blend)

¼ tsp. black pepper

½–1 tsp. Mineral Salt

1 ½–2 tsp. garlic powder

1. Throw onion chunks in a food processor and pulse for 5 seconds. Repeat until you have your desired onion size for your salsa. Remove the onions from the processor and put them in a medium-sized bowl.
2. Repeat this same pulse process with the tomatoes and cilantro and then add them to the bowl as well.
3. Add the lemon juice and the remaining spices to the bowl. Stir everything together; taste and adjust seasonings if need be.

For Pineapple-version (Still FP) Add:

2 tsp. Pineapple Natural Burst Extract
3 Tbs. Gentle Sweet

For Mango-version (E) Add:

1 ½ mangoes (diced small)
2 Tbs. Gentle Sweet

QUESO DIP

(S)

Makes Multiple Servings

Queso dip is life, am I right??? Aside from the ideas I give on page 346 to have with this dip, you can also have this as part of a main meal, spoon it over cauliflower rice and chicken, or it even tastes great over salad! Want to Crossover? Great over brown rice or with blue corn chips.

1 cup salsa (any store-bought kind or my R's Fresh Salsa from page 353)
1 cup light sour cream
1½ cups cheddar or Mexican blend cheese (grated)
¼ cup unsweetened almond or cashew milk (or use water)
¼ tsp. Mineral Salt
¼ tsp. black pepper
Optional, but yummy, ¼ tsp. crushed red pepper

1. Put everything into a small saucepan set to medium-high heat. Bring to a boil and then simmer for 7–10 minutes, stirring every few minutes.

FOR THE LOVE OF PESTO

Makes Multiple Servings

The whole reason I grow basil in my garden now is due to my love affair with pesto. I know you can buy pesto in a jar, but there is nothing like the fresh! I grew up making ginormous batches of it in the spring and summer months for our big family and I would even freeze it to have in the winter, as I couldn't be without it. This is that same, simple recipe I developed as a child and it has never steered me wrong my whole life through. I love having veggies or crackers to dip in it, but also adding it to zucchini noodles . . . so scrumpts!! Also, you can use this on the Pesto Pizza from page 200, on a sprouted sandwich for a good ol' XO, or just plop some on your salad.

Note: If you don't have a garden, you can go to Walmart and buy a little, organic basil plant in the grocery section for only $1.99. You'll need to give it some love so it can grow more significant, but hey it will look so cute growing in your house or apartment next to a window. If you really don't want to grow your own, farmers' markets have basil for way cheaper than grocery stores.

2½ cups basil leaves (tightly packed)	1 tsp. black pepper
1 cup walnuts*	1 tsp. Mineral Salt
3–5 fresh garlic cloves	½ cup lemon juice (bottled or fresh)
½ cup Parmesan cheese	½ cup olive oil

1. Go down the list, throwing everything into a food processor, process until smooth. BOOM!

*Note: You can use any nut, just please NOT peanuts! You can even use sunflower seeds for a less expensive option. I have done that multiple times and it works great.

HIT THE SPOT GUAC

Makes Multiple Servings

My Aunties are making me say something about this recipe. Hmmm . . . well, it is so creamy and good . . . the cilantro knocks it out of the park. I mean, doesn't the title say it all? Just try it! I have nothing else . . . hope they're satisfied with that.

3 avocados	1 tsp. garlic powder
Juice from 1 medium lime	½ cup fresh cilantro (chopped)
½ cup Greek yogurt (any fat %)	1 cup chopped tomatoes (about 1 large
½ tsp. Mineral Salt	tomato)

1. Put avocado flesh in a bowl, mash with a fork, and then mix with the Greek yogurt. Add the remaining ingredients, stir together, and tweak if needed.

DADDIO'S JALAPEÑO SALMON DIP

S

Makes Multiple Servings

My dad was the inventor of this basic recipe, although the one he made was a lot heavier, full of full-fat cream cheese and full-fat cottage cheese. He'd go through stages of making this every week, and we'd all have it with veggies from our garden and good homemade bread. I have lightened it up a bit, as I don't have a big need for heavy fats … but it is still so super tasty.

1 (14 oz.) can wild Alaskan salmon (drained)	2½ cups low-fat cottage cheese*
3–4 jalapeño peppers (deseeded and diced; you can leave a few seeds, if you are heat lover)	1 cup sharp cheddar cheese (grated)
	⅓ tsp. black pepper
	Optional ¼ tsp. liquid smoke

1. Add salmon to a medium bowl and mash well. Add all the other ingredients, mix well, and you're done.

*Note: If you don't love the texture of cottage cheese, you can process or blend it smooth first. It's a super creamy dip this way.

REAL THING HONEY MUSTARD

Makes Multiple Servings

Some people are under the impression that honey is not part of the THM plan. It sure is! Raw honey has so many health benefits, but it is just important that we not overdo it since it can raise blood sugar. Raw honey can help with allergies and boost your immune system. My aunties have always said a teaspoon of raw honey a day is awesome … and you can have more once you're at goal weight, of course, and it is excellent for children over a year of age. You can use this as a dressing or as a dip or on a sprouted sandwich … super yummy! My husband loves it with my Southern "Fried" Chicken from page 128, which would be a XO, or my Golden Fries from page 233—with those you'd still be in E-mode.

½ cup yellow mustard	½ cup 0% Greek yogurt
¼ cup raw honey	Optional doonk Pure Stevia Extract Powder
½ tsp. creole seasoning	

1. Mix well in a small bowl. Refrigerate leftovers.

R'S TARTAR SAUCE

Makes Multiple Servings

My utter hatred for mayo includes me avoiding anything else in the mayonnaise family like tartar sauce. Here's my FP Tartar Sauce that I can dip into with the peace of mind knowing it has no mayo-like ingredients. Even though we don't obsessively count calories on THM, you still don't want to overdo them. Since mayonnaise is super calorie-heavy, it is easy to overdo. So, try this much lighter tartar sauce version sometime, even if you're partial to mayo. You can have it with my Southern "Fried" Chicken from page 128 or the Fried Pickles from page 236. But, best of all is having it with the Fish Sticks from page 142. Some people even like it on the side of their steak!

1 cup 0% Greek yogurt	2 Tbs. pickle juice (yes, juice from a dill
¼ tsp. dried dill	pickle jar)
¼ tsp. Mineral Salt	Juice from ½ a lemon
⅛ tsp. black pepper	

1. Mix everything in a bowl, stir, and start dipping.

ORANGE SESAME DRESSING

Makes Multiple Servings

This dressing is so full of zesty flavor, you'll forget it is even FP! I like to always have it on hand and thanks to the citric acid being a natural preservative . . . it keeps well in the fridge. It's perfect for salads, marinating meats, and veggies. Or, go try the Hawaiian Salad (page 210) or the Orange Sesame String Beans (page 250) that use this dressing.

1 cup water
¼ tsp. citric acid
⅛ tsp. cayenne pepper
½ tsp. Mineral Salt
½ tsp. paprika
½ tsp. garlic powder
½ tsp. onion powder
½ tsp. black pepper
½ tsp. Gluccie or xanthan gum

1 tsp. blackstrap molasses
1 tsp. sesame oil
2 tsp. pure orange extract (or try 1½ tsp. Apricot Natural Burst Extract, if you don't have orange)
¼ cup Gentle Sweet
¼ cup Baobab Boost Powder
¼ cup Integral Collagen
¼ cup balsamic vinegar

1. Add everything to a blender and blend until smooth.

TANGY WANGY DRESSING

Makes Multiple Servings (you can halve amounts first time, if desired)

If you like the taste of fresh cilantro, you're going to love this dressing! I like to have it on sliced cabbage, bell peppers, and chicken or fish. You can't go wrong with what you put this on... unless, of course, you have a crazy idea of putting it on your PB&J sandwich.

1 bunch cilantro
3 fresh jalapeño peppers
½ cup MCT oil
½ cup olive oil
¼ cup apple cider vinegar
½ cup lime or lemon juice (fresh or bottled; but to me, fresh is always best)
3–4 garlic cloves
¼ cup Integral Collagen
1 tsp. Mineral Salt
1 tsp. black pepper
1 tsp. ground cumin
1 tsp. dried oregano

1. Remove seeds from jalapeños (I like to wear gloves for this . . . oh, and if you are a heat lover you can leave a few of the seeds in). Add everything to a blender and blend until smooth.

RASPBERRY VINAIGRETTE

Makes Multiple Servings

I already sent in a short intro with this recipe, but my aunties told me I have to sell this recipe more or barely anyone will make it. Okay, Ladies and Gents (if there are any Gents reading), you'll like this a lot if you're a fan of raspberries and sweet tangy toppings for your salad. And another FP dressing to boot . . . win-win! We all need more slimming, dairy-free FP dressings in our lives! There . . . how did I do?

1½ cups frozen raspberries
1 cup water
¼ cup balsamic vinegar
¼ cup Gentle Sweet
¼ tsp. black pepper

½ tsp. citric acid
1 Tbs. soy sauce
¼ tsp. blackstrap molasses
½ tsp. xanthan gum or Gluccie

1. Put raspberries and water in a small saucepan set to medium-high heat. Cover and cook for 7–10 minutes.
2. Remove from heat to let cool for a few minutes.
3. Put mixture into a blender and add all other ingredients. Blend until smooth.

SPUNKY GINGER DRESSING

S

Makes Multiple Servings

This is my all-time favorite homemade dressing (other than my go-to simple combination of hot sauce & olive oil dressing). It combines the metabolism-boosting abilities of MCT oil and ginger

with the anti-inflammatory properties of olive oil for a Deep S powerhouse! Do you remember all the metabolism-boosting benefits of ginger that I told you about in my Spicy Candied Ginger recipe? Didn't read that? Turn to page 306 and give the intro a read and you'll be even more inspired to make this dressing recipe. My mom used to make one very similar to this when I was growing up (but without the MCT oil), and I absolutely loved it. I enjoy this on any salad, meat, stir-fry, even for dipping bell peppers or cukes into. SOOOOO GOOD!

3 oz. fresh ginger
3 garlic cloves
½ cup extra virgin olive oil
½ cup MCT oil
½ cup apple cider vinegar
¼ cup Gentle Sweet
3 Tbs. Integral Collagen
½ tsp. Mineral Salt
½ tsp. black pepper
Optional ¼ tsp. cayenne pepper

1. Put everything into a blender and blend until smooth.

SUN BASKING BASIL DRESSING

Makes Multiple Servings

I told you in the introduction to my For the Love of Pesto recipe what a sucker I am for anything with fresh basil in it. So, you bet I had to make a nice, creamy basil dressing for this recipe book.

Here ya' go, if you're nuts about basil like I am. You can read my "how to get fresh basil" in the introduction on page 355. Speaking of basil, I better stop typing and go plant some of my basil seeds.

- ¾ cup tightly packed basil leaves
- 2–3 fresh garlic cloves (peeled)
- ¾ cup water
- ¾ cup fresh lemon juice (about 6 medium or 4½ large lemons)
- ¼ cup MCT oil
- ¼ cup extra virgin olive oil
- ½ tsp. black pepper
- ½ tsp. Mineral Salt
- 1 Tbs. Unflavored Pristine Whey Protein Powder (leave out if DF)
- 3 Tbs. Integral Collagen

1. Add all ingredients to a blender and blend until smooth.

APRICOT WOW-SPREAD

Makes Multiple Servings

This goes great on my Handy Naan Bread from page 262 or the Overnight Biscuits from page 94. It is also an awesome spread on pancakes or even as a topping for ice cream. Of course, you can have some on your sprouted bread, sourdough toast, or even on Light Rye Wasa crackers.

Pearl Chimes In My niece is a genius, I tell ya'! This stuff tastes and feels like you are spreading full-on real apricot preserves on your bread...but there's no fruit in this (other than incredible, health-boosting baobab). This means it is FP and can go with so many things... even on my Freezer Waffles or Wonderful White Blender Bread (from the Trim Healthy Table book) with butter! I love this stuff so much that I told Rashida..."We must start making this at our THM manufacturing center to have it available for all my fellow Drive-Thru Sues!" If you're like me (a tad lazy and would rather buy than make), you'll want to purchase oodles of it and spread it on everything. But for now...until we ever get around to manufacturing this stuff...just go make it!

2⅔ cups water	1 Tbs. Super Sweet Blend
½ cup Baobab Boost Powder	¾ cup Gentle Sweet
¼ tsp. Mineral Salt	1 tsp. Gluccie
1 tsp. citric acid	2 Tbs. liquid pectin
2 tsp. Apricot Natural Burst Extract	1 Tbs. + 2 tsp. Just Gelatin

1. Place everything but the Gluccie, pectin, gelatin, and ⅔ cup of water into a small saucepan set to medium-high heat. Bring to a boil and then reduce heat to low.

2. Whisk in remaining ingredients. Once Gluccie and gelatin have dissolved, cook for another 5 minutes. Then, place in small glass jars to cool off. Cover with lids and then transfer into the refrigerator to set. Due to the citric acid, this keeps well in the fridge.

BERRY WOW-SPREAD

Makes Multiple Servings

As I mentioned in the intro to this chapter…yes, you can buy all-fruit (no added sugar) jellies and use them on THM, but you sort of have to be stingy with amounts as they contain concentrated fruit juices, which can mess with blood sugar. For me, limiting amounts really takes the fun out of them. Well, with this spread, you can pile it on high and deep and your blood sugar will only love you for it. Try it on my Overnight Biscuits from page 94. Enjoy it on a turkey sandwich made with sprouted bread and Light Laughing Cow cheese, in yogurt, on a healthy on-plan ice cream, or on THM's Shameless Crackers-Classic Toppers or Light Rye Wasa crackers (with a smear of Light Laughing Cow Cheese or Cheesy Wow-Spread page 370). There's a million ways you can use this stuff! It sets really well and has a lovely texture, but if you want you can always warm it up for a nice syrup to have on your healthy pancakes or waffles.

---

12 oz. frozen blueberries, raspberries, or
    strawberries (or a berry mix)
1 cup water
2–3 doonks Pure Stevia Extract Powder
½ cup Gentle Sweet

3 Tbs. liquid pectin
1 Tbs. Just Gelatin
½ tsp. Gluccie
½ tsp. citric acid

---

1. Put all ingredients into a saucepan, bring to a boil then cook uncovered for 12 minutes on medium or just so that you have a nice soft bubbling action going on. Stir well and then put a lid on it. Turn heat to low and cook for 5 more minutes. Pour mixture into small glass jars, screw lids on, and then refrigerate until set. Keep refrigerated.

CHEESY WOW-SPREAD

Pearl Chimes In   I was so inspired by Rashida's spreads and have been using them so much that I thought it would be a great idea to try a dairy free, savory, cheesy version. It turned out great and since it is FP, I have been using it in place of Light Laughing Cow Cheese and other cheeses in so many of my meals and snacks lately. (I still enjoy dairy sometimes, but since I'm about to turn 50 and my hormones have changed . . . my weight these days appreciates me not eating too much dairy.) This goes great on a sprouted grain sandwich with turkey and/or tomato! It is a mild, smoky Gouda-type of flavor and it also works well on crackers and on veggies. As written, the flavor here is mild. If you want to kick the flavor up . . . go way higher on the garlic, onion, and paprika, and add a little cayenne. You could even do a Mexican-version with chili powder and cumin, but perhaps try this milder version first before going wild. I know Serene did a dairy-free cheese alternative in our Trim Healthy Table book, but it called for agar-agar to help it set, which most people don't have . . . so the recipe didn't get the love it probably deserved. Thankfully, this just uses pectin and gelatin, which you can find at most grocery stores, and this recipe is really easy to make. If you don't have Gluccie, just sub it out for xanthan gum.

1 cup unsweetened almond or cashew milk
⅓ cup water
¼ cup Oat Fiber (or use ground old fashioned rolled oats or cooked white beans, if you don't have this)
2 Tbs. Nutritional Yeast
½ tsp. plus another ⅛ tsp. Mineral Salt
½ tsp. Bragg Liquid Aminos (if you don't have, add just a pinch or two more salt)

⅛ tsp. smoked paprika
¼ tsp. onion powder
¼ tsp. garlic powder
½ tsp. lemon juice (bottled or fresh)
½ tsp. sesame oil
1 Tbs. liquid pectin
1½ tsp. Just Gelatin
½ tsp. Gluccie

1. Add all ingredients to blender in order (meaning end with Gluccie). Blend well.

2. Pour mixture into a small saucepan and heat until hot, but not boiling (whisking well a few times).

3. Pour into a pint jar, leave on the counter to cool a little for a few minutes, and then put a lid on and transfer to fridge. It should thicken up over several hours . . . Best after 4–6 hours.

Note: If you want this to last longer in your fridge, try adding ¼ teaspoon citric acid.

CREAM CHEESE ICING

Makes Multiple Servings

This icing goes with my R's Carrot Cake from page 280 and Pumpkin Muffins from page 272. You can use it on any of your own special baked goods, too, if you like.

8 oz. ⅓ less fat cream cheese (softened at room temperature)	½ cup Gentle Sweet
4 Tbs. butter (softened at room temperature)	½ tsp. Vanilla or Maple Natural Burst Extract

1. Add all the ingredients to a food processor and process until creamy.

CRANBERRY POMEGRANATE SAUCE OR

This goes on the side of Thanksgiving dinner with your turkey, but I can eat this stuff like a dessert! I have it with Greek yogurt, on-plan ice cream, or even on pancakes! It is, of course, excellent on a turkey sandwich made with sprouted bread, too.

---

1 (12 oz.) bag cranberries (fresh or frozen)
3 cups water (divided)
1½ tsp. Gluccie
2 tsp. Just Gelatin
¼ cup Gentle Sweet

2 Tbs. Super Sweet Blend
2 pinches Mineral Salt
½–1 tsp. pure orange extract
Optional seeds from 1 large pomegranate
    (leave out for FP)

---

1. Add cranberries and 1 ½ cups of the water to a medium saucepan set to high heat. Cover and allow to come to a rapid boil. Whisk in Gluccie and boil for 2 more minutes.

2. Reduce heat to medium-low and add remaining ingredients, ending with the pomegranate seeds (if using). Turn off the heat and let cool.

BREAD PUDDING SAUCE

Makes Multiple Servings

This was created for the Breakfast Bread Pudding (page 113) from the Brilliant Breakfasts Chapter, but you can use it for pancakes or on any E or FP muffin or cake that you want to make taste even more delicious without the use of fat.

1⅓ cup unsweetened almond or
  cashew milk
⅓ cup Gentle Sweet
2 Light Laughing Cow Cheese wedges
½ tsp. Vanilla Natural Burst Extract
½ tsp. Caramel Natural Burst Extract
½ tsp. blackstrap molasses
2 large pinches Mineral Salt
¼ tsp. Gluccie or xanthan gum

---

1. Add everything but the Gluccie to a small saucepan and set to high heat, whisk well. Once it starts to bubble, reduce heat to low. Whisk in Gluccie and let simmer for 3 more minutes.

CREAMY BUFFALO SAUCE

Multiple Servings

A creamy Buffalo sauce that is FP . . . life just got better! Jack has always loved creamy Buffalo sauce, so I decided to make a healthy version and thankfully he's super happy about this one. Our girls love it, too. The cottage cheese creaminess balances out some of the heat, so it's not crazy spicy (you can add cayenne pepper if you want more heat). Go make the "Best Buffalo Wings" on page 167 using this. Or, just have it over your grilled chicken or fish and veggies or whatever else you would like to have a creamy Buffalo sauce on without adding a lot of fat.

2 cups low-fat cottage cheese
1¼ cups hot sauce (I use Louisiana Hot Sauce.)
½ cup water
1 tsp. onion powder
½ tsp. garlic powder
¼ tsp. black pepper
1 Tbs. smoked paprika
½ tsp. Gluccie or xanthan gum

1. Put everything into a blender and blend well. Once smooth, transfer to a medium saucepan set to medium-high heat. Bring to a boil while stirring here and there.

2. Once it has reached a boil, reduce heat to low and let simmer for 7–10 minutes.

GO TO GRAVY

FP

Makes Multiple Servings

Pearl Chimes In Serene and I grew up Down Under so that automatically means we are both gravy lovers. You can't have a good dinner without gravy poured over everything if you were born and raised in New Zealand! Gravy is the ultimate of comfort foods for me so this means I have played around with lots of gravy recipes over the years of my THM journey, trying to turn it from fattening to trimming in the tastiest possible ways. This easy recipe is now my favorite and thankfully it is a FP so it can go with any meal. I almost always have some sitting in the fridge ready to quickly reheat for many meals. If you've tried some of my gravies before and didn't love Gluccie as the thickener . . . never fear, it is not used here. This is thickened with oat fiber and a small amount of oat flour and to me it is just right. I enjoy it over non-starchy veggies, especially done with a water sauté method (check out how to do that in the New Way Veggies recipe on page 254) meats, brown or cauli rice, and of course over my Mashed Potatoes from page 202.

¼ cup plus 1 Tbs. Oat Fiber
¼ cup ground oat flour (oats ground into a flour in the blender, measure after grinding)
2 Tbs. Nutritional Yeast
2 pinches Mineral Salt

Sprinkles of dark chili powder for color
2 cups water (divided)
Bragg Liquid Aminos to taste (be generous)
Cayenne pepper to taste (start with a light sprinkle)

1. Put all the ingredients, minus one cup of the water, in a small saucepan set to high heat. Whisk well and then bring to a quick boil. Turn heat down to a simmer. Add final cup of water. Whisk again and simmer until thickened.

2. Taste and see if it needs more seasonings. (I use quite a lot of cayenne pepper, you don't have to, but a little bit does bring a richer, bolder flavor to this gravy . . . so if it is not flavorful enough, try another small sprinkle. You can also add onion and garlic powders if you like those. After tasting, I usually end up giving another squirt of Bragg Liquid Aminos which is really needed for this recipe.)

INSTANT CHEESE SAUCE

E , **FP** , **XO** OR **S** (YUP, ALL OF THEM!)

Makes Multiple Servings

Pearl Chimes In   The title of this recipe is actually part fib and part truth. The truth is that it is instant (cue the Hallelujah Chorus). The fib is there is actually no cheese or dairy of any kind in this sauce. Hallelujah once again, because I promise … it still packs a wonderful, yet slimming cheesy punch! Along with my *Go To Gravy* (page 376), this sauce has become a staple in my home as it is so easy, tasty, and versatile. I almost always have some made up and sitting in my fridge.

The E-version of this sauce uses golden potatoes and the FP-version uses cauliflower rice. Those two versions, using the smaller amount of nuts option, are what I make the most often for my husband and myself. I've found lots of pure E meals are my ticket to slim and happy in this new season of my life (I'm about to turn 50) and the lower fat versions of the sauce help turn my E's into pure indulgence! Really … even just using the measly 2 Tbs. of nuts, this sauce tastes so creamy I keep thinking there must be more fat in it! Having said that, your family members might prefer the S or XO-versions (using more nuts), as my teen-agers do.

I suggest trying the E-version using the potatoes first. You're going to love it. And if you want to get your family on board with it … it is a great way to pull them in. In fact, I suggest making the Crossover version of this sauce for your kids … that would be using the potatoes, but using the larger amount of nuts or nut butter with it. If you want to keep yours true E, just make the recipe your way (with less nuts). Take half out for you and then add more of the cashews or nut butters to theirs. I think you'll love the cauliflower version, too … but perhaps try it second, not first. The cauliflower version is FP with just the 2 Tbs. of nuts and if you add the larger amount of nuts to it, then it becomes a delicious, creamiest of creamy S.

Many people eating vegan make veggie-based cheese sauces similar to this, so you can find lots of different versions online. There's no reason we can't utilize some vegan brilliance and tweak it to fit the THM plan … we take the best of all food approaches! The problem with most of these sauces is that they are too labor intensive for a lazy cook like me … I don't want to have to boil veggies first! My friend Karen who helped me perfect Super Slimming Porridge page 102 (she fought and beat aggressive breast cancer and is thriving with a more plant-strong approach to THM) came up with the brilliant idea to use canned or pouch veggies to make things so much quicker . . . all we have to do is blend! You can boil your veggies from fresh if you prefer but I love the ease of just opening a can, throwing contents into a blender then viola! It is the "instantness" of this recipe that keeps me making it over and over again. Karen also helped tweak the seasonings in this recipe to perfection so big thanks to her.

I enjoy Instant Cheese Sauce over the following:

1. Steamed, baked, or water sautéed non-starchy veggies (check page 254 for that "New Way Veggies" method)
2. Zucchini noodles (or any noodles)
3. A mix of cauli and brown rice together
4. Steamed golden, red, or purple potatoes
5. Any lean meats such as fish or chicken
6. Low-fat baked corn chips or other veggie based chips
7. My kids love it with regular blue corn chips, using the option of adding some Rotel-style chili and tomatoes to the sauce . . . it becomes like a spicy Velveeta dip, but actually even tastier and so much healthier for them!
8. We also enjoy it for Mexican pizzas. I found 100% fat-free baked tostadas (Charras brand . . . they were at Kroger) and we top them with refried beans, salsa, some taco seasoned chicken or black beans for protein . . . bake in a 425°F oven for 10 minutes and then top with finely shredded lettuce and lots of this sauce . . . amazing meal! You can add avocadoes for Crossover family members.
9. Please also try this sauce on the Cheesy Rice and Chicken skillet recipe (page 120).
10. Aside from pouring it over steamed potatoes, another way we often enjoy this in my home is for Stuffed Potato Night. I bake up a bunch of potatoes . . . Idaho for my kids and husband. I prefer golden or sweet for my season of life, but I also do some baked yellow squash for this meal (just for me) as I don't want to overdo potatoes but I also want to have a big plate of food! I put the squash in the oven half way through, as it takes less time to cook than the potatoes. My husband and teenagers like some meat with their stuffed potatoes, so I sauté up some grass-fed beef or turkey and then rinse that super well under very hot water to get all the excess fat out of it to make it E friendly. I return it to the skillet and add cauli rice and/ or processed mushrooms, then chili powder, mineral salt, cumin, and smoked paprika. They never detect the addition of the veggies to the meat. I use just a small amount of this meat on my potatoes though as these days I usually prefer fish or plant proteins as my go-to protein sources but I still enjoy red meat from time to time. Now the whole family gets to choose from a bunch of stuffings/toppings for their potatoes and squash and we all end up swamping them with this amazing cheese sauce.

1 (15 ounce) can whole or diced golden potatoes (drained) for E or 2 (8–8.5 oz.) shelf stable (ready to heat) pouches cauliflower rice for FP*

1 (14.5 ounce) can sliced carrots (drained)

1/4 cup Nutritional Yeast

2 Tbs. raw cashews or 1 Tbs. Tahini or almond butter for E or FP versions (use 1/2 cup cashews, or 1/4 cup Tahini or almond butter for XO or S versions)

2 tsp. Mineral Salt

1 Tbs. lemon juice

1 tsp. onion powder

Optional 1–2 tsp. garlic powder (I don't add this as my husband doesn't like it, but you probably will.)

Small sprinkle of cayenne pepper (gives added sharpness, but you don't need too much)

1¼–1⅓ cups just off the boil water (or heated broth)

Optional 2–4 Tbs. Rotel-style chilies and tomatoes (drained)

1. Put all ingredients except for optional Rotel in blender (using just 1¼ cups of the water). Blend very well until perfectly smooth. Taste and adjust seasonings if needed . . . perhaps after tasting you want to get creative and add a little squirt of liquid smoke seasoning, or a sprinkle of smoked paprika, or even 1 Tbs. of Apple Cider Vinegar as my friend Karen enjoys (I prefer it without the ACV). Add a little more of the water or broth if you want a thinner, more pourable sauce.

2. Add drained Rotel, if using and stir into sauce. Use whatever you want of this sauce for your meal and then put remaining cheese sauce into a jar with a lid and refrigerate the rest (it is easily reheated if you prefer it warm).

*Note: You've heard Serene and I say golden or red potatoes are the most blood sugar-friendly for you, but if you can't find canned golden potatoes you can use regular, white canned potatoes depending upon how you personally react to them. My blood sugar seems to do just fine with them these days, going by how I feel and they don't negatively affect my weight. If you're still having blood sugar troubles with this sauce using the potato version, add a little more water to it (another 1/2–3/4 cup) and about 1/2–3/4 tsp. Gluccie and/or 1–2 Tbs. of baobab. These two ingredients can really slow down the rise of blood sugar and help stabilize it. If you're not having protein in other parts of your meal . . . you can add a little collagen to this sauce, too.

Karen and I both use Nature's Earthly Choice brand of cauliflower rice and it works well in this recipe and doesn't have that strong cauliflower rice smell when you open the packet.

TAZINCY DIPPING AND SMOTHERING SAUCE

(SORTA FP-ISH IN SOME SETTINGS)

Makes Multiple Servings

Serene Chimes In My turn again, finally! I get the last recipe of the book, but don't skip this one thinking it is some loser … just a shove at the end type recipe. This is a must make winner! On how to pronounce this name … it is a hard "c" as in zinc … not soft as in Leonardo Davinci.

Alright, let's get to it … Pearl and I are both Tahini fans … I mean die-hard fans! You've heard of it, right? It's that creamy, sesame seed butter stuff … basically ground sesame seeds. You can find it in the international aisles of your regular grocery store or at natural grocery markets. Tahini is rich in many vitamins and minerals and is an excellent source of zinc, which supports the immune system and is necessary for a healthy metabolism. In times of stress, we need extra zinc as well as during pregnancy and breastfeeding seasons. Children also need ample zinc to flourish and this recipe is a simple, yet scrumptious way of "zinc-ing" up your whole family. Use it for dipping, for pouring over veggies, for salads and sandwiches. Use the sweet version for toppings for baked goods or for enjoying over berries or Greek yogurt.

Our sister Vange, (Rashida's Mom) lived most of her 20's in Israel and she introduced us to Tahini and other foods and flavors that are favorites of the Middle East. I recently took a trip there, with my family, where we so enjoyed celebrating Tahini at most of our meals. Once I got back, I was so inspired by all things Tahini that I made a Trim Healthy version of a dip called "Tahinah" that we had enjoyed in Israel. I put that delicious (if I do say so myself) recipe and video in our Trim Healthy Membership site (www.TrimHealthyMembership.com), so check it out if you are a member. But I can't and don't want to stop playing with Tahini and this new Tazincy Sauce is lighter in calories and fat than my other recipe, yet still bursting with flavor. So, get dipping and smothering with it and get your immune system thriving!

Notes to Read Before Making: While I labeled this an S due to Tahini being a seed butter, you can still eat some with E meals, especially the boosted versions. If you divide the basic version up into 6 servings (about 1 Tbs. or so per serving) you can have some on a sprouted E sandwich or perhaps use the sweet version as a topping on an E muffin and still fit into the E fat amounts. This basic version is divinely lovely so do give it a try, but mostly I make the boosted versions in my home. They are boosted in both nutrition and flavor and because they have more volume and less fat, you can have a bigger serving for E and really dig in generously for S. Oh … and feel free to add 3-4 Tbs. Pristine Whey Protein Powder or 1 Tbs. Integral Collagen to any of these versions for more protein if desired.

Tazincy Basic-version:

2 Tbs. Tahini
¼ cup water
3 pinches Mineral Salt
Shakes black pepper

For a Basic Sweet-version add...

1 Tbs. Gentle Sweet or 1–2 doonks Pure
  Stevia Extract Powder
Optional ¼ tsp. Vanilla Natural Burst
  Extract

1. This recipe only creams up properly
    with a hand-held blender. Find a mug
    that allows your hand-held blender to
    fit inside and reach the bottom. Place
    all your ingredients in the mug and blend until perfectly creamy. Store leftovers in the refrigerator.

Boosted Savory-version:

In addition to the Tazincy Basic-version add...
1 Tbs. Baobab Boost Powder
2 Tbs. water
1 Tbs. lemon juice
3 more pinches Mineral Salt

For a Boosted Sweet-version:

In addition to the Basic Sweet-version add...
1 Tbs. Baobab Boost Powder
2 Tbs. water
1 Tbs. lemon juice
1 more doonk Pure Stevia Extract Powder
Optional ¼ tsp. more Vanilla Natural Burst Extract

Acknowledgments

Firstly, I am thankful to God for this opportunity and a beautiful home dynamic that allowed me to pursue my passions and see this dream come to fruition.

To my parents who have always encouraged and allowed my passion for cooking to grow and mature from a young age. I am sure it took a lot of patience and wasted ingredients!

To my siblings who were brutally transparent food critics growing up. I am sure I learned a thing or two from all of the honesty!

Of course, a big thanks to my sisters Tiveria, Sahara, Iqara, and to my mother-in-law, Teresa Simpson, for all of the time you sweet souls supervised my darling little rascals so I could work on this project!

To my aunties, Serene and Pearl, where do I even start? Thank you immensely for such an opportunity to be a part of the THM world and for not just allowing, but for encouraging it (vehemently, I might add)! You have opened my eyes to the freedom of food and health, as you have done for so many other women, and I am forever grateful for all of this! Aunty Pearl, specifically, you have the patience of a patron saint and the work ethic of a machine! You answer every one of my inquisitive phone calls at all hours of the day (or night…), and you always have the solution to my "foodillemmas!" I have had such a grand time working on all of our edits, reviews, do-overs, etc. The pleasure has truly been all mine, and I thank you graciously!

Autumn Barrett, you are the star photographer who snapped all of our family "glamour" shots and the book cover. You have done an incredible job, and are always the calm in the storm. Thank you for all of your countless hours helping me look through photos to choose and upload for the book. Thank you also for your patience with my husband's inability to smile normally for a photo.

Thank you to Lisa McReynolds and Melissa Lockett for always loaning me your dishes to use in my photographs at the drop of a hat (or a text)! You both have been my personal encouragers and have always blessed me with your taste testing of my recipes!

Shout out to the awesome editing crew … Jessica Myers, Stephanie Copeland, Esther Smith, and Cindy Young. You guys rocked it with your eagle eyes making sure everything looked just right. Thanks again!

My darling husband, Jack . . . thank you for always being my greatest cheerleader and supporter—even when the chips were down (presumably down in your belly). And thank you for always being the smile I needed when things didn't go my way! You never complained when the kitchen looked like a bomb had gone off in it and you never let me get down on myself! I truly could not have done this without your constant encouragement!

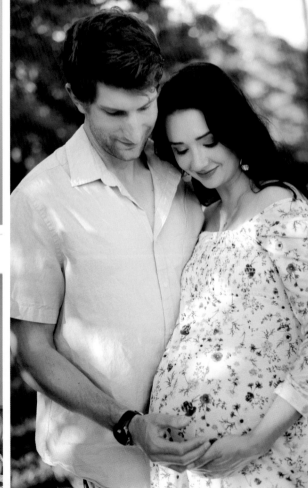

A new book from Pearl Barrett
and Serene Allison:

I'm That Girl

Change Your Identity . . .
Change Your Life!

Index